Automated Perfoı

Automated Performer Flying: The State of the Art shares the secrets of performer flying in entertainment history and provides step-by-step instructions on how to create a performer flying effect from scratch.

This book sheds light on all aspects of performer flying, covering its history, explaining concepts like mechanical compensation versus electrical compensation, providing guidance on how to calculate stopping distances and forces, and sharing tips on how to build successful relationships with performers. Case studies of prominent productions featuring performer flying, including Cirque du Soleil and Beyoncé, are included throughout.

Written for technical directors, theatrical riggers, and students of rigging, technical direction, and stagecraft courses, *Automated Performer Flying* takes readers through the process of creating a performer flying effect from the first spark of the idea to opening night.

Jim Shumway is a Senior Project Manager at TAIT, where he consults on and executes the most advanced performer flying effects in the world. Prior to joining the TAIT team Jim travelled the world with Cirque du Soleil for five years on four shows, working on two creations and reaching the role of Head Rigger. He is an annual guest lecturer at Yale University's School of Drama, speaking on Performer Flying and Acrobatic Rigging.

Automated Performer Flying

The State of the Art

Jim Shumway
Illustrations by Phil Caminiti

Focal Press
Taylor & Francis Group

NEW YORK AND LONDON

First published 2020
by Routledge
52 Vanderbilt Avenue, New York, NY 10017

and by Routledge
2 Park Square, Milton Park, Abingdon, Oxon, OX14 4RN

Routledge is an imprint of the Taylor & Francis Group, an informa business

Library of Congress Cataloging-in-Publication Data
Names: Shumway, Jim, author. | Caminiti, Phil, illustrator.
Title: Automated performer flying : the state of the art / Jim Shumway;
illustrations by Phil Caminiti.
Description: Milton Park, Abingdon, Oxon ; New York, NY : Routledge, 2020. | Includes
index.
Identifiers: LCCN 2019027785 (print) | LCCN 2019027786 (ebook) | ISBN
9780815352136 (hbk) | ISBN 9780815352143 (pbk) | ISBN 9781351131513
(ebk)
Subjects: LCSH: Stage flying–Handbooks, manuals, etc. | Stage machinery–Handbooks,
manuals, etc. | Stage management–Handbooks, manuals, etc. | Theaters–Safety measures–
Handbooks, manuals, etc. | Theaters–Stage-setting and scenery–Handbooks, manuals, etc.
Classification: LCC PN2091.F58 S58 2019 (print) | LCC PN2091.F58 (ebook) |
DDC 792.02/4–dc23
LC record available at https://lccn.loc.gov/2019027785
LC ebook record available at https://lccn.loc.gov/2019027786

ISBN: 978-0-8153-5213-6 (hbk)
ISBN: 978-0-8153-5214-3 (pbk)
ISBN: 978-1-3511-3151-3 (ebk)

Typeset in Bembo
by Swales & Willis, Exeter, Devon, UK

Contents

Acknowledgements

A special thanks to Catherine Rosano and Cindy Simmel-Devoe for inspiring kids to make a living in the entertainment industry through hard work and dedication. Even if not in our industry, kids whose lives you've touched are better adults for having known for each of you.

McLane Snow, Andy Schmitz, Scott Levine, Neil Mulligan, Bill Sapsis, and countless others who suffered through early versions of this book, I thank you.

And of course, thank you to Trish Shumway, my wife, for putting up with my constant self-exile in the office while I wrote and wrote and wrote.

Preface

Hello and welcome to *Automated Performer Flying: The State of the Art*! I wanted the title to be *Everything You Ever Wanted to Know About Automated Performer Flying But Were Too Afraid to Ask*, but alas it was decided that title wasn't keyword-searchable enough; such is the world in 2019. That alternate title really sums up what is trying to be achieved with this book. It seems very few books have been written exclusively on the topic of performer flying. Over the generations, and much like circus families, many of the secrets of performer flying have been handed down from competent technician to competent technician, often with similar last names. Back when performer flying was limited to only the highest-level productions, this was a sustainable plan for the industry. But in the current era, where almost every show seems to need, or at least want, a performer to fight the pull of gravity, it is crucial that more people be exposed to the do's and do-not's of this slice of our industry. The lack of textbooks on this specific topic is particularly vexing when considering that in the last 20 years the technology being used to execute these effects is constantly changing and improving. How on earth are we all to execute these effects safely, let alone improve what is considered the norm, if certain fundamentals are not out there to be studied, understood, and acted on?

The goal of this book then is to take you on the journey of creating a performer flying effect from scratch. Everything from the first spark of the idea to the finer points of working with performers and everything in between. This is not a book about manual performer flying. While much of the information contained herein applies to both manual and automated systems, this book focuses on the broad and finer points of automated systems. Part of the reason for this is certainly the fact that my background is not in manual performer flying, but rather in automating such effects. The thesis of this book is that there is a thirst among students and working professionals alike for more knowledge on the current state of the art. If that is true, it seems only responsible to be accused of leaning too hard in the automated direction.

Much like Jay O. Glerum's *Stage Rigging Handbook* could be considered the manual for the Entertainment Technician Certification Program's (ETCP's) Theater Rigger certification, and Harry Donovan's *Arena Rigging* could be considered the same for ETCP's Arena Rigger certification, I hope this book will underscore the need for an Automated Rigger certification. All too often in our industry we draw a hard line between the rigging of our increasingly complicated stage machines and the control of those machines. This, in my opinion, is the cause of most of the accidents and incidents resulting from the use of these creations. Instead of drawing that hard line in the sand between Automation Technicians and Riggers, we as an industry have to push ourselves to develop Automation Riggers to continue succeeding with the amazing effects artistic teams challenge us to create, and to do so safely.

How Did We Get to This Point in History?

Many people think performer flying was invented for Cathy Rigby and her famous performances of *Peter Pan* on Broadway. While this was certainly a giant leap for the art form into the public consciousness, this is certainly not where it started. Anyone who has taken a Theatre History class could probably point to the Greeks and their Deus Ex Machinas as the earliest known performer flying effects. These, as best we know, were single-axis gags allowing performers to appear over the scenery and be lowered to the stage. As with so much of our industry these are the earliest *known* uses of performer flying. That said, I'm sure someone prior to the Greeks tried to make their show better by suspending a performer on a rope. Without any documentation though, the Greeks get to keep this crown too. After the Greeks, the next big advance in performer flying is during, you guessed it, the Renaissance. During this period we begin to see the first documented instances of many of the same tricks we use today. John A. McKinven's excellent book *Stage Flying: 431B.C. to Modern Times* is a wonderful resource to see some of the great minds of the era's drawings of their creations. These productions were funded almost exclusively by the Church, meaning we were mainly flying angels, saints, and devils. From there, very little has changed other than staggering improvements in size, cost, complexity, repeatability, and most importantly safety.

One could argue we are currently living through another such period of exponential leaps forward in stage machinery, and specifically performer flying, with the introduction of not only automated equipment, but also increasingly advanced and nuanced custom software with which to control them. As recently as 15 years ago the machines we were using to fly people, and even more so the software, could best be described as "farm equipment". Today's machines are Swiss watches compared to those systems of the not too distant past. Just imagine what that same leap forward will make us feel about the systems we are so proud of today!

Acrobatic Rigging versus Performer Flying

So, what is the difference between "performer flying" and "acrobatic rigging"? When I refer to an effect as performer flying, I mean that we have the performer attached to the rig via a harness of some kind. To put that differently: the performer is attached to the rig to the point that they are along for the ride. They will continue to be part of the rig, once attached, whether they want to be or not. This covers most theatrical flying instances. Any time someone is in a harness, or connected to a prop with a waist belt, I would consider that performer flying. By contrast, in acrobatic rigging we are relying on the performer to stay attached to the rig. This covers most circus arts flying. If there is nothing keeping the performer in the air other than their own hands, feet, hair, teeth, etc., then we are working on an acrobatic rigging situation. This distinction is important as we talk about certain aspects of flying effects. This can effect certain design criteria, to say nothing of the codes you may be required to adhere to. Keep this difference in mind as you read the pages that follow.

The Five Cardinal Rules of Performer Flying

The last thing I will leave you with before I stop using the word "I" is my Five Cardinal Rules of Performer Flying:

1.   If it's not 100%, it's 0%.

This is to say that performer flying and acrobatic rigging is an all-or-nothing kind of industry. There is no "She's got one more in her" when talking about our systems. The *Go* or *No-Go* decision is a digital output; it is a 1 or a 0. This is not an analog output; it is not a 70% decision. Either we are 100% confident that our system will perform flawlessly, or we don't use it in this performance.

2.   Don't become the manufacturer.

While portions of this book are written to advise you of best practices as if you are making various parts of a performer flying rig from scratch, if you are not a professional manufacturer you should avoid inadvertently becoming one. That may sound confusing, but simply put, if you are buying a component from a company to use in your rig make sure you understand everything about how that component is meant to be used. Further, do not unintentionally violate that, thereby becoming the manufacturer. If you are going to void a warranty or otherwise make that component your own in a court of law, make sure it is a conscious decision to do so!

3. The performer gets the final say.

You are going to go to great lengths to make sure that your rig is 100% and ready for the performer. You are going to do everything in your power to make sure that your rig is ready for opening night and every subsequent performance. "The show must go on" is one of those antiquated phrases that can make us lose sight of the fact we are putting performers in potentially dangerous, or even life-threatening, situations. As such, the performer *always* gets the final say as to whether or not the effect happens. To be clear: they do not need to have a "good" reason to not get on the rig. In fact, many of the reasons people would consider "not good enough" to skip a run are in fact the best reasons not to put a performer in the air. These can be things like not being mentally stable in that moment, a recent personal issue, or not feeling safe on the rig. Other more inarguable reasons might include feeling one's harness is loose, a very recent injury, or light-headedness. The point is: it doesn't matter why the performer doesn't want to go – they get the final say.

4. If you don't know how to get down, don't go up.

Simply put, you must have a rescue plan. This will be covered thoroughly later in the book, but it is unacceptable to put a performer in the air, where they could be stranded in an emergency situation, without a practiced written plan to get them promptly on the ground.

5. If you don't know how to stop, don't start.

This is usually a simple one to follow with manual performer flying systems, as your means of starting is the same as your means of stopping. That of course being a living, breathing human. But in an automated system it is crucially important to make sure you have a surefire means of stopping the system immediately in the event of something going wrong. This is usually in the form of "the big red button", better known as the E-Stop button. Make sure it not only exists, but that is within reach of at the very least your operator, and preferably also several other people watching the effect intently. These machines, despite how safe we have made them over the years, do not care about you or your family. We *must* be able to stop them at the first sign of trouble.

Who Is This For?

I hope this book will find an audience with everyone from students to riggers to automation technicians who want to know more about performer flying. I equally hope it finds an audience with both new and seasoned aerialists who want to know more about the nuts and bolts of what is going on above and around them. I hope parts of this book will help the dads who are asked to run the fly rig at the middle school's production of *The Wizard of Oz*. To that end, each topic will be eased into to make sure the least experienced among us can understand what is being discussed, then get detailed enough to warrant the time of even an experienced professional who wants to know more about performer flying or acrobatic rigging.

Each chapter will wrap up with a summation of what you should take away if you are a beginner, and a separate list if you are a professional. This might mean that the beginnings of some chapters are very basic for professionals, and the later pages are too much for beginners. To the professionals I would argue that everyone could always use a refresher on the fundamentals. It is not enough to know *what* the fundamentals are. You must also know *why* the fundamentals are what they are. Hopefully this will help baseline us as an industry as to why we do the things we do. To the beginner I would say don't be afraid to bail out of a chapter if it's getting too technical! Feel free to jump to the end of the chapter to review the list of what you should have learned to evaluate if you've succeeded.

The information contained herein is the result of my journey through years of executing these effects. While I started in community theatre, most of my performer flying experience has come in service to Cirque du Soleil and TAIT. As such, my views are seasoned with a particularly corporate, for-profit, viewpoint. My views of how we should do these effects tend to err on the side of more staff, more time, more training, and more paperwork. Such luxuries are not always available to everyone at all tiers of our industry. That's okay too! The goal of this book is not to prescribe exactly what should be done in every scenario; each performer flying effect is different from the last, and the next. What I am hoping to impart to you is enough information for you to evaluate whether or not you are doing your effect as safely as you can. Similarly, I only mention a small handful of companies in this book. Those companies should not be considered flawless, and unmentioned companies should not be considered unworthy. I am hoping to leave you with the vocabulary and the tools to evaluate if whatever company you are working with has staffed your project adequately on its end, and is maintaining a requisite baseline of safety.

I hope this book helps illuminate where we are at as an industry today. I hope it helps everyone from the community theatre all the way up to the biggest productions to better understand how to plan, execute, and maintain these effects. I hope this book sparks conversations and even debate about where we should be going as an industry and how best to get there. Most of all though, I hope this book helps us all be safer. I hope that it helps spread the knowledge of what these systems are doing, and how, in the hopes of having more educated eyes out there in the field making sure we all stay safe. At the end of the day, we are just telling stories. It is infinitely more important that everyone gets to go home at the end of the day than that the show goes on.

So, without further ado, let's jump into the very beginning of the lifecycle of a performer flying effect, that moment you get the call.

Thanks for reading. I hope you enjoy it.

Part 1

The Flying Effect Lifecycle

We may well want to jump right to a discussion of types of winches, kinds of rope, or everyone's favorite carabiner. Those are 1-foot-off-the-ground kind of decisions and topics. We need to start 30,000 feet above the ground to make sure we are seeing the whole picture before we can concern ourselves with such details. In this first part we will cover how to think all the way through your effect early and often, focusing on the important parts of the Design, Fabrication, and Administrative phases of any performer flying effect.

1 Proper Prior Planning

Where else to begin but at the beginning? Usually these endeavors start with someone calling and saying something to the effect of "I have a terrible idea", and you responding, "I'd love to help!" From there begins a long and winding journey that requires equal parts knowledge, skill, patience, luck, and perseverance.

Before we get too excited and dive in head-first we should ask, "Should we do this?" or even, "Can we do this?" For people employed at companies that do this every day, obviously the answer is "Heck yeah!", assuming your best-suited staff are available to work on the project. But for others who may have limited or no prior flying experience, this is an important question to ask both as an organization and as individuals. As an organization it is important to decide if you have the skill internally to handle an effect that can, without exaggeration, kill someone. While unpleasant to think about, it is important not to approach these effects with rose-tinted lenses. Do not make this decision exclusively in the conference room. Get out there and talk to your staff whom you will be thrusting this responsibility on, and make sure they agree that they can do this and do it safely. Certainly, flying a person should not be your organization's first foray into defying gravity. If you are deciding to do your first in-house performer flying effect then at the very least your organization should have a recent history of successfully flying inanimate objects!

What to do though if you decide your organization is ready to take this step into flying people, but you recognize you don't have the skills in-house? The good news is there are many reputable companies out there that specialize in performer flying; Foy, ZFX, and TAIT immediately spring to mind. They, and others, will be more than happy to take your call, hear what you are trying to achieve, and help you do so at your budget. Depending on your precise needs these companies can do as little as cold-rent you gear, if you feel you have staff to run the effect but not to design and manufacture it from scratch, all the way up to being a member of both your artistic team and your technical staff, helping you reach your goals safely.

Now, if you as an individual are having this responsibility thrust upon you and you don't feel prepared or capable, say so, loudly and often. This is not the time to push your comfort zone. You should make sure your boss or bosses understand that you do not feel ready for such a gig. Hopefully this will help them realize that your organization should get some advice and help. This can come in the form of bringing in a whole company to help, or bringing in an individual with a work background to supplement your skills. Either way, the point remains the same: bring in some reinforcements!

Whether you decide to bring in some help or take on this challenge with your team in-house, it is critical to recognize that the most important part of any phase of a performer flying effect is communication:

- Making sure you fully understand the artistic vision.
- Making sure you are clearly communicating how that vision is being translated into reality.
- Making sure your mechanical designers (that may be you) understand both what is required and what is not.
- Making sure the fabrication team (again, this may be you) is paying ample attention to details that matter.

Making sure the end users (and again, this may be you too) know what they are doing. Keeping all these people on the same page can be a monumental task, even if you are singularly all these people. Each of the above-mentioned roles are not necessarily different people. In plenty of organizations in our industry one person could wear several of those hats, if not all of them at the same time. While that does make miscommunication between the parties harder, it does not negate the need for an introductory meeting to make sure all parties are on the same page, in the same book. Do not be lured into thinking though that one meeting is enough over the full lifespan of creating such an effect. Never forget that creating from a blank page is far harder than editing something that is sitting in front of you. Even with the best intentions and the most qualified staff by your side, the waters will still muddy over time and therefore need periodic sifting.

Client Meetings, or Extracting Information

"Client" is one of those words that may have you thinking, "This book wasn't written for me." A lot of performer flying in the US is done by a few companies who rent out their skills, and as such "client" is an apt word for their relationship with their customers. That said though, there are many homebrew rigs out there created by perfectly capable regional, community, or educational theatres. In this context your client can be your boss at your theatre who has assigned you this project, your theatre's resident Artistic Director, or even the artistic half of your own brain if you are wearing all the hats! Our client is the person we are trying to impress with all our efforts going forward, and the quality of the final effect.

The first meeting that you should arrange after accepting to take on a performer flying effect is one with the person or persons who will determine the artistic success or failure of the gag. Usually this will be with the Show Director, but depending on how large and/or complicated the production is, this meeting could be with or include the input of client project managers, composers, technical staff, performer management, safety officers, or others. It is important to set aside time to only talk about the performer flying effect. Do not let this meeting be rolled into some larger meeting, or be a single bullet point on a long agenda. This is your first opportunity to get the people you will be working with, or reporting to, to understand the attention to detail that is required to successfully execute this effect. One way to do this is to circulate a detailed agenda a day prior to the meeting.

Hopefully you already had some basic conversations before you agreed to take the helm this performer flying ship in the forthcoming high seas, but it is always best to go over everything with everyone involved one more time. Maybe someone with an important opinion is unaware of the timelines involved, or doesn't know that this is happening at all! After this meeting everyone will (very briefly) be standing on the same point on the map. And immediately after, everyone will start running in different directions until the first rehearsal, when all the parts meet again. This meeting is your first and last chance to document everyone's needs and desires, and your plans to achieve them. Remember that no question is too broad or too specific at this juncture. All that said, your agenda should include items like:

What is the effect, or, put differently, what are we trying to achieve?
Is this performer flying or acrobatic rigging?
When is the first rehearsal?
When is opening night?
How long will the production run?
Is it a touring production, a permanent install, or a one-off?
How many performers will be flying?
Do they have prior experience flying?
Is the effect used once per performance or repeatedly?
Is the performer flying in a harness or on a prop?

That is usually enough to get the conversation started. Depending on your client's ability to verbalize their vision, or their level of prior experience with such effects, it can be helpful to have some footage ready for the meeting to spur the conversation and get everyone speaking with the same vocabulary, both verbally and visually. In an ideal world, this would be footage of your previous very successful work; however, not everyone has the ability to film everything they do so don't be afraid to use YouTube to find work that is illustrative of what you're talking about. The important thing, however, if you're going the YouTube route, is to have those videos bookmarked and handy. There is nothing that slows a meeting down quite like waiting for someone to remember the title of the video in their head. This should help your client be able to answer the questions above, the hardest of which is likely the first one: "What is the effect?" Based on the answers to those questions you should have many follow-ups, which will help you create a specification, or "spec" as it is often called.

Creating a Specification to Define Success

Having all concerned parties agree to the "spec" is crucial to success. A more technically inclined client might well provide you with a spec to meet. Even in this case, however, it is always worth going over it with their representative to make sure the spec is actually achievable. There is nothing worse than putting in all the effort needed to create one of these effects, only to have the client be dissatisfied with your work because it doesn't do something they wanted it to, or thought was needed, when that particular was never achievable in the first place. For example, if your client wants a performer to launch out of a trap in the stage high into their rafters very quickly, let's say at 20 feet per second (normally abbreviated as *20ft/sec*), but their ceiling is only 20 feet tall, then that 20ft/sec is likely not achievable. With time to accelerate to and decelerate from top speed there is not enough room to run to get up to that speed. Our system will only be able to accelerate so fast to our chosen top speed, to say nothing of the limitations of the human body. These are important things to consider before blindly agreeing to a spec that might not be possible. (For a more detailed discussion of acceleration and forces, please see Chapter 4.) If this speed is allowed to be a measure of success, however, your client may end up disappointed even if your gag does everything else it needed to. This is the kind of thing that you should be looking for in the very beginning and getting out in front of.

Another example not rooted in speed would be not thinking through the choreography of the show as it relates to your flying machine; many productions of *Peter Pan* come to mind. You may have a situation where you want to use the same machine for multiple effects throughout the show. There is no problem with this, as long as you and the creative staff have talked through the choreography of the show. If you intend to use the machine to have Peter fly through the window, then logically the line needs to be preset there from the top of the scene. It seems obvious, but details like this are often missed. Make sure the creative team understands that flying lines cannot preset themselves! Put differently, the line cannot disappear up into the rafters one moment, and suddenly be strung through a set piece the next without some intervention.

These are the kinds of things you want to discover in your initial meeting with the client. Both of the given examples are too specific to put on an agenda, but are emblematic of the kinds of things you will need to read between the lines about as they answer your more basic questions. In our first example about a specific (unachievable) speed being spec-ed by the client, right then and there is your opportunity to explain why that specific parameter is unachievable, and propose an alternate one that they find acceptable. In our second example of one machine not being able to be everywhere at once, this is your opportunity to point out that we need more systems than we were planning, or need to rethink the flow of the show. In all these instances this is also an opportunity for you to show your understanding of the big picture and willingness to help your client see their vision through. While it may seem tedious in the moment, having these conversations early and often will always result in less drama (the bad kind) along the way. So much of a successful performer flying effect is the execution of soft skills in working with various kinds of people in our industry. This meeting is your first big hurdle and test of your soft skills.

By the end of this meeting you should feel confident that you know exactly what is expected of you and how you are going to execute it. Your client should feel they were heard, understood, and have found the right person for the job. You should know exactly what your scope is, both where it begins and where it ends. So many difficult conversations happen on the first day of rehearsal because of a "scope gap". This is what happens when one vendor understood their spec to be providing A through C, and another vendor understood their spec to be providing E through G, but no one was ever planning on providing the D in the middle. Having this meeting with your client may not prevent scope gap from rearing its ugly head, but at least you will have excellent documentation showing that you have showed up with everything you and your client had agreed to previously. Having this documentation also puts you in a great position to be able to be seen as bending over backwards to help your client by filling this scope gap, should it exist and should you choose to.

A tricky conversation at the initial meeting will be when the Creative in the room wants to talk about the "feel" of a flight instead of a recognized unit of measurement. It is only "tricky" because is it not a black-and-white, easily understood, same-page-same-book kind of metric to be held to. It is not a bad thing that creative people want to talk in those terms; quite the opposite in fact: it's how they enter the world and we want them to be able to relate to us in a way that makes them comfortable. It's important then to know who on your team can translate "feel" to speed, height, flight envelope, and other more technical measurements. It might not be your strong suit, and that's okay. You want to make sure you have your artistic-minded tech in the room when the conversation turns this way. This is another time when having videos of effects that were designed to elicit different moods can be very helpful. Another technique that has proven variably successful is to equate the speed of your machine to various driving machines most people are familiar with. For example, a riding lawnmower travels at roughly 3ft/sec. Whatever your strategy, the goal is to find common ground and make sure the artistic voice feels heard and understood too.

With these steps taken, you are ready for the next step: figuring out how to deliver what you've promised.

The Big Question: Manual or Automated

Right from the onset, we have a big decision to make about our effect: manual or automated? We likely had an idea about the answer to this before we scheduled our big meeting with Team Creative, but it's okay to let the answer come to you over the course of this meeting. Sometimes there is no clear obvious winner in this debate for your given effect. In that case, we should always default to what this company of players is most comfortable with. Sometimes a decision has already been made before you were brought on to the project. All those scenarios are fine, but you should be prepared to discuss the "whys" and "what-ifs" of both paths in the wood.

There are pros and cons to both types of systems. This book is entitled *Automated Performer Flying*, so you can likely guess which flavor will be gone into the most detail in the pages that follow. Nothing that follows should be read as suggesting automation is always better or always right. Automated systems and manual systems are equal tools; we want to make sure we use the right tool for the job at hand. Your choice will likely be most influenced by budget and the skills your staff are trained with. Manual systems are certainly cheaper to fabricate. Generally speaking, removing electricity (more specifically, electronics) from anything will make it cheaper. And since we've removed all the fancy electronics from the system, there is also significantly less to stop the system from working night after night. Now, that said, most of those electronics we've removed are safety monitoring devices, so manual systems are arguably less safe than automated ones. At the very least, it can be argued that manual systems are less "safe" than the automated ones. (The difference between *safe* by itself and "safe" with air quotes around it being compliance with various codes.)

Manual systems require a physically fit operator who can "dance" with the performer on the other end of the line. Many people will claim that manual systems also require less training to use than automated ones. This is a common misconception. It's not accurate to say that it requires *less* training. The point being made is that the skills required to be able to operate a manual system are easier to teach and be absorbed by more people than an automated one. But this is only true if we compare apples to oranges. Manual systems are very popular for high school productions because after they are installed by a trained professional that same professional can train a person (usually a dad) to use the system in an afternoon. The skills that need to get taught mainly relate to pulling on a rope. Beyond that, the use of a manual system is all about finesse and timing. That said, a similar point can be made that a dad can be taught to hit a G–O button in the same amount of time. In neither case is the situation particularly safe. One should never discount the amount of time and training that should be invested in teaching anyone, much less someone with no prior theatrical experience, how to fly a person. The goal of "training an operator in afternoon" should not factor into your decision of manual versus automated, because it is not actually an achievable goal when safety is included in the equation. Perhaps a better way to think about your choice would be to consider it in a frame of ease of making changes. Changes to the routine can be very easily made to the manual system: just tell the dad what you want. Now you are relying on his ability to remember the changes and perform them similarly every night. Changing the routine in an automated system does often require someone with greater familiarity with the system, but once you change the cue it will be the same every single time the button is pressed, at least at the machine. In either case there are of course countless other variables that will affect the precision of the flight. All that said, it is commonly accepted that manual systems are a great choice for simple routines that are in short-running shows or shows of a particular budget. The barrier of entry on cost is just lower. Again, however, this does not excuse you from scheduling an appropriate amount of time for training and rehearsal, as the system you are installing will only ever be as good as the person operating it.

Manual systems are said to be more of a dance between the operator and the performer than automated ones. This does in fact prove to be true. Like any partner dance endeavor though, it involves countless hours of rehearsal to be at its best. When a manual system operator and performer are in sync it can really be something to behold. There is a natural movement and flow to the routine that is much harder to achieve with an automated system. The tradeoff for the often more mechanical visual outcome of an automated system is consistency. It may only be 90% as natural as a manual one, but it will be 90% every time, instead of a manual system which may vary from 110% beautiful to 75% based on everyone's output that run. All that being said, an automated system can also be a gorgeous thing to watch; it just requires advanced programming and sufficient time to make it look so.

There are pros and cons to an automated system as well, of course. Automated systems are the obvious choice for very complex flying. Do not, however, equate axis-of-motion count with complexity. As we will discuss later, a single axis moving up and down can often be the hardest flight to make safe, consistent, and pretty. Consistency is automation's biggest selling point. You will know that every time the G-O button is pressed the exact same motion will occur. An oft-cited con of automated systems is that they are "complicated". It's not so much that they are complicated but that they are interdisciplinary. Very few single individuals are able to understand both the rigging (inherit to both manual and automated systems) and also understand the controls system. This is in fact one of the great crises facing our industry. While they are very different skill sets, some of the biggest companies in our industry do us no favors by drawing hard departmental lines between those that understand rigging and those that understand controls. This unwarranted segregation seeps down to the rest of the industry, the result being that you would be hard-pressed to find panels or classes at the various conventions we all attend covering the overlap of these two skill sets. If you want to be absolutely invaluable in the future of this industry, start becoming an expert in *both* these fields instead of just one.

Some see little value in adding these interdisciplinary complications to their lives, but think about what all those electronics are providing you. Most of the complicated electronics that are party to automated performer flying are there to ensure the machine is always operating correctly and accurately. As such, these complications should give you peace of mind. In Chapter 5 you will find a more precise dissection of these individual components, but items like limit switches, encoders, cross-groove sensors, slack line detectors, and load cells are all there to monitor the machine's status and performance hundreds of times per second. While all these devices can make it hard to get the machine moving, they also give you the peace of mind to know that if the machine is in fact moving a lot of processing is telling you that everything is running correctly. All this fancy check-back equipment does mean you will want staff familiar with its operation and troubleshooting, which is certainly a factor to take into consideration.

Ultimately, very few organizations actually get an opportunity to sit down and flow-chart out this decision. Money being what makes the world go round often makes this decision for you as automated systems are quite simply at a higher price point than manual ones. If you are in the small minority of people or organizations that are on the fence but can afford either, do consider the above points. Wanting to challenge yourself or your organization to move to an automated system is a wonderful opportunity for growth in your staff. Just know, as you likely already do, that the first time you do anything new is the most difficult it will ever be. If this is to be your organization's first performer fly routine of any kind, consider and plan for an extended rehearsal period. If you are renting a working solution from a vendor, do not plan on having their assistance in training your staff for the shortest possible amount of time to have the smallest possible effect on your budget. While it can be expensive, keeping them around for an extra day or two can go a long way towards a successful, and most importantly safe, execution of your effect.

Risk Assessment/Risk Reduction

Possibly even before making the decisions we've laid out earlier in this chapter, you must start the process of risk assessment/risk reduction, also known as "RA/RR". This is a process that most technical entertainment types do in their heads, constantly, every day. However, for high-risk elements such as performer flying this must be formalized into a written document. While this can seem like a time-consuming, butt-covering, never-to-be-read-again, waste-of-time kind of document, the process of creating it often illuminates problems that would otherwise go undiscovered until far later in the process, or, even worse, not until the related accident happens.

The process seems rudimentary on its surface. Simply write down every imaginable risk associated with your system, categorize each risk's likelihood and severity, enumerate mitigations for each risk, and re-evaluate the likelihood and severity. The goal of this document is to show that you've really thought through every conceivable problem and found a way to reduce how likely it is to happen and how bad the incident will be if it does. This seems like a waste of time to people who always think this way, but again, getting your team in a room and setting aside time to produce this document almost always results in great forethought and progress. It can be most productive to separate the enumerating of the hazards (the risk assessment) from the solving of those problems (the risk reduction) into two distinct efforts. This may already seem like too many meetings to you for such a butt-covering kind of document, and for your organization you may well be right. It is not important exactly how this document is created, but rather that it exists at all. This process, formal though it may be, really separates those who practice proper prior planning, thinking through their system early and often, and those who quite simply do not.

Many of the risks you will come up with are not unique to the particular system you are working on. Performer flying rigs have huge swaths of risks that are common to all of them, whether you are doing a high school production of *Peter Pan* or the Olympics Opening Ceremony. Some of these risks are things like "What if the limit switches fail?", or one not even unique to automated systems: "What if the lifting media breaks?" After the first time you go through this process, you will have a great boilerplate document to build off of for future systems. Unfortunately though, the first time you do this you still need to sit down and enumerate all these hazards and their known solutions.

Most of the risks in your RA/RR process, and certainly nearly all of the boilerplate ones, are mitigated by 30,000-foot-view concepts that the performer flying industry holds close and has handed down from generation to generation.

1. Large Factors of Safety
2. Redundancy
3. Fail-Safe Architecture

Through these three concepts most risks can be mitigated to a comfortable level without further intervention. To use our examples above, the common mitigation of the limit switches failing is that they are normally-closed switches. By making this component selection we have constant monitoring of the switch's health instead of finding out when we needed it that it was broken all along. This would fall under "Fail-Safe Architecture". By monitoring the safe state, instead of waiting for something dangerous to happen to actuate the switch, we have created a fail-safe system. The switch being actuated in the normal course of events breaks the circuit, triggering the automation system's response. Since the switch is normally closed though, removing power from the switch in any fashion causes the same response as physically triggering the switch. So, for example, if the wire supplying power to the switch is cut for some reason, the switch indicates as struck. In a normally-open design, you wouldn't know the wire was cut until you needed the switch to trigger and it didn't. Since the severity of this event is serious injury, we want additional mitigation to further reduce its likelihood. This is why we have two limit switches at each end of travel of a performer flying machine. By having two switches, both fail-safe, and both normally closed, we have introduced "Redundancy" to the system. With both these mitigations in place we can sleep easier at night knowing we have grossly reduced the likelihood of the winch being able to run past its limits and into the first obstruction. (Please see Chapter 6 for a more detailed discussion of limit switches.)

For our second example, the common mitigation for the lifting media breaking is that we employ a large factor of safety. Common practice in the industry is to employ a factor of safety of at least 10:1. This means the minimum breaking strength of the lifting media (or rope) is 10 times higher than the load we intend to put on it. (This is an oversimplification of how we employ factors of safety, but a sufficient definition for the moment. For more on this topic continue reading further into this chapter, and Chapter 13.) By spec-ing rope in such a manner, we grossly reduce the likelihood of the lifting media breaking. We have created a lot of headroom in our design between what we intend to do and the point at which the rope will break. But, just as with the limit switch example, given the severity of the event occurring, we want to further reduce its likelihood. Most commonly, this is achieved through mandating thorough inspections at frequent intervals. Yes, mitigations can, and should, include operational processes to help solve these problems! Again though, neither of these mitigations *eliminates* the hazard; that's not the point of this exercise. No risk can be completely eliminated. The goal here is to reduce their likelihood and, where possible, their severity. In both of these examples the severity if these events occur is high. Someone will get seriously injured or possibly die. As a result, since we have decided we cannot reduce the severity, we want to make sure we've made the likelihood as near to zero as is possible.

And so the process goes until you and your team feel you've recorded every imaginable risk there is, no matter how unlikely, and for each risk a severity and likelihood is assigned. These are usually quantified as numbers in a given range. For example, you could assign severities from 1–5. It is important to create a legend or key defining the scope of each number in your ranking. Once you get to this point it can be helpful to walk away for a day or two and ruminate on the compiled list. Then get the team back together and begin to discuss what mitigations exist for the compiled risks, and once again assign a new, post-mitigation severity and likelihood. Lastly, we want to compare the two columns full of severities and likelihoods and make sure everyone involved is comfortable with where we've landed. In the above examples, without this last review you might have felt comfortable enough with only using normally-closed switches without also having redundant switches. It is important to remember there are no completely "right" answers, and there is no island of "safe" we're trying to arrive at. The point is to document our work to mitigate our known risks, and for everyone involved to be aware of and comfortable with those risks.

If your clients are particularly on top of this kind of paperwork (think: the largest entertainment conglomerates in the world) they may come with their own RA/RR processes and/or documents. Just like the first time we create our in-house documents, the first time you interact with another company's paperwork will take longer than every subsequent interaction. You will need to copy all your boilerplate risks and mitigations into their sheets, and you may find its categorization scheme may deem some of your stock fixes not good enough. While this can be frustrating, it can also be a sign that your thinking has become stale. These challenges are always, and should be viewed as, an opportunity to make your systems even more fool proof or to invent the new standard!

An ever-growing oversimplification spouted in meeting rooms with fancy chairs is "I want a SIL-3 system." SIL stands for "Safety Integrity Level" and is an RA/RR method defined by the IEC 61508 standard. SIL ratings run from 1–4 with 1 being the least safe and 4 being used for nuclear power plants. Mercifully no one in our industry is yet asking for SIL-4 systems, but keep your seatbelt buckled; it's probably coming someday soon to a theme park near you! The part that is often missed, which leads to the errant comment above, is that SIL is not something you buy off a shelf. You do not go and buy all SIL-3 components and end up with a SIL-3 system. SIL is a particular way of doing your risk assessment, through which needed SIL ratings per component are revealed. The process is designed to remove some of the arbitrary categorization that can happen in other forms of RA/RR paperwork, and instead use math to determine needed mitigation level. So if you fill out an RA for your show with SILs method some components will turn out needing to be SIL-1 or SIL-2, and yes some will end up needing to be SIL-3. These will be your single-point-of-failure kind of components. So, there is nearly no such thing as a "SIL-3 system". Rather, we can say we will be evaluating our system to comply with SIL ratings.

Site Surveys

A well-executed site survey is critical to the success of your project. A site survey is a visit to the place where you will be installing your system, before design begins, for the sole purpose of seeing, experiencing, and most importantly measuring the space. It is worth mentioning that unfortunately you may not have the opportunity to actually visit the space your rig is to be installed into. It is important to advocate for this visit as it often helps solve problems before they even work their way into existence. If, however, it is simply not possible for good reason, you will still want your client to give you information about the venue just as if you were there. Being able to articulate to them the level and style of information you are expecting will still go a long way towards educating you about the space.

Site surveys are often done before the initial meeting with the client, or are sometimes done during the meeting. Walking the space with the creative team can be very fruitful, especially if it is a space they are very familiar with and you are not, or vice versa. That said, even if you know the space well, even if it is the theatre you work in every day, it is best to do a site survey specific to your forthcoming performer flying adventure. If you are fortunate enough to walk the space with the creative team you will be in a great position to talk through the technical choreography of the show. You can get everyone on the same page about often overlooked items like where the operator will work from. Needing line of sight is obviously crucial for the operator and is often easily accommodated. But the later these kinds of requests are vocalized, the tenser the conversation can be. It is also critical to remember during the site survey that this may be the only chance you get to document the "as-built" that is the actual space. This of course depends on how far you are from the venue and how busy they are in the interim between now and the load-in, but even if it is a space you have daily access to, it can be helpful to behave as though this is your only shot at this. Thinking this way will force you to think your process all the way through earlier in the process than you might otherwise. This is a huge part of proper prior planning. While this might seem like obvious advice, you would be surprised how many completely avoidable mistakes are made simply by not thinking the process all the way through, early and often. These are two phrases you will read many times over the course of this book. "Proper prior planning" and thinking through your system "early and often" will eliminate a vast majority of the most common errors. The site survey is your first check-in point to make sure you have done just that.

Having a well-packed site survey kit will put you on the path to success, and have you looking very professional. A Pelican case or similar is a very appropriate container. You will want something that is robust, has wheels and handles, and can protect your gear. Here is a list of suggested gear, with a brief explanation for each item's inclusion:

- Laptop with drafting software – you will want to reference real life to your digital models.
- Building drawings loaded on laptop – you will forget otherwise. Or the building will not have Wi-Fi. Or you will forget your Dropbox password.
- Power cord for laptop – you will want more time than the battery will provide.

- Mouse for laptop – because no one enjoys, or is good at, drafting with the trackpad.
- Printed drawings on paper of building and/or show – you will want to sketch and take notes in context.
- Vellum – so you can draw lots and lots of options on one set of printed drawings.
- 25 ft or 50 ft extension cord – the outlet will be far away.
- Gaff tape in two or three colors – for marking survey points or tapping out your areas.
- Sharpies in two or three colors – for labeling the gaff tape.
- Pens in two or three colors – for sketching on the drawings or vellum.
- Sketch pad – for when the vellum just won't do.
- Pencils – because we all make mistakes.
- Mark-out chalk or soap stone – to write on the building with.
- Index-card-sized whiteboard (or stack of index cards) – for labeling your pictures. More on this below.
- Thin-point whiteboard markers – for your tiny whiteboard.
- Four 100 ft soft tape measures – for measuring large, critical, dimensions, like the size of the wing of a theatre.
- Two imperial/metric 30 ft tape measures – for measuring smaller, but still critical, dimensions.
- Two Disto Laser measuring devices – for measuring even lager critical dimensions, like the distance from the stage to the underside of the grid.
- Two or three laser plumb bobs – for transferring marks you make on the stage up to the grid, or vice versa.
- Spare batteries for the lasers – because the batteries in the lasers will be dead.
- 200 ft of thin, bright, string – you can lay out anything with enough string and a working knowledge of geometry; ask the ancient Egyptians. Also, with string and any weight (like a stack of washers) you can make an analog plumb bob.
- Digital camera (if you're not going to use your phone as such) – because you can't remember every detail you will see.
- Charging cord for digital camera or phone – you will forget to charge it the night before.
- International travel adaptor – for when you're not in Kansas anymore.

Your list may vary depending on your specific situation, but this a good starting place. For example, if you are going to be outside in bright sunlight, you shouldn't be relying on the lasers to be your main way to measure long distances. In that situation you may want to pack longer soft tapes. Or if you know the nearest outlet is going to be 300 feet away then you should probably pack more extension cords. You should modify this list as needed to suit the specifics of your situation.

Measurements Worth Taking

Now that we have all our gear and we're in the space, what do we do? Simply stated, we want to make sure the documentation of the space that we've been provided with (if any) is accurate, or we want to gather enough information to create that documentation from scratch. For the sake of describing this process we will assume you are surveying a theatre. That said though, the same ideas apply if the space is an arena, stadium, hotel ballroom, or a found space. Depending on the scale of the venue you might simply need more friends or higher-end measuring devices.

One should start by verifying large overall dimensions. Get your gaff tape and your 100 ft soft tapes and measure the width of the proscenium opening. Measure the depth of the stage. Measure the overall size of the wings. Hopefully this all matches what you had been previously given, but more often than not you will already have had your first surprise of the day. This is a great time to break out the vellum and lay it on top of your printed drawings of the theatre to start recording actuals. (For all you readers who have only ever drafted digitally, this is where the concept of "layers" comes from.) Of course, you should also be recording the info into your drafting software of choice. This can sometimes be too time consuming to do *in situ*, so drawing on top of your printed drawings can be much quicker. Be smart though: use the vellum like you would layers in your drafting software. If you don't, by the end of the survey it will be very difficult to read the document anymore!

The next thing you'll want to do is establish a datum point, or a "zero-zero" point. In a theatre the intersection of the proscenium line and the centerline is usually your best bet, but it can vary from situation to situation. Ultimately it doesn't matter where your datum is, as long as you know where it is and you use it in the same way for each measurement. Once this location is established, label it with gaff tape and a Sharpie. Next we'll transfer this datum point up to the grid so we know we're measuring from the same spot up there too. Grab one of your laser plumb bobs. Place it on the dot you made on your datum gaff tape and shoot the point up to the grid. If you're having a very lucky day the dot will be between grid slats, allowing your friend in the grid to find the dot, place a piece of gaff between the two neighboring slats, and mark the same dot on his or her piece of tape. If you're having a more normal kind of day, you will need to direct your friend with your below-the-grid viewpoint to find the slat under which your laser dot is shining.

Next you'll want to shoot a few more points up to the grid to establish three points for the proscenium line and the same for the centerline. This is because you should never ever, under any circumstances, assume the grid was installed square to the stage. Frequently they are not square to each other, and unfortunately most drawings of theatres have them drawn as square. Now, in the grid you can start measuring where critical structures lie. You'll want to measure things like where the loft block beams are, where the headblock beam is, where the grid wells are, if where you're planning on dropping through the grid is actually open, and the location of any immovable obstructions. Take the time to make sure you are measuring square to your two datum lines. This will require some extra friends, but it will pay dividends in the end.

Back on the ground, you can be measuring for smaller and smaller details. If your system will be interacting at all with the counterweight system, figure out if the counterweight rail is parallel to the centerline. Is it on 6 inch or 8 inch centers? T-Track or J-Rail? How tall are the arbors?

Also, at this point on the ground you can lay out the space your system will take out on the stage with gaff tape. This can be very helpful if you are delivering a system to be part of larger show. Showing the Technical Director or Head Rigger the amount of space your system is going to take in the air (by taping it out on the stage floor) can be very illustrative. This can then equip them to have any difficult conversations that need to be had with other individuals or departments that might be affected by our system. Similarly, if you are planning on installing a manually operated system, you should measure and tape out the area in the wings your operators will need. This can be very helpful to show the Technical Director, Stage Manager, or on smaller productions the Show Director, how much of the wing you are going to need. Again, sometimes these conversations can be tense, but it's always far better to have them early.

This should continue until you are satisfied you have collected every dimension you are going to need, and several you don't think you will need. Why do that? Because no matter how many dimensions you record, there will be at least one more you wish you had. It is impossible to enumerate specifically every dimension you will need, if for no other reason than every rig is different than the last and the next. Be thorough, be vigilant, be smart, and you'll succeed.

Taking Pictures Worth Taking

A huge advantage we have these days is the ability to take a nearly limitless number of photos of the space and be able to review them instantly. This advantage should not be disregarded. You should take pictures of everything, everything, everything. This approach, however, can have an unintended consequence; a lot of parts of theatres look the same! You will later, when reviewing your photos, be sitting there wondering if you were facing stage right or stage left when you clicked this one. Or which lineset is being shown as having a critical difference. It can be hugely helpful to have a small, index-card-sized, whiteboard with you (Figure 1.1). You can quickly jot notes on it and hold it in the frame of the camera.

Less is more on these labels, for sure. You just want enough info to jog your memory of the vantage point of the photo. For example, "Facing SR" could

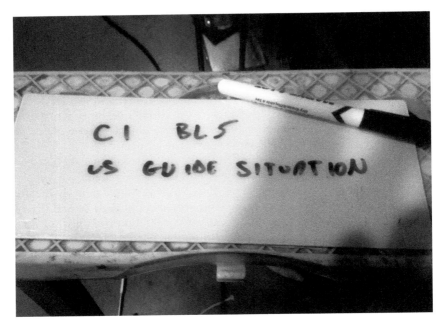

Figure 1.1   Whiteboard in Photo

be exactly the kind of thing you might want clarification on later. Or "SR1 Beam". Or "Lineset 32, Well 3".

Another common mistake in site survey photos is the classic disembodied tape measure showing a critical dimension (Figure 1.2).

This is so very close to being helpful. Sadly though, we don't know where the measurement is being taken from! Was it from the outside edge of the piece? Or was it from the inside face of the outer-most part? Or the datum? Or that bar across the street with all the cheesy stuff on the walls? We may never know! Always either back the camera up to include the starting point of the tape measure, or use your mini whiteboard to enumerate this detail. Remember when taking these photos that, besides your memory, these images will be all you have to find some details you didn't know to look for at the time of the survey.

Conclusion

All this planning can seem daunting. Frankly, it can be! Again though, simply by thinking through our system early and often we are at least half-way to successfully executing on proper prior planning. All of these steps help us turn unknowns into knowns. Don't be afraid to come out of this planning phase with a solid list of unknowns. Instead, be afraid of coming out of this part of the process *without* a list of unknowns. Unknown unknowns are a very dangerous thing indeed. But if we know the things we haven't yet figured out, we can set on figuring out answers to those too.

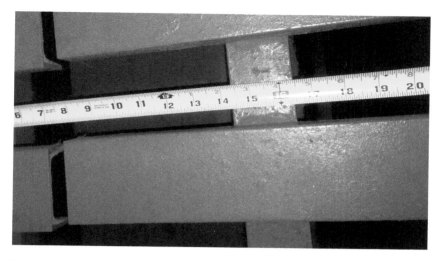

Figure 1.2 Disembodied Tape Measure (this is not helpful)

Takeaways: Beginners

- Take the time to decide if you should do a performer flying effect at all, and if you decide to move forward, should you get help?
- Be secure in verbalizing what you don't know. Take active steps to fill in those gaps.
- Think through the system early and often.
- Never underestimate or underthink the risks of a performer flying system.

Takeaways: Professionals

- Don't be afraid to call meetings with everyone involved to baseline expectations. Write them down and circulate them as a "spec".
- Plan hard. Plan early. Plan often.
- Risk assessment/risk reduction is a crucial part of a well-executed performer flying rig.
- "A Sil-3 System" is a gross oversimplification of a complicated process.

2 Design and Fabrication

Now that we've spent all that time meticulously planning our rig it's finally time to go design and build it! You may well be your own mechanical designer and fabricator for your effect, but making sure you have the requisite knowledge and skills to design and build such a system should be as stringently applied to yourself as you would apply it to someone else you are hiring to do this work for you. Don't let ego get in the way of recognizing there are things you don't fully understand, if that is the case. This is not an area of entertainment where we want to bite off more than we can chew. Assuming that you might have a team you are directing, or a vendor you've hired to design and/or build this system, you will want to make sure that both halves of that equation are involved early and often. Constant open communication across the entire team, but particularly between the design and fabrication teams, is key to success.

The Design Spiral

Do not make the mistake of thinking of the creation of a flying effect as linear. It cannot and should not be thought of as progressing in a straight line as time passes, or as you might draw it out as a simple timeline. Think of it instead as a spiral getting smaller and smaller as it gets to the center; the center in this case representing completion of design. During each trip around the circle all parts of the design need to be thought about and developed equally, the details getting further refined on each concentric trip around the spiral. To put it artistically, you want to paint with finer and finer brushes as the design goes on without having to pick up a bigger brush you were otherwise done with. If Assembly 1 is at the chip brush level of detail, you better not still have the roller out for Assembly 2. It can be helpful to make a chart with different colored circles to help you make sure you are not over-developing one part of your system while neglecting another (Figure 2.1).

This does not have to be a particularly fancy chart. Just something quick and dirty to help you keep your eyes on the bigger picture while keeping your

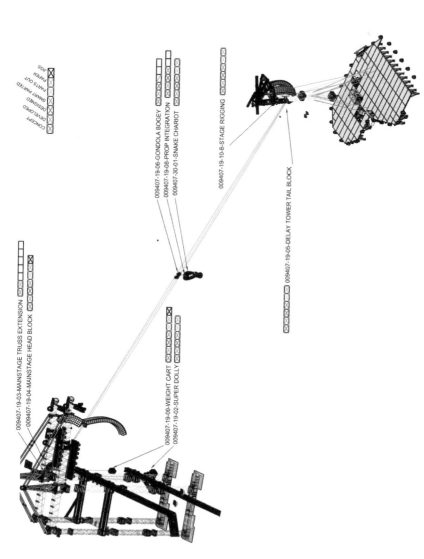

Figure 2.1 Progress Chart

head down and focusing. The reason for this approach to design is simple. If you fully develop one part of the system without regard for the rest, you will inevitably box yourself into a corner with what was a seemingly benign decision you had made previously. You will then find yourself designing a very-silly-looking assembly or making what you know is a less-than-optimal design choice in the name of accommodating an earlier choice that is already too developed to change now.

These kinds of mistakes can be avoided simply by reimagining spatially our view of design. It is not, or should not, be considered a continuous march through linear time. Instead we want to equally develop all parts of the system at the same time. Avoid the temptation to have blinders on when thinking about design this way. Do not have a spiral going for the lifting machine and a separate spiral going on for something as seemingly innocuous as the packaging of your system. You might think these two items don't really affect each other and that these spirals can be separated from each other, each sitting at different moments on a timeline. This is a classic mistake. Your Design Spiral, to be as effective as possible, should include every single part of your system. Each decision and compromise will inform another on another assembly or phase of the project. Thinking of them all together and keeping them all equally developed will only serve to make your final product a better solution.

Machine Design/Selection

While dissecting every possible decision along the way through design would be an encyclopedia-sized book on its own, there are several key concepts that inform each of those decisions. The most common mistakes found in the wild are results of forgetting, or willfully ignoring, these fundamentals. The value in frequent, fervent, and thorough design reviews along the path from blank sheet to finished design cannot be overstated. These are easy to blow off, or not even think of, as they can be seen as a waste of time. This can be especially true if you are wearing all the hats, and are therefore reviewing your own work! Assuming you work with at least one other human, it is important to foster a culture of peer review among your performer flying team. No one knows everything, and no one is incapable of being wrong. If you start believing either of those things of yourself, you are quite simply no longer of any use to this industry. This is a serious risk among riggers in particular and must be kept in check!

When your team believe in the value of peer review you can run periodic design reviews without the fear of anyone's feelings being hurt. Having reviews at all is important enough, but the demeanor of these meetings is just as critical. It is important to run these meetings with an expectation that the design doesn't work. If you run these meetings as though everything is great and we're all geniuses, details will be glossed over and mistakes will be missed.

If, instead, you run the meeting as though the design has no hope of ever working, you will succeed in picking it apart to a reasonable level of detail, increasing your odds of success.

Fundamental #1: Factor of Safety

A factor of safety is the relationship between the forces we will exert on a component and the force at which that component fails. There are many feelings out there as to which term is the best to use to express this idea. Some use "factor of safety", others use "safety factor", and still others use "design factor". The reasons for these affiliations are usually semantic in nature. "Factor of safety", for example, is the "correct" textbook verbiage for this concept. "Safety factor" is a shortened version of this used colloquially in the field. Some, rightfully, point out that using the word "safety" in any term to describe this concept may give the uninitiated user of this equipment a false sense of safety if these concepts are followed, and so land on "design factor". Regardless of your term of choice, this concept is usually expressed as a ratio. So, when we say we're using a 10:1 factor of safety, this means the load we will put on the component in question is one-tenth of its minimum breaking strength. It's important to emphasize the last part of that sentence: factors of safety are calculated off a component's minimum breaking strength, not their working load limit (commonly abbreviated as "WLL"). The difference between the WLL and its minimum breaking strength is the safety factor from the manufacturer. If you then apply your 10:1 safety factor to the manufacturer's WLL, that is how you end up with a shackle the size of your head to fly a 90-pound acrobat. You have made an unnecessarily huge safety factor by not fully understanding the math you were doing. Instead, working from the manufacturer's published minimum breaking strength, we then apply our 10:1 safety factor. Normally our WLL will now be less than the manufacturer's published WLL. This means we are applying a larger safety factor than the manufacturer; always a good sign.

Does every component need to have a 10:1 factor of safety? The short answer is no, but it's important to fully understand what you are talking about before making such a blanket statement. According to the Entertainment Services & Technology Association's (ESTA's) E1.43–2016 Performer Flying Systems standard (which is also known as ANSI [American National Standards Institute] E1.43–2016), harnesses, quick-release hardware, load-bearing hardware, and flexible lifting media should all be designed with a 10:1 on the WLL, 6:1 for characteristic loads, and 3:1 for peak loads. Static load-bearing components, however, need only be designed at a 6.67:1 for the WLL, 4:1 for characteristic, and 2:1 for peak. Static load-bearing components are parts of your system that will be loaded by the rig, but are considered more redundant in nature. Examples cited by ESTA are things like winch frames, sheave block support frames, and support trusses. So, clearly, simply starting with a mandate like "Everything will be 10:1" can result in unnecessarily heavy, cumbersome, and/or over-built components. Another common error is to only focus on the 10:1 portion because it's the biggest number. In reality, the mandate for a 3:1 factor of safety on peak loads can often be the main driver for sizing components. This is because peak loads include the maximum e-stop force your system can create. Multiplying that force by 3 is often a bigger number than multiplying your WLL by 10! (A deeper discussion of e-stops and forces can be found in Chapter 5.)

Fundamental #2: D:d Ratio

Another key ratio to keep an eye on is that of D:d. This is the relationship between the diameter of the lifting media (represented by the lowercase *d*) and the diameter of the sheave, drum, or other objects around which it is bending (represented by the uppercase *D*).

There's some big vocab in that last sentence; don't be intimidated. *Lifting media* is just a fancy way to say "rope". That said, using the term "lifting media" casts a broader net. This means we are talking about wire rope or fabric rope or literally any form of rope you are using. *Sheave* is a fancy sailing word for a pulley. It is quite simply a wheel which we are using to redirect the path of our lifting media.

This ratio is also often expressed with a slash between the letters, as "D/d", which happens to also be exactly how to calculate your D:d ratio. How convenient! So a quarter-inch rope bent around a 5 inch-diameter sheave has a D:d ratio of 20:1. The recommended minimum D:d ratio varies by manufacturer and material, but there are some universal truths regardless. Long story short, the biggest D:d ratio that you can reasonably accommodate should be used. The smaller the D:d ratio, the faster the rope will wear out. At small enough values it can also start to reduce the breaking strength of the rope! To take it to an edge case, if you bend our quarter-inch rope from above around something that is quarter-inch in diameter, which would mean you have a D:d ratio of 1:1, the strands on the outside of the rope have much farther to stretch then the strands in the middle. The strands on the inside of the bend are equally and oppositely being crunched. This difference in material reaction causes the rope to break at a lower breaking strength than published. This is, needless to say, very bad.

Common D:d ratios in performer flying are in the 20s or greater. As we can see in Figure 2.2, this is around the point at which we do not see huge gains for increasing the size of our sheaves and drums.

(Please note: Figure 2.2 is not for any particular rope; instead it is meant to be illustrative – and illustrative *only* – of an exponential curve common to many popular performer flying ropes in use today. When designing a system, the specific chart for your chosen lifting media should be used.)

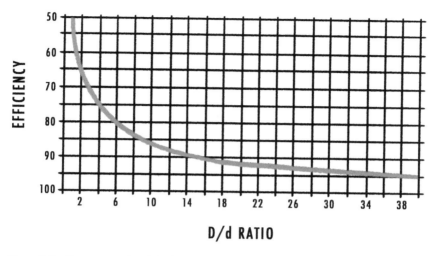

Figure 2.2 Representational D:d Chart

So why would you ever drop below these numbers in the 20s and greater? Well, sometimes these machines need to fit in smaller spaces than those that would be considered ideal. Reducing the D:d should always be on the last-resort list, but can be done. What is important is that the decision to reduce the D:d ratio below a normal range be an intentional one, and only used after all concerned parties are aware of that change. In this case you would want all concerned parties in your design group to agree to the change as well as your Flying Director. Again, you may be wearing all those hats for this production. Just make sure your current self and your future self agree with the decision. As this design choice is adding a risk that would otherwise not exist, this choice should be added to the RA/RR paperwork, and mitigations for this decision clearly enumerated.

While not explicitly related to D:d, one other common design mistake that can be exacerbated by it is reverse bending. This is where the lifting media is wrapped one direction around one sheave and then bent in the opposite direction around a neighboring sheave (Figure 2.3).

Wire rope manufacturers will tell you that the minimum distance between the exit of the first sheave and the entrance of the second sheave is one lay of the cable. A lay is the distance down the cable it takes for one strand to wrap all the way around the outside of the cable. This is true when a reasonable D:d is employed. The smaller your D:d the larger the distance you will need between sheaves to avoid the ill-effects of reverse bending, among which are reduced breaking strength, decreased rope lifespan, and birdcaging. (For a deeper discussion of wire rope construction, please see Chapter 10.)

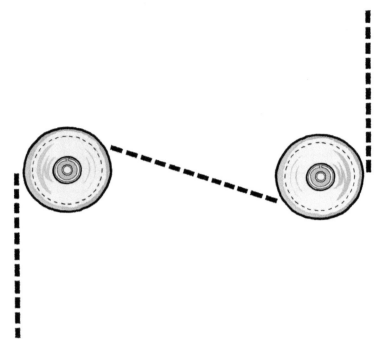

Figure 2.3   Reverse Bending

Fundamental #3: Duty Cycle

How long is the production to go on? How many minutes or hours does the rig run per show? How many shows per day are expected? These are the kinds of questions that are important not to lose sight of when designing. While no dangerous decision should ever be made, if you are designing a machine for a one-off it may be more acceptable to dip below your usual D:d because the effects on the lifespan of the rope are irrelevant to this application. Flipping the same coin over, looking at a rig that will be used many times per day, every day, forever (better known as a theme park show), you may want to consider the material interactions of your sheave material against your lifting media more than you would for a one-off. Nylatron against Amsteel rope, for example, is no big deal when the rope is being changed every 40 hours of run time on an arena touring production, but take that same material interaction to a theme park show, where the rope will be changed once every six months and the rig is run 27 times a day, and you will learn that Nylatron may not dissipate heat well enough to not degrade the rope slowly over time. In this specific case aluminum sheaves would be a better choice.

There are no hard and fast rules about managing the results of duty cycle. It is simply another design criteria to not lose sight of while you're down in the weeds of design. Unfortunately, the effects of duty cycle are often best studied after the rig exists. Sending rope out for break testing *after* it has been through the wringer on your rig is one of the best ways to know how well (or poorly) your system was designed for how it's being used.

Fundamental #4: Redundancy

To be succinct: single points of failure are dangerous and should be avoided in the design phase. Sometimes this is obvious. It is doubtful, for example, that anyone would draw a plate mounted to a grid with a single bolt, even if that one bolt could hold it. It makes our collective Spidey Senses tingle. Instead we draw these plates with two or more bolts. It just looks and feels better. As a result, if a technician in the field forgets to tighten one of the bolts, we're still covered. Redundancy at work! A less obvious example though might be avoiding welds that will be held in tension. This design concept results in more accidents than can be accurately expressed. It is a common error in video wall headers, for example. These welds are in a situation where as long as they are all there and working, everything will be okay. Yes, any one weld can hold the load it will see locally. Incorrectly, its neighboring welds are often seen as adding redundancy to the system. In fact, we've created a situation where we have no redundancy at all. If one weld fails, the load per weld goes up on the failed weld's neighbors. As a result, they fail, adding even more load to their neighbors, who fail even faster. This failure mode is often referred to as "unzipping" and eventually results in the load falling from the sky. Instead of relying on welds in tension, we should design those connections so that the welds are in compression, or are backed-up (or replaced) by a bolted connection.

If we are mounting our system to a truss and lifting it with chain motors, we should also think about redundancy in our motor spacing on the truss. What happens if one of the motors we're using to lift our truss in place fails and the technician continues to move with the rest of the motors? If the answer is "It falls out of the sky" then we have a problem. As you are might be aware, this is a situation that happens with some regularity out on the road. As such, we should design the system so that it doesn't collapse if the prescribed span becomes longer. This doesn't mean we need to design for the system to fully function when missing a motor (although if possible, do it!), but rather that the system doesn't fall out of the sky if it's missing a motor. In that case you only need to concern yourself with the self-weight of the system and the stopping force of the chain motors, but not the e-stop force of your performer flying rig.

Fundamental #5: Serviceability

Can you get that wrench into the machine where you need to? How about after we put the winch in its truss? Can you still get that wrench where you need to? That belt that needs to be replaced every so often: can it be removed without taking the whole winch apart? It's not that hard, you say? Why don't you come up here 60 feet in the air and do it by *yourself* without dropping anything? Long story short, friends: don't forget that people need to interact with your creation! Make sure hands and tools can get to where they need to. Make sure parts can be removed without taking the entire machine apart. Make sure the critical parts identified in your RA/RR can easily be seen so they can be inspected on the regular interval you are prescribing.

Don't think that you need to come up with all these fixes and catch all these mistakes on your own. This is why you do regular and robust design reviews! Get your friends, peers, and critics in a room and have them pick apart your design. Don't take it personally; rather, use these meetings as motivation to catch these things before the rest of the team. And if you miss one, simply take the note and don't make the same mistake again in the future!

Automated Machine Selection, or Chain Motors versus Winches

If you decide to make the leap to an automated system, the very next debate will be "Chain motors or winches?" Chain motors usually jump out to an early lead in these debates as they are often cheaper, simpler, and more people understand how to troubleshoot them. More people also understand how to set up a system of chain motors, as this is common practice for most entertainment riggers. When you start to dig into the situation though, chain motors are rarely the right solution. For starters, very few chain motors are compliant with current codes for performer flying. While you would be correct in saying, "I've got well more than a 10:1 safety factor when I hang a 90-pound acrobat from a 1-ton chain motor", the requisite factor of safety is not the only thing that makes a machine worthy of performer flying. Chain motors often are missing features a performer flying machine is supposed to have. Most notably in this scenario: dual brakes. While a detailed explanation of why performer flying machines have dual brakes can be found in Chapter 6, the reason is quite simple, and has already been discussed in this chapter: redundancy. Everything about performer flying design is set up to mitigate catastrophic failure. Most chain motors, aside from being specifically enumerated "not for performer flying" by their manufacturers, only have one brake and are therefore unfit for service of this kind. That said, certain manufacturers do make chain motors specifically with performer flying in mind. They are usually then bought and modified by other companies to run natively on the second company's automation platform. Surely then, these are good to go, right? As these machines are expressly designed to meet various performer flying codes across the world, they are *acceptable* for performer flying from a code-compliance standpoint, but they might still not be the right tool for the job. They are often like using a flat-head screwdriver to open a paint can. It's not that it won't work, but perhaps there is something out there more suited for the task. If you have sold yourself on the concept of using a chain motor as a performer flying machine, what is your rescue plan? No chain motor manufacturer has a way to bypass the brakes to lower a stranded performer (in a controlled fashion) in the event of a power outage. This is one of the go-to rescue plans for power outage scenarios and as a result if one is to use chain motors for performer flying, one must also have a plan to get a stranded performer down in this scenario. (A more detailed discussion of rescue can be found in Chapter 12.)

Speed is also often an issue with chain motors. If the effect in question is to be quite dynamic, a chain motor is rarely the right choice. The overall idea of a chain motor is to lift something heavy, slowly. Samples that have been converted for performer flying then follow a similar path. They will reliably lift a lot of load, but rarely do so quickly. So, if speed is what you're after, look elsewhere. Also, generally speaking, if a swinging flight is what you're after, look elsewhere. Chain motors are designed to lift something straight up and down. They are not made to handle pendulum flights at all. So, while their simplicity can be attractive, it is also often their undoing.

Chain motors also do not store their lifting media in a particularly refined way. The unused chain simply piles into a bag connected to the motor. As we have all seen with motors that are simply lifting inanimate objects straight up and down this chain can, in the right circumstances, "run" out of the bag. A loud yell of "CHAIN RUNNING" is made in this scenario and all the workers nearby run away from it to avoid getting hit by the falling chain or whipped by the end of the chain should it also come crashing down. Now imagine how that same scenario might play out if you were in mid-air connected to the chain motor with the running chain.

None of this is meant to rule out chain motors. There are instances where the time and money savings are not outweighed by their drawbacks, or those drawbacks can easily be mitigated in this specific use case. Just like every other decision in a performer flying rig, it's important to understand the full picture before starting down a path. See the whole board; nothing is "just" anything.

Winches, or "hoists" as ESTA prefers they be called, from reputable flying companies do not come with such concerns. Unfortunately though, there are plenty of people and companies that purport themselves to be reputable when in fact they are not. For a detailed discussion of every feature a proper performer flying machine should have please refer to Chapter 6, but to speak briefly and broadly here, your winch should have a grooved a drum for positional accuracy and repeatability, fail-safe limit switches at both ends of travel, redundant fail-safe brakes, a servomotor, and redundant encoders. To be even more succinct, the winch in question should not be a product mainly advertised for dragging vehicles out of ditches.

Properly designed winches also allow for the most freedom in the design of your system. Like chain motors, winches are only designed to lift things straight up and down. Fortunately, there are common and easy design solutions to allow for pendulum and conic flight patterns with winches. (A full discussion of these features can be found in Chapter 7.) Winches can be placed nearly anywhere in a venue, with the lifting media coming off of them then routed to wherever in the venue their services are needed. The usefulness of this feature cannot be overstated. A well-designed system will have the winch placed somewhere equally accessible for the gag to function as for maintenance, cable runs, and rescue. The only limiting factor here can be something known as "fleet angle". Since all proper performer flying machines have grooved drums to allow for positional accuracy and repeatability, the management of the lifting media as it moves across the drum is a crucial design factor.

Fleet Angle

Fleet angle, as far as the rigging wing of the entertainment industry is concerned, is the angle at which the lifting media hits a deviation point. This can be the angle at which the media hits a grooved drum, enters or exits a sheave, or other deviations. This should be kept to less than 1.5 degrees to maintain the full breaking strength of the rope, for its full lifespan, without damaging the rope or the deviation point it is in contact with. Exactly what wears first, and how quickly, will vary depending on the two materials coming into contact with each other. For example, steel wire rope hitting an aluminum sheave at an excessive fleet angle will have a different failure mode than a fabric rope hitting a steel sheave with the same excessive fleet angle. The combinations are endless; what's important is to know the symptoms

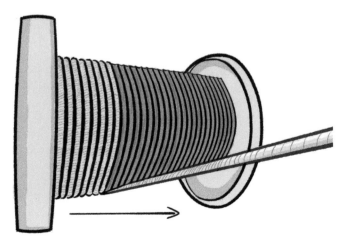

Figure 2.4   Rope Travel on Grooved Drum

and outcomes of your system's particular pairing. Excessive fleet through the rigging system, from sheave to sheave, can almost always be eliminated by a good site survey and building extra adjustment into your sheave's mountings. But this is not the problem this section is here to discuss. Instead, we are talking about the moving target that is the position of the rope on your grooved drum. How much physical distance the rope will traverse across the drum is a function of how much lift you need and the diameter of the drum itself (Figure 2.4).

The bigger the diameter of the drum, the more rope it can take up in a single rotation. The more rope that drum can take up in a single rotation, the fewer wraps the rope needs to make around the drum to achieve your full travel. The fewer the wraps around the drum, the less distance the rope will travel down the length of the drum. The opposite is true of smaller-diameter drums. Of course, there are often limiting factors for the diameter of a drum, "Where does the winch have to fit?" being the first one that springs to mind. If your winch needs to fit through a standard doorway at any point in its life, then your drum can only be so big! Once you establish the diameter of drum, taking into account factors like D:d ratio and the overall size constraints of our machine, it is important to know how far the rope will travel across the drum so that you can mitigate the fleet angle throughout its travel. This is simply a matter of making sure the first sheave the rope will contact after it leaves the drum is far enough away that, at the most extreme angle of contact, you are still below 1.5 degrees. This can be achieved with simple triangle math (Figure 2.5).

The first trick here is to plan for the first sheave to be in the middle of the rope's travel across the drum instead of off to one side of it. This sets you up to have zero fleet angle in the middle of the drum's travel, which will likely be where the machine will spend most of its time working. Secondly, this means the sheave only has to be half as far away as it would have to be if you mounted it in line with the extreme end of the drum. Since you know the length of the drum (or half the length, in this case) you can then determine

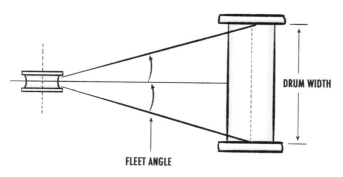

Figure 2.5   Fleet Math Illustration

Figure 2.6　Mod Winch Drum
Credit: Jason Shupe

the minimum distance away the sheave must be to keep the angle the rope hits the drum at below 1.5 degrees. You now know how far away your winch and your sheave must be! Depending on the size of your drum and needed travel, this can be quite a distance. For example, if you have an 8-foot-long drum (Figure 2.6), and you will be using all 8 feet of it, you would need to be more than 150 feet away to maintain an acceptable fleet angle. Clearly, this would be an important fact to know early, and to plan around!

But what if this minimum distance we've discovered is too great? Are we doomed to replace our lifting media all the time because our system will eat it at a rapid pace? Fortunately, there is a fix for this: the zero-fleet winch. Conceptually, a zero-fleet winch's special power is that the lifting media always exits the winch in the same place, negating the need to solve the fleet angle issue by placing the first sheave a specific distance away from the machine. While there are many different ways to achieve this particular brand of magic, all the solutions tend to fall into two camps.

The first (Figure 2.7) adds additional sheaves to the winch that run back and forth along the drum via a lead screw tied to the drivetrain of the winch. This internal zero-fleet then moves automatically every time and any time the drum moves. Through a precise design process, the lead screw and sheave size are designed to stay perfectly in time with the grooves of the drum, ensuring there is never any fleet between the drum and this first sheave.

Figure 2.7   Internal Zero-Fleet Winch

The end result is that the lifting media always exits the winch in the same spot in space, the winch having internally resolved its own fleet angle issues. Downsides to this plan include the increased complexity in design as well as the additional sheaves, and other components, needed to achieve it. The additional deviations the lifting media takes results in additional line weight needed on the performer end of the line to ensure the winch runs flawlessly without the performer load on it. Similarly, every additional component adds friction to the system, causing the same need for additional line weight, which can be quite an eyesore for the artistic team.

The second solution is far more obtuse, but achieves the same effect. You can use the same concept of a lead screw to drag the entire winch back and forth in a track. For example, in Figure 2.8 all of the machinery highlighted moves back and forth in the aluminum track being driven by the motion of the drum bearing on the lead screw. Here, instead of the grooves of the drum forcing the rope to move back and forth, as would be the case in a non–zero-fleet winch, the winch drags its whole self back and forth so the rope can stay in the same place in space. Downsides of this design include additional maintenance of the track system and the overall length of the winch. Since the whole drivetrain has to move back and forth the full length of the drum, the total length of your machine is nearly double what it would otherwise need to be.

Figure 2.8   External Zero-Fleet

While neither design is perfect, both having their unique idiosyncrasies, a solution in either family is far more malleable than a non-zero-fleet winch. Zero-fleet winches can be packaged into smaller machines and into smaller spaces than their less complicated brothers. Since these machines internally resolve the whole problem of fleet angle they also remove one of the greatest risks to the health of your lifting media.

Engineering Review

When designing a system from scratch it is important, critical in fact, to have a third-party engineering firm go over your design with a fine-toothed comb. Aside from the obvious reason that we all make mistakes and it's nice to have someone review your work, the reality of today's litigious society cannot be ignored. A huge benefit to having a third-party, licensed engineer review and stamp your work is that you have now spread the liability around should something, God forbid, go horribly wrong. All current performer flying standards also require an engineer's stamp on some or all components/systems to be considered good to go and compliant. The addition of this wrinkle to the plan can often frustrate people. It can be seen as adding undue cost, time, and/or complexity to a project. People who build props for performers to be flown on are often the most put off by the suggestion of their element needing to be engineered. The bottom line is, inarguably, the entire chain of custody of the flying performer must be engineered to the standards of the day to withstand the force the system will put into it. This goes from the facility impact all the way to the performer and encompasses everything in between. As the saying goes, "A chain is only as strong as its weakest link", and in this case all the links must be verified to be of sufficient strength.

A great way to know if you or someone else truly understands the performer flying system is to ask yourself/them, "What is the weakest link in the system?" Even after engineering review and even if all the components are of a sufficient strength, there will still be a weakest link. If the person you are asking this question of, yourself included, cannot immediately answer this one it means they/you have not thought through the system well enough yet. Being able to cite this component rapidly, and at will, is a sure sign you know your rig.

It is important to understand what kind of relationship you have established with the engineering company on a given project. Often they are contracted to review strength of materials and code compliance. They are not by default going to check whether or not your machine will actually work. They can, and gladly will, provide that service for an additional fee but will not automatically be reviewing to that level of detail. Make sure you know what they are providing versus what you are expecting. Put another way: this is another area where scope gap can be an issue. If you want or need their help with a mechanical evaluation, talk about that early and often to make sure everyone is on the same page. It is best to get them involved early and often. In fact, a check-in with your engineer should be considered part of every trip around the Design Spiral we spoke about earlier. This is helpful for two main reasons:

1. One of the biggest hurdles in working with engineers is getting them to understand the conceptual design of your plan. It is obvious to you because you have been involved in every decision that got us to this point. Your engineer, though, only having whatever documentation you've produced to this point, may not immediately understand how you are achieving your design intent. The earlier you involve them, and the more revisions they see, the better chance they have to really understand what you are attempting.

2. If you've started walking down a path that will never work, it's best to know as early as possible. For example, if you decided to build a component out of quarter-inch plate, but that is going to fail no matter what you do to it, it's better to know after one trip around the Design Spiral than after four trips. Needing to change a plate thickness by some amount is among the top causes of needing to all but start over in machine design.

The cause of most people's issues when working with engineers is that they have no vocabulary with which to defend their design choices. Not every organization is blessed to have engineer on staff to pre-check their decisions, in fact very few are, but the more math you can do in advance of showing your work to an engineer, the better off your design will be. Engineers, understandably, approach a new design from a very "This will never work" point of view. As a result, they almost always will want various material and component choices to be beefier than you have chosen. If you have an educated comeback as to why you have chosen a given material or component it can go a long way towards avoiding redesigning your initial choice. Eventually though, even with your homework done, you may hit a wall where an engineer says that something will absolutely 100% fail if you even look at it wrong, when in fact you have been using that same something for years successfully and safely. The good news here is engineers love real-world data to supplement their assumptions. Talk with your engineer and agree on a set of testing parameters and how to record them. Then execute and document those tests. Assuming you were right, that a given material/component/assembly/machine can take whatever test you throw at it, your engineer will gladly acquiesce to your original plans. If, on the other hand, your chosen item fails the tests, you get to feel like the money you are paying your engineer is money well spent.

In the end, the goal of this relationship is to have a stamped set of drawings. This will give you, your client, your performers, and Authorities Having Jurisdiction peace of mind that your system will perform safely. All this discussion of design and engineering may seem like it doesn't apply to you if you only ever rent a system from a vendor. While the particulars of the design may be above your head, insisting on receiving a copy of the stamped engineering book from your vendor will show them that you know what you're talking about. If they cannot provide it, this is your opportunity to move on from a clearly unsafe or overwhelmed vendor.

Fabrication

After we've spec-ed every nut and bolt and our plans through the design and design review process we can finally start building it! Having a pool of experienced fabricators to draw from is an asset that cannot be overstated. At the very least, your fabrication team leader should have experience with all of the components he or she is expected to oversee, as well as an excellent foundational knowledge of the concepts being applied in this particular design. Bringing your fabrication lead into your design review meetings with your designers is a huge asset, allowing your fab lead to understand what he or she is looking at before the drawings arrive on the floor. Such reviews can also lead to catching designs that cannot physically be assembled (more common than you might realize), bolts which tools cannot reach, and excellent suggestions on how to streamline the fabrication process.

Certified Welding

Certified welding is not currently a requirement of all relevant standards (ANSI E.143–2016 does require it, for example) but having certified welders can certainly help you sleep better at night whether they are explicitly required. At the very least, having welding standards that closely mirror those of organizations like AWS (the American Welding Society) can help to standardize the documentation and execution of structurally critical welds throughout your system. At the very least, all critical welds should be inspected by a third party. This can be as superficial as a visual examination of each weld but by having a third party, who is theoretically unbiased by your process or timetable, inspect and sign off on your fabricator's work helps to keep everyone honest. Further, since we have elected to become the manufacturer of this assembly, it helps to spread the liability related to the welding performed. This, however, should not be our main motivation in electing to have a third-party inspection of our welding. The value in having an unbiased judge inspect your welds is worth its weight in gold. We all know how timelines in our industry can get, and we are extraordinary at working together towards a common goal. Unfortunately, this can cause us to take an "It'll hold" approach to questionable execution of work in the closing hours of any phase of the project. Someone disinterested in those constraints, with only the quality of the welds as their concern, will always give you honest advice.

Testing: FAT and SAT

Before we send all this equipment out into the world we want to thoroughly test it and make sure it behaves the way we expect it to. This pre-shipping testing is called Factory Acceptance Testing, or FAT for short. This is the formal process of testing and documenting that your machine and system meet a minimum standard for shipping. What is described here is a highly regimented process used in large shops. If you aren't in a position to generate this much paperwork that's okay, although it is highly recommended to do so. What is important is that the spirit of an FAT is followed. We want to make sure we have successfully built the machine according to the design and that the design functions as expected before we ever let it leave our shop!

Prior to being ready to perform the FAT you will need to spell out, on paper, all of the criteria your machine needs to meet to be okayed to be sent out the door. Much like the process of RA/RR, in which we write down every conceivable thing that could go wrong, here we want our FAT to include very obvious things. Sometimes it can seem silly to write down and check that these features are functioning, because they are such basic functions. Some examples in this category are:

Does the disconnect switch kill power to the machine?
Does commanded motion happen correctly?
Does the E- switch show as *E-* in the control software?

Perhaps some less obvious things that should be included in an FAT are:

How much amperage does the machine draw at max speed with max load?
Does each brake, by itself, meet or exceed the needed holding force to be code compliant?
What is the stopping distance when hitting each limit at full speed?

Of course, you are going to check these things, so why do we need to write them down? If we write these things down and have a form to fill out, first and foremost it becomes very difficult to ship a machine *without* all these checks being performed. Even the best of us can forget a step of the process from time to time, and having a sheet with blank spaces waiting for us when we think we're done is very helpful at preventing that simple mistake resulting in an injury later. Further, these filled-out FAT sheets become important legal documentation. If something were to go horrifically wrong while the gear was in use, having filled-out sheets that show a systematic testing procedure exists and was followed can be a very wonderful thing.

In Figure 2.9 we can see a stock FAT sheet for a TAIT T-Winch. The beginning of the sheet, which is a multi-page document, asks the tester to get the identifying numbers off the winch, and to call out what configuration will be tested. (The TAIT T-Winch can do multiple load/speed configurations based on its gearing, which can be changed in the field. As such, this is critical to record.) The sheet then goes through a number of basic function tests, followed by speed testing, dynamic stopping, and brake tests. The last field on the sheet allows the tester(s) to agree that the machine is ready for use, or that it has failed and needs certain repairs before further testing. The sheet also requires the tester(s) to sign their name. The motivation for this comes from the document's future legal use, and to remind the tester(s) that they are personally signing that these tests were completed, and the results recorded accurately.

TAIT TOWERS	**Test Documentation**		
T - Winch			
	FAT Document		

Date				
Axis Name				
Device Type		**T - Winch**		
Tait Employee		Unit Serial Number		
Config		300# @ 10ft/sec or 540# @ 5ft/sec		

All testing should be performed in a safe manner with proper precautions taken to protect those working in or around the testing area. Winches may be configured slightly differently from one another and fields that do not apply to a particular Winch should be marked N/A in the pass fail column.

Test/Inspection Item	Tested Value	Pass/Fail	Notes
1: Physical Inspection - Pre-Power Up			
General Construction inspection			
All mounting hardware is present			
All external labels are applied and			
All wiring is routed cleanly and appropriately secured			
All electrical connections are secure			
Beckhoff Slices			Installed Beckhoff slices match the schematic and have been addressed properly
Hot glue or silicone has been applied Beckhoff cards to secure them			
One NAV:COM port is present free of			

Figure 2.9   Sample FAT Document

Winch frame is free of visible defects			Inspect winch frame for cracked welds, or bent sections that may pose a risk to operation
Power LED is present, free of damage, and clearly labeled			LED should be blue in color
Four limit LEDs are present, free of damage, and clearly labeled			LEDs should be Red or Yellow in color
Rating Label			A label specifying rated speed and capacity is present and easily read
2 : Input Testing - General Motion			
E-Stop Limit Minus *Enter strike Position Above*			When struck triggers the proper alarm and inhibits motion in either direction
Hard Limit Minus *Enter strike Position Above*			When struck triggers the proper alarm and inhibits motion in the negative direction
Soft Minus *Enter Soft Limit Position Above*			When struck triggers the proper alarm and inhibits motion in the negative direction
Soft Plus *Enter Soft Limit Position Above*			When struck triggers the proper alarm and inhibits motion in the positive direction
Hard Limit Plus *Enter strike Position Above*			When struck triggers the proper alarm and inhibits motion in the positive direction
E-Stop Limit Plus *Enter strike Position Above*			When struck triggers the proper alarm and inhibits motion in either direction
Brake Lift			Brakes lift when commanded to-do so from Navigator and Brake Sense Status changes
Brake Release			Ensure when 24VDC is applied to pins 1 and 2 of the Brake Release port, the motor brake releases
General Motion Testing			Axis, starts, stops and moves in the intended direction when commanded to do so from Navigator
Jogging: Speed and Travel			Unit can jog at rated speed in both directions smoothly and without error
Primary Encoder Scaling *Enter Scale Factor Above*			Physical distance traveled matches reported distance in navigator
Secondary Encoder Scaling *Enter Scale Factor Above*			Physical distance traveled matches reported distance in navigator
Velocity Reference *Enter Scale Factor Above*			Physical Speed achieved matches reported speed in navigator
Load Cell Scaling *Enter Scale Factor Above*			Record the scale factor used to achieve an accurate load reading
Unit Achieves Full Travel *Enter Travel Distance Above*			Record the scaled distance travelled through full stroke of the winch
Position Error Window *Enter Position Error Setting Above*			Ensure the position error window is not bypassed and record the maximum allowed position error
Position Error Window			Ensure the position error window is not bypassed when testing is complete
Zero Speed Enable			The unit should enable and not move while fully loaded

Figure 2.9   Sample FAT Document (Continued)

3: Motion Testing		
Gear Ratio 1		
Rated Speed	**20 FPS**	
Safe Working load	**#150**	
A: Low Speed Testing		
Control Mode	Trapezoidal Cue	
Load		Load should be equal to winch's rated safe working load
Speed Setting		Low Speed Motion is defined as 10% of the units rated speed
	FPS	
Accel	FT/sec^2	
Decel	FT/sec^2	
General Motion Testing		Axis moves smoothly and quietly through full stroke
Travel Distance of Unit in Feet		
Positioning Accuracy		
Forward Travel		Move a distance of at least 10 feet in the forward direction, pass is defined as being within the target window distance of the intended position
Target Window +/- .010 feet	*Record Largest target Error Above*	
Forward Position Achieved		Record the ending position
Reverse Travel		Move a distance of at least 10 feet in the reverse direction, pass is defined as being within the target window distance of the intended position
Target Window +/- .010 feet	*Record Largest target Error Above*	
Reverse Position Achieved		Record the ending position
Positioning Repeatability		
Test #1		Repeat the above forward move 10 times. Pass is defined as being within the baseline window of the 'Forward Position Achieved' on all moves.
Baseline Window +/- .005 feet	*Record Largest target Error Above*	
Test #2		Repeat the above reverse move 10 times. Pass is defined as being within the baseline window of the 'Reverse Position Achieved' on all moves.
Baseline Window +/- .005 feet	*Record Largest target Error Above*	
B: High Speed Testing		
Control Mode	Trapezoidal Cue	
Load		Load should be equal to winch's rated safe working load
Speed Setting		High Speed Motion is defined as 100% of the units rated speed
	FPS	
Accel	FT/sec^2	
Decel	FT/sec^2	
General Motion Testing		Axis moves smoothly and quietly through full stroke
Travel Distance of Unit in Feet		
Positioning Accuracy		
Forward Travel		Move a distance of at least 10 feet in the forward direction, pass is defined as being within the target window distance of the intended position
Target Window +/- .010 feet	*Record Largest target Error Above*	
Forward Position Achieved		Record the ending position
Reverse Travel		Move a distance of at least 10 feet in the reverse direction, pass is defined as being within the target window distance of the intended position
Target Window +/- .010 feet	*Record Largest target Error Above*	
Reverse Position Achieved		Record the ending position

Figure 2.9   Sample FAT Document (Continued)

C: Stop Testing

All stop testing should be performed with load moving in the down direction, please capture a motion graph which clearly shows the point the stop was initiated, time between the stop being initiated and the load coming to a stop. Paste a screen shot of each stops graph in the area provided at the end of each section.

E-Stop

Control Mode	**Trapezoidal Cue**		
Load			Load should be equal to winch's rated safe working load
Speed Setting	FPS		Speed is defined as 100% of the units rated speed
Accel	FT/sec^2		
Decel	FT/sec^2		
Distance Traveled After Stop was Initiated			
Axis Came to a Safe Stop			

Place screen shot of E-Stop graph here, resize picture or cell space as needed

4: Motion Testing
Gear Ratio 2

Rated Speed	**10 FPS**
Safe Working load	**#300**

A: Low Speed Testing

Control Mode	**Trapezoidal Cue**		
Load			Load should be equal to winch's rated safe working load
Speed Setting	FPS		Low Speed Motion is defined as 10% of the units rated speed
Accel	FT/sec^2		
Decel	FT/sec^2		
General Motion Testing			Axis moves smoothly and quietly through full stroke
Travel Distance of Unit in Feet			

Positioning Accuracy

Forward Travel			Move a distance of at least 10 feet in the forward direction, pass is defined as being within the target window distance of the intended position
Target Window +/- .010 feet	*Record Largest target Error Above*		
Forward Position Achieved			Record the ending position
Reverse Travel			Move a distance of at least 10 feet in the reverse direction, pass is defined as being within the target window distance of the intended position
Target Window +/- .010 feet	*Record Largest target Error Above*		

Figure 2.9 Sample FAT Document (Continued)

Forward Position Achieved			Record the ending position
Reverse Travel			Move a distance of at least 10 feet in the reverse direction, pass is defined as being within the target window distance of the intended position
Target Window +/- .010 feet	*Record Largest target Error Above*		
Reverse Position Achieved			Record the ending position
Positioning Repeatability			
Test #1			Repeat the above forward move 10 times. Pass is defined as being within the baseline window of the 'Forward Position Achieved' on all moves.
Baseline Window +/- .005 feet	*Record Largest target Error Above*		
Test #2			Repeat the above reverse move 10 times. Pass is defined as being within the baseline window of the 'Reverse Position Achieved' on all moves.
Baseline Window +/- .005 feet	*Record Largest target Error Above*		
B: High Speed Testing			
Control Mode	**Trapezoidal Cue**		
Load			Load should be equal to winch's rated safe working load
Speed Setting	FPS		High Speed Motion is defined as 100% of the units rated speed
Accel	FT/sec∧2		
Decel	FT/sec∧2		
General Motion Testing			Axis moves smoothly and quietly through full stroke
Travel Distance of Unit in Feet			
Positioning Accuracy			
Forward Travel			Move a distance of at least 10 feet in the forward direction, pass is defined as being within the target window distance of the intended position
Target Window +/- .010 feet	*Record Largest target Error Above*		
Forward Position Achieved			Record the ending position
Reverse Travel			Move a distance of at least 10 feet in the reverse direction, pass is defined as being within the target window distance of the intended position
Target Window +/- .010 feet	*Record Largest target Error Above*		
Reverse Position Achieved			Record the ending position
Positioning Repeatability			
Test #1			Repeat the above forward move 10 times. Pass is defined as being within the baseline window of the 'Forward Position Achieved' on all moves.
Baseline Window +/- .005 feet	*Record Largest target Error Above*		
Test #2			Repeat the above reverse move 10 times. Pass is defined as being within the baseline window of the 'Reverse Position Achieved' on all moves.
Baseline Window +/- .005 feet	*Record Largest target Error Above*		
C: Stop Testing			
All stop testing should be performed with load moving in the down direction, please capture a motion graph which clearly shows the point the stop was initiated, time between the stop being initiated and the load coming to a stop. Paste a screen shot of each stops graph in the area provided at the end of each section.			
E-Stop			
Control Mode	**Trapezoidal Cue**		
Load			Load should be equal to winch's rated safe working load
Speed Setting	FPS		Speed is defined as 100% of the units rated speed

Figure 2.9   Sample FAT Document (Continued)

Accel	FT/sec^2	
Decel	FT/sec^2	
Distance Traveled After Stop was Initiated		
Axis Came to a Safe Stop		

Place screen shot of E-Stop graph here, resize picture or cell space as needed

5: Motion Testing		
Gear Ratio 3		
Rated Speed	5 FPS	
Safe Working load	#540 D/P	
A: Low Speed Testing		
Control Mode	Trapezoidal Cue	
Load		Load should be equal to winch's rated safe working load
Speed Setting	FPS	Low Speed Motion is defined as 10% of the units rated speed
Accel	FT/sec^2	
Decel	FT/sec^2	
General Motion Testing		Axis moves smoothly and quietly through full stroke
Travel Distance of Unit in Feet		
Positioning Accuracy		
Forward Travel		Move a distance of at least 10 feet in the forward direction, pass is defined as being within the target window distance of the intended position
Target Window +/- .010 feet	*Record Largest target Error Above*	
Forward Position Achieved		Record the ending position
Reverse Travel		Move a distance of at least 10 feet in the reverse direction, pass is defined as being within the target window distance of the intended position
Target Window +/- .010 feet	*Record Largest target Error Above*	
Reverse Position Achieved		Record the ending position
Positioning Repeatability		
Test #1		Repeat the above forward move 10 times. Pass is defined as being within the baseline window of the 'Forward Position Achieved' on all moves.
Baseline Window +/- .005 feet	*Record Largest target Error Above*	
Test #2		Repeat the above reverse move 10 times. Pass is defined as being within the baseline window of the 'Reverse Position Achieved' on all moves.
Baseline Window +/- .005 feet	*Record Largest target Error Above*	

Figure 2.9   Sample FAT Document (Continued)

B: High Speed Testing

Control Mode	**Trapezoidal Cue**		
Load			Load should be equal to winch's rated safe working load
Speed Setting	FPS		High Speed Motion is defined as 100% of the units rated speed
Accel	FT/sec^2		
Decel	FT/sec^2		
General Motion Testing			Axis moves smoothly and quietly through full stroke
Travel Distance of Unit in Feet			

Positioning Accuracy

Forward Travel			Move a distance of at least 10 feet in the forward direction, pass is defined as being within the target window distance of the intended position
Target Window +/- .010 feet	*Record Largest target Error Above*		
Forward Position Achieved			Record the ending position
Reverse Travel			Move a distance of at least 10 feet in the reverse direction, pass is defined as being within the target window distance of the intended position
Target Window +/- .010 feet	*Record Largest target Error Above*		
Reverse Position Achieved			Record the ending position

Positioning Repeatability

Test #1			Repeat the above forward move 10 times. Pass is defined as being within the baseline window of the 'Forward Position Achieved' on all moves.
Baseline Window +/- .005 feet	*Record Largest target Error Above*		
Test #2			Repeat the above reverse move 10 times. Pass is defined as being within the baseline window of the 'Reverse Position Achieved' on all moves.
Baseline Window +/- .005 feet	*Record Largest target Error Above*		

C: Stop Testing

All stop testing should be performed with load moving in the down direction, please capture a motion graph which clearly shows the point the stop was initiated, time between the stop being initiated and the load coming to a stop. Paste a screen shot of each stops graph in the area provided at the end of each section.

E-Stop

Control Mode	**Trapezoidal Cue**		
Load			Load should be equal to winch's rated safe working load
Speed Setting	FPS		Speed is defined as 100% of the units rated speed
Accel	FT/sec^2		
Decel	FT/sec^2		
Distance Traveled After Stop was Initiated			
Axis Came to a Safe Stop			

Place screen shot of E-Stop graph here, resize picture or cell space as needed

Figure 2.9   Sample FAT Document (Continued)

6: Brake Testing		
Static Load Testing		
Load		Load should be equal to 150% winch's rated safe working load
Primary brake	*Enter slip distance Above*	With the other brakes released, allow the rigged load to be held by the remaining brake for a period no less than 2 minutes, record slip distance if any.
Secondary brake	*Enter slip distance Above*	With the other brakes released, allow the rigged load to be held by the remaining brake for a period no less than 2 minutes, record slip distance if any.
Dynamic Load Testing		
Load		Load should be equal to 125% winch's rated safe working load
Primary brake	*stopping distance*	With the other brakes released, allow the rigged load to be held by the remaining brake for a period no less than 2 minutes, record slip distance if any.
Secondary brake	*stopping distance*	With the other brakes released, allow the rigged load to be held by the remaining brake for a period no less than 2 minutes, record slip distance if any.
6: Final Steps		
Appropriate backs have been taken and saved to the show file		

Notes

☐ Equipment accepted as constructed

☐ Equipment accepted with notes

☐ Equipment not accepted, corrections and re-testing required

Accepted by:

Name _____

Signature _____

Figure 2.9   Sample FAT Document (Continued)

Now that we've successfully tested our gear at our shop, we can take it to site and fly people on it, right? Not so fast! After we install it, we need to do Site Acceptance Testing, or SAT. This process can vary wildly based on what kind of job you are doing. At its most stringent the SAT is a thick binder of tests in which you will do everything you did for the FAT again, plus all manner of system testing too. This scenario is common in theme park attractions where the gear is expected to have a heavy duty cycle per day, every day from now until the end of time. As a result, it can be lengthy and tedious to get through. That said, by the end of these SATs everyone is supremely confident in the gear. This, however, is an extreme example. Most SATs need not be this intense; in fact, you may well author your own SAT. This is especially true if you are wearing a lot of, or all, the hats. Much like the FAT, we want to make sure that we have put the system through its paces once installed, and that we have thoroughly documented that testing. Even if your client does not require it, having such documentation to share with them can make you look very professional and make them feel very at ease with your attention to detail. Where FAT often focuses on the individual machines, SAT's unique addition is that of the system as a whole. For example, if you were doing a lift/travel rig of some kind, your FAT would likely only record the correct behavior of the lift axis and the travel axis separate from each other. Your SAT documents would then retest all those functions of the individual machines and then cover their interactions on top of that. In an electrically compensated system, for example, the SAT sheets might be the first place you formally document that you've tested that you can't pull the lift axis through your traversing skate with either axis. (Electrically compensated systems are covered thoroughly in Chapter 8.) Even though the *S* in *SAT* stands for *Site*, it can be helpful to think of it as also standing for *System*.

Installation

Installation of a performer flying system will vary wildly based on all kinds of factors. Is it outdoors or indoors? Is it climate-controlled? Does it have a roof? Does the venue have a dock? Who is getting whatever heavy equipment we might need? Who else's gear are we interacting with? Will they be there? How long do we have to install? What time does the venue go dark for lighting programming? Can we work through it in the dark if we so choose? The list goes on and on. The important thing is to think through your installation process before showing up at the venue. Every single thing is in play here. Think through every step from the gear coming off to the truck to the end of the SAT process. Remember to plan with three criteria in mind:

> Safety
> Sanity
> Comfort

If you think through every step with these criteria as a guiding light, you will be successful every time. Let's break those down further.

Safety is an easy one to remember. Clearly we need to make sure that each step of the install is safe for our staff, everyone else's staff, and the equipment itself. Over-stressing an assembly of our creation while hoisting it up to where it goes because we didn't think all the way through the process is just as bad and unsafe as putting a climber at risk of a fall without a harness. Remember, all we are doing is facilitating the telling of stories. No schedule, deadline, or payday is worth not sending everyone home under their own power at the end of every working day.

Sanity is often forgotten in our industry in the name of time. Or at least it's often blamed on time. In reality, the true culprit is often a lack of proper prior planning. While we, as an industry, pride ourselves on our ability to always come through no matter the circumstances (the show must go on, after all) wouldn't it be great to not have to use those skills all the time? As you are planning your install, really think about how you are going to achieve each step. Don't rely on "That's how we've always done it" thinking. You may well always install this machine this way with these steps, but maybe there's something you saw in your site survey that, upon further review, could reveal to you in advance that your normal plan won't work. Then instead of relying on your masterful problem-solving in the moment, you can plan a sane and safe solution to this anomaly. Often in our planning we also make rash decisions to try and save a buck. Sanity is often lost in the name of not wanting to pay for an additional day with the crane, or not wanting to rent an extra chain motor distro. Rarely does this line of thinking factually pay off. Err on the side of sanity and enjoy a reasonable install period.

Comfort can be a dangerous word in our industry. Used flippantly, people could think you mean that your team will only work six hours a day, and that all your meals must be Kobe steaks. But this is not what we're talking about when we mention comfort. If you are going to be outside, get some sunscreen in advance and put it in the workbox. Also, think about shelter from the sun. Should we get a cheap easy-up tent? We should probably get some tarps in case it rains. Will there be catering the first day we're there? Maybe we should bring some water in a cooler. Is it going to be crazy cold? We should get some hand and foot warmers and throw them in the workbox. Environmental factors are what we should be thinking through, and covering for, when we think about comfort. Thinking about these things in advance will keep your staff happy and rolling no matter what the gig can throw at them. You will end up needing to do these things anyway, so by planning in advance for them you won't be a person down when you send one of your installers out on a run to go pick these items up on Day 1. Equally important when we're talking about comfort is to consider what tasks will be needed, on which days, and for how long. This may seem obvious but especially during the installation phase, when single team members may be wearing multiple hats, you can end up in a position where you are expecting one of your people to work 20 hours a day over and over. This most usually happens with your controls person who, after spending a full day of installing electrical equipment, might then be expected to work all night commissioning machines for the forthcoming SAT. This is not healthy, safe, sane, or comfortable. Noticing these flaws in the schedule early can allow you to spread the installation out over a longer period, or to plan on bringing extra help so you can run a day shift and a separate night shift.

Programming

To this point, we have mainly been concerned with the physical reality of the rig and its impact on the building that will support it. These issues are worthy of a huge portion of our attention, but often leave us with one huge blind spot. All too often we forget that once we get all this equipment safely designed, beautifully constructed, and meticulously tested, we then need to use it to put on a show! The precise process of cuing a show is covered in great depth in Chapter 14, but it is worth discussing broadly here as well. Long story short: programming takes time. To further that point: programming takes the time it takes. Whether it is a manual or an automated system is somewhat irrelevant to remembering to allot for, and constantly advocating the need for, appropriate and focused time for these endeavors.

The first concept to understand is that you will need an adequate amount of time from the end of your SAT to the first time you are to work with the performers. The moment testing is done, it's all too easy to think you are instantly ready to put performers on the rig. This could not be further from the truth! First we need to program (in the case of an automated system) or practice (in the case of a manual one) our show moves as we currently understand them. We want to have adequate time set aside for these technical rehearsals so that we have an opportunity to learn the idiosyncrasies of our system and, further, do so with an inanimate object on the end of our system, namely a sandbag. We don't want a living, breathing, human to be the first object on our rig. Of course, we did everything to this point flawlessly and everything is going to function perfectly, but on the off chance that's not entirely true, wouldn't it be better to find out with a big sack of sand instead of a big sack of organs?

Not only do we want to find out if we've made any critical errors, but we also want to make sure anything we are going to put a performer on has been tested and validated as safe first. Never, under any circumstances, do we want to be in a situation where we are editing cues or changing the plan while we have a human on the line. Needing to make changes is a normal part of creating a piece of art, so by no means do we want to take the position of "We program it once, and that's it!" But what we do want to make clear is that we do not make changes on the fly. Manual operation and digital programming both require time and testing after alterations are made to ensure the performer will be safe. You wouldn't get on a brand new roller coaster before it had been tested, right? And while you ponder that analogy, also remember that roller coasters are installed by people who had at least a full eight hours off since their last shift; we are rarely so lucky. Any change that is requested to known-safe programming should first be tested with our dear friend Sandy (the sandbag). She can take more punishment than any person, although we should still attempt to avoid it. We all know the hours that are common in our industry. When operating manually, any small confusion in the expected sequence of events can result in a serious injury. When operating an automated system, it only takes one errant number or decimal point in the wrong place to result in a dramatic event. As such, we always want to test any change with Sandy, and not a human.

Thinking Ahead When Programming

Specific to automated systems is the existence of a rigid, but extremely repeatable, cue structure. The huge advantage, versus a manual system, is that the cues will be executed exactly the same way, every single time they are run. The equal and opposite disadvantage is that this can make changes to that cue structure difficult. To put a finer point on that, it can be a disadvantage *if* the need to be able to make changes isn't thought about until the end of the process. Just like so many other things in the lifecycle of a rig, if we don't think all the way through at the beginning, we are doomed to box ourselves into less-than-ideal circumstances later. It is not enough to simply get the cues into your software as quickly as possible. Rather, we want to consider how we will operate this show as we begin to program. The specifics of your choices will vary based on how your chosen automation software works, and are beyond the scope of this book, but any modern software will be capable of skinning a cat more than one way. Think about how you want to structure your cue stack so that is easily editable, sufficiently flexible, and readily operated.

Think through, thoroughly, how the show will be run. A huge function of this is who is calling the show, if anyone, and what their sight lines on the action are. If there is a show caller, then conversing with them on what cues they want to call before you start programming would be wise. If there is no show caller, and the automation operator is to take the cues on his or her own, then the operator should be consulted on how they like to run. There are also structural decisions to be made about what, exactly, will constitute a cue. For example, some feel strongly that any cue that lifts a person off the ground should also contain the part that brings that performer back to the ground. This is a perfectly valid point of view, and is good practice in certain circumstances. But, for example, if we already know the performer will go up and then stay there for a long time, perhaps we'd rather not have a cue sitting there running on a long delay before they come down. Also, having multiple moves residing in a single cue can make bailout cues more plentiful, harder to write, and more difficult to access quickly when needed in a hurry. The flip side to that same coin, though, is the reality of having too many cues to trigger all on top of each other. The fact of the matter is that there is no default correct answer that works 100% of the time. It is incumbent on you and your team to understand what you are trying to achieve, and how best to go about it with the software you've chosen. If you are renting a system and operator from a vendor, these are the kinds of things you want to think through before they arrive in your building. Having thought through how you want your show to run will save you significant time with your vendor. Additionally, they will also feel like you are putting them in a position to succeed.

The real point of all these examples is to drive home the idea that programming takes longer than you think it does. When securing time for this phase of a project, do not underbid yourself. You will never have all the time you want to program even in the most ideal of scenarios. Don't forget the programming is the only part of all your hard work that the audience gets to see! It takes the time it takes, so make sure you've campaigned hard for all the time you think you'll need. Similarly, don't forget that your team needs to sleep too. If your programmer is also your winch technician and is also your Flying Director, expecting that person to come in early in the morning to do mechanical notes, work all day during rehearsals, and then program all night will not likely yield the stellar results you are after. If, to get the time you need to program, you need to work around the clock then make sure you are staffed in a way to support those efforts. While it can be costly, don't be afraid to have more than one programmer so that everyone can get some sleep and stay sharp for the next day.

Conclusion

Wow, that's a lot of information on a lot of topics! The design, fabrication, installation, testing, and programming of your system is a lot to think about. Just as was emphasized in the last chapter, thinking all the way through your system early and often will help alleviate most of the common pitfalls in these phases. Don't silo these phases off from each other! Make sure you are thinking about how decisions in each of these phases will affect the others, especially if you are wearing all the hats in your organization.

Takeaways: Beginners

- Don't be afraid to admit you don't know enough to execute one or all of these phases.
  - Hire someone who does!
- Don't make decisions based solely on saving money.
  - Chain motors versus winches.
  - Time and staff required for safety and sanity.
- Third-Party engineering review is an absolute must.
  - If a vendor you've hired is unwilling to provide proof of engineering review, this should be considered a huge red flag.

Takeaways: Professionals

- Factors of safety, D:d ratio, duty cycle, redundancy, and serviceability are among the many concerns you need to balance in the design phase of a project.
- Rigorous design reviews are incalculably valuable.
- Engineering review must happen for every component that supports the load of the performer.
  - This includes props built by those who may not be used to such review.
  - Not having stamped engineering drawings is a non-starter.
    - While this may not be actively required by existing standards it is best practice.
- Plan your installation and programming phases to make sure you have enough staff for the output you are expecting.
- Programming takes the time it takes.

3   Administration

At this point we have completed a nearly impossible run of work. We have managed to drag a performer flying effect into existence, likely kicking and screaming. Now we enter a less sexy, but ultimately very important, phase of the project: documentation. Simply teaching people how to do their job is not enough to ensure safe operation for the whole run of the show. In the entertainment industry we lean far too heavily on an oral tradition of training, meaning we rarely write anything down. This is simply not acceptable when we are dealing with machines that can cause serious injury. The level and detail of said documentation can, and should, vary between a show that is running for a weekend versus one that has an open-ended run. To be perfectly morbid about the situation, we should be making sure that if you walked outside and got hit by a bus all the knowledge you had between your ears exists in written form for someone else to catch up on. We also want to have living documents to record all the work we are going to put into maintaining the system. This is critical, unfortunately, in the event of an accident. It is important while creating, and subsequently insisting upon the usage of, these documents to realize there may come a day when they will be Exhibit A in a court of law. While these can be uncomfortable events to think about, it is important to remember that, when used improperly, these effects can lead to accidents, court cases, and lifelong ramifications. But instead of being intimidated by such thoughts, we are going to use our knowledge of these possible outcomes as serious motivation not to forget this most often overlooked phase of a performer flying effect: administration.

There are two rules of paperwork that are almost always missed when we create these documents:

• Make Only Functional Paperwork
• Put the Information Where the Team Needs It

By following these two simple rules we can alleviate nearly all the trepidation of keeping our needed paperwork in order. So, what qualifies as needed paperwork? This can vary wildly based on the details of a particular production. Most situations will dictate the need for:

- Inspection sheets
- Cue track sheets

Some examples of long-running production-specific documents might include:

- Training plans
- As-builts
- Yearly improvement plans

Inspection Sheets

The most important documents, after the engineering book, for any performer flying rig are the inspection sheets. This is your proof that the system has been thoroughly checked at the predetermined regular intervals you laid out in your RA/RR paperwork. It is also your checklist of what needs to be checked at those predetermined regular intervals. To be clear, not everything needs to be inspected every day. It is critical to identify what parts of the system need to be checked daily versus weekly versus monthly versus annually. If you have engaged a vendor that you rented a performer flying effect from, you should be expecting them to provide you not only with the data of what to inspect when, but also the inspection sheets themselves. If you have conceived and built the system on your own, that means you have become the manufacturer, and therefore need to create this documentation.

How frequently performer flying rigs are inspected will vary based on how much they get used in a given time period. Generally speaking, setting aside a few hours a week to do a deep-dive inspection is sufficient. A common mistake in creating inspection sheets is to think that we can use the same sheet for our daily inspection as we do for our less-regular deep-dive sheet. The goal being both usability and information dissemination, we need two separate documents here.

Every single day we are going to use our rig we need to give our system a pre-use inspection. Taking our cues from the procedures governing fall protection, this inspection does not need to be particularly lengthy, but it should still be performed with intention and seriousness. This is our last opportunity to find a potential issue before we strap performers in. First and foremost, we want to make sure we inspect the entire length of our lifting media, from the attachment to the performer all the way to the termination into the drum of our lifting machine. In doing so, we will check for any new abnormalities since our last daily inspection. When installed properly it's hard to imagine our system eating the lifting media in just one day's use. Rarely though is our system the cause for such distress. It is often caused by outside factors we hadn't considered. Think about the effects of an errant pyro blast on synthetic ropes, or birds' beaks and talons. Certainly a wacky suggestion, but it has happened. We also want to pay particular attention to any other single points of failure in the system; things like carabiners, swivels, or other connecting hardware should be checked for proper function and condition. The goal is to give the whole system a once-over while paying particular attention to the single points of failure.

Our weekly inspection sheets should be more detailed than our daily sheets. Here we want to spend more time really getting into our machines and systems. This is our opportunity to find, for example, bolts that have vibrated themselves loose in the course of regular use. Or notice belts that might need re-tensioning. This is also a prime opportunity to check, and clean, things like fan filters and electrical connection ports. As you can see from the above example inspection sheets, the weekly inspection is simply a more detailed version of the daily inspection. This line of thought should seem obvious; anything ever we need to inspect we should be at least glancing at every day. After we've been looking at it quickly every day, we then want to make sure once-a-week-ish that we are really getting in its business with a fine-toothed comb.

The first two examples of inspection sheets were clearly designed to be more broad reminders of what should be inspected than they are a detailed instruction manual. Another, more detailed approach is to have each element broken down into every single thing that must be checked. Such a sheet would better show the mental approach we must have while executing our weekly inspection. We want to have peace of mind that we have really gotten into each system and feel strongly about its structural integrity until the next inspection. While this more detailed weekly inspection sheet better reflects our thought process, it also might seem to be difficult to actually use. It won't feel as though it was designed with the end user in mind. We must, as we create and use these documents, remember they serve two purposes. One of course is to document our inspections, but the other is to be a useful tool to the end user.

Functional Paperwork

Sadly, these documents are often an afterthought, if a thought at all. They are often thrown together quickly, with the only worry being that they don't exist. Very little, if any, thought is given to how these documents will be used. This starts a vicious cycle of inspection being viewed as a chore, instead of the necessity that it is, because no one wants to deal with the paperwork. Having paperwork for paperwork's sake is not and should not be the goal of the administration of a performer flying effect. But, knowing that there is a certain amount of administrative responsibility that goes hand in hand with these kinds of effects, we should invest time in making the needed paperwork functional. Yes, the most critical function of this paperwork is to prove due diligence in a court of law, God forbid it ever came to that. It is, however, equally important that the end user has a document that helps them *do* the inspection, which will prevent us from ever being in court in the first place. For example, there is often a strong desire to have the whole inspection sheet fit on one side of one piece of paper. From 30,000 feet that seems like a great idea, and for a small production, say a high school production of *Peter Pan*, that idea seems very reasonable. Our first two examples of inspection sheets (Figures 3.1 and 3.2) both show that in the right circumstances this can be achieved. But if you're

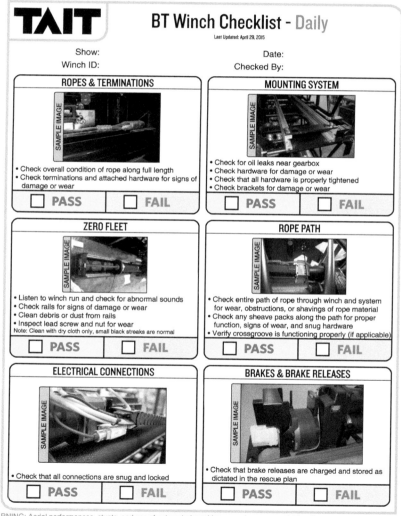

Figure 3.1   Daily Inspection Sheet Example

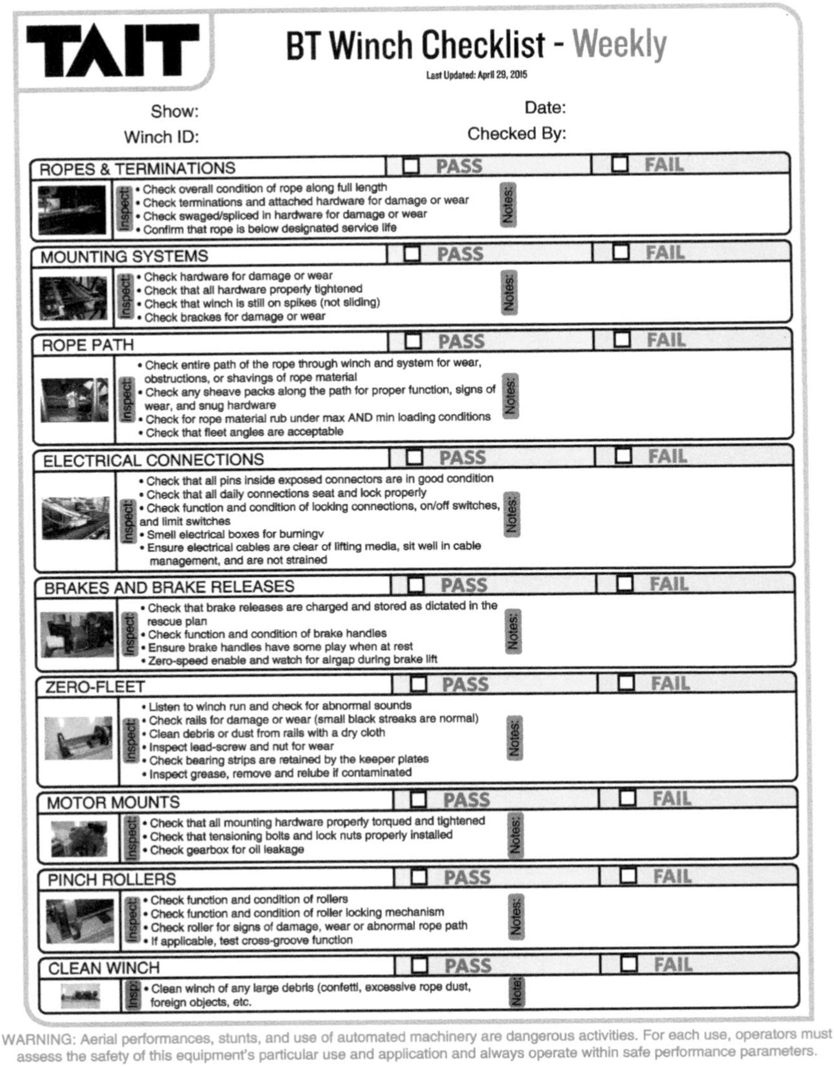

Figure 3.2 Weekly Inspection Sheet Example

a full-scale Cirque du Soleil production, that same desire to have it fit on one piece of paper will lead you to create a document that is unreadable and un-fill-out-able. While the desire to have all the information one would want or need to fit on a single page can be a great idea, it's important to decide if it's a good idea for *this* circumstance. We should always be prepared to do things differently than "how we always do it" to make this unique scenario in front of us safer, more repeatable, and enjoyable for all involved.

Clarity of language in inspection sheets is also often an issue. Again, this is a rare problem for a small production that might only have one axis of motion, but the lesson can still be applied. In larger shows there are often pairs or more of similar machines that need to be separately inspected. There are often multiple assemblies with the same name. Perhaps those distinctions or delineations come naturally to the team who installed them, but what happens when those employees move on? The new employee will likely be handed the same piece of paper and be expected to have the same depth of understanding that the previous employee had. Again, one of our goals here is to create documentation that future-proofs us from tribal knowledge loss when people move on. How can we overcome this? Why not add photos of the to-be-inspected parts to the inspection sheets? Yes, it will take more time to create the sheets initially, but you will have the peace of mind of knowing that the information is where the team needs it. In the not-too-distant past not only adding these photos to our sheets would be difficult, but *taking* the photos was inconvenient too. Now that we all have 12-megapixel (or better) cameras in our pockets all the time, there is simply no excuse to not add this level of clarity to such an important document for everyone's safety and peace of mind.

If you have the time and the budget, don't be afraid to research some of the digital platforms for performing and recording your inspections. There are too many to mention by name here, but they all follow the same theme. Most are web-based applications through which you can enter inspection criteria per element. You then put a unique identifier on each piece, like a barcode or an RFID tag, which triggers a handheld device to bring up the pertinent form. The inspector then fills it out, signs it, and submits it. You now instantly have a filled-out and filed inspection sheet with an indisputable tag for which person performed the inspection. Most of these systems can also be set up to send emails or alerts when elements have an overdue inspection. These systems are very slick once they are up and running. That said, they require a fair amount of time and effort to get up and running to the point of being described as "slick". They can also require a decent monetary investment in startup costs in the form of barcodes, RFID tags, and handhelds. They also usually have a recurring monthly service charge from the organization hosting your data. For the large, long-running production this can be a great investment. For the smaller or one-off production the juice is simply not worth the squeeze.

Put the Information Where the Team Need It

If we are not so blessed as to walk into an organization that already has the fanciest digital solution up and running, how do we manage all this data we're creating with all our inspection sheets? Daily sheets, weekly sheets, monthly sheets, yearly sheets! We used to have to physically print these sheets and then physically save these sheets forever! Imagine being on tour and having to drag around an extra file cabinet just for all this paper. Largely thanks to the cameras we all have in our pockets, this is no longer an issue. While simply printing the sheets every day, or every week, and filling them out with pen can be the fastest and easiest thing, a little outside-the-box thinking can make everyone's life easier. Why not print out one sheet, laminate it, and leave it at the site of the inspection with a dry erase marker? Then the information is where the team need it! Now you don't need to call your IT department when the printer doesn't work, you don't need to be upset that the printer ran out of yellow ink, and you don't have to file a physical piece of paper. Just have the team take a picture of their marked-up laminated sheet and email it to you. Then you simply digitally file it away! A wonderful knock-on effect of putting the inspection sheets at the inspection site is that people will read them when they're bored. They will become more familiar with the sheets and, by extension, the machines.

This is a great way to have the information where your team need it. Now, on a more detailed sheet, perhaps even the finest-point dry erase marker will be too thick to use on the sheet. We can either re-think the way we've built our sheet to work better with the writing utensil of choice, or perhaps this plan won't work for us on this show. That's okay too! It is crucial not to get stuck in a "This is how we've always done it" mindset. You should always be doing whatever is the best for this specific scenario. Draw on your past experiences to help solve today's issue, but don't be limited by yesterday's solutions.

Training Documents

So far, we have been discussing the need for, and strategy of, inspection sheets. But as stated above, there are other very important documents we need to create and monitor. Number two on the list is training documents. These too will vary in content from situation to situation. The goal of these documents is to lay out how the system functions, idiosyncrasies specific to this system discovered the hard way, and key points to teach the manipulator of the system at a given post. Sometimes, and often, these documents are as simple as cue sheets for each person involved in the running of the show. Sadly, this step is often skipped on the smaller, shorter-running productions, but it is just as important for them as it is for the production that is planned to run in perpetuity. Remember, our goal here is to make sure we have adequately documented how we run the show in the event the "usual" person who runs the show can't be there. This applies even to the dad running the fly rig for the middle school musical. If he got sick or injured and couldn't perform the second weekend of shows, the stand-in dad #2 who will be asked to run the rig would hugely benefit from having a document written by dad #1 on what he's doing, how, when, and most critically why. The act of writing these documents can often reveal discrepancies in the understandings of the person performing the cue and the person calling the cue. As such, it is always best to create these documents in conjunction with the calling Stage Manager.

These documents are specific to running a particular show. The larger, more complex, and longer-running a production, the more you will find a huge use for documents detailing training required outside the show. They can also be helpful in defending spending on outside training to your superiors. For example, if you have a document approved by the company that says each person running the show must have an Industrial Rope Access Trade Association (IRATA) certification, then you have clear cover for sending a new employee to get Ropes Access training, regardless of the cost. These documents can also come in handy when selecting candidates for cross-training into new positions.

There are few ways as straightforward to find new, easier ways to do things than training someone new into an existing role. Fresh eyes almost always find a new way to do it because they aren't burdened by the knowledge of how we got here in the first place. At worst, they will ask their trainer a question that will spark a new idea in the trainer, and the same result is achieved. This is reason enough to train people without experience into some of your easier show tracks. Performer flying is one of those specialties where we have a chicken-and-egg problem. We want the people we hire to have experience proving they know what they are doing before they get to us, but they need one of these positions to get the requisite experience we seek. Cross-training individuals you see potential in can help break this cycle. Hopefully they will see the opportunity they are being presented with, and treat it as such. The benefit to you is that you can now worry less about who would cover Rig 2's cues if they are sick or, as we so dramatically often put it, get hit by a bus.

Given that you know you are intentionally giving someone with less (or no) experience a chance, it's important not to rush the training process and to make sure you are prepared for said training to go on longer than you anticipated. These training episodes usually go something like this on long-running productions:

- The trainee follows the trainer for two full shows, watching the cues and asking questions.
- The trainee then begins doing the easiest and least critical of show cues with the trainer watching. The trainee continues to watch the other cues.
- Outside of the show, the more complicated and critical show cues are practiced with the trainer and other technicians if required by the situation.
- The trainee then begins doing all the show cues with the trainer breathing down their neck.

- The trainee then does all the show cues with the trainer far enough away for the trainee to mess up, but not far enough away for the show to be stopped.
- Finally, the trainee does a proper solo show.

While this does not guarantee you clean shows all the way through training, this has been proven time and time again to be the correct balance of live-fire training and quality control.

As-Builts

Often, in the heat of getting a show open, we alter, modify, change, trick, move, re-wire, add, or otherwise adjust the gear on site different from what was drawn. The longer-running the show, or the more you intend to rely on support from the manufacturer, the more you should invest in making sure those drawings are updated to reflect reality. This can seem like a time-consuming waste in the moments following a successful opening night, but this should be viewed as the last step in your Design Spiral. Frequently troubleshooting via satellite has been complicated, extended, or resulted in an unneeded house call by the vendor simply because the as-builts, those being updated drawings reflecting any changes made during fabrication, were not updated. If not for your current self, consider investing in as-builts for your future self. If you don't document how you solved the problem under duress this time, you are likely to end up under the same duress in the future. This point stands as much for the high school renting a flying rig as it does for the large-scale, long-running, hyper-custom production. If you are the renter of gear from a flying company, you should make sure before their installer leaves that he or she has documented anything unique about the installation in your venue. This way, if you need support later from their head office there will be pictures and/or paperwork for their reference so that they are in the best position to solve your problem in a timely fashion.

Exit Information

Along the same line as as-builts, but unique to automated systems, is recording exit information (Figure 3.3). Once the show is open, you will want to document a great many things about the setup of the system for all the same reasons you want accurate as-builts of the physical gear. The meanings for the following terms are covered later in the book so don't be intimidated if the following doesn't make sense just yet! You will want to record the Category 0 and Category 1 stopping distances at full available system speed. You will want to record, per axis, what the first obstruction is. The "first obstruction" is the first part of the system that will crash or bottom out if run continuously without limits. Speaking of limits, you will want to record the distance from the first obstruction that the E- (pronounced "Eee Minus") is set, as well as the distance from the E– to the H– limit. You will also want to record the location of any slow zones that are employed on a given axis. Lastly, you will want to save a "golden" copy of the show file, along with all drive configurations, in case of emergency in the future. The important point to come away with right now is that taking the time to record the specifics unique to your system so that you have that information should you ever need it in the future is critical to success and the last step in your Design Spiral.

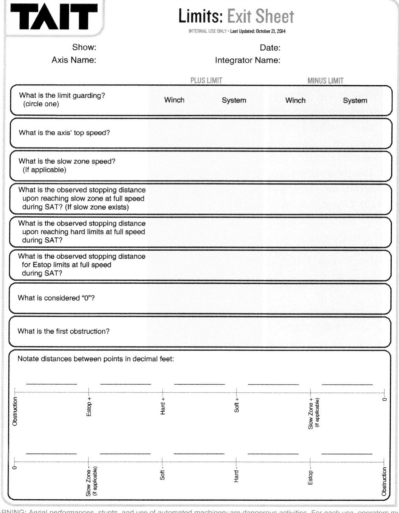

WARNING: Aerial performances, stunts, and use of automated machinery are dangerous activities. For each use, operators must assess the safety of this equipment's particular use and application and always operate within safe performance parameters.

Figure 3.3   Exit Information

We want to record this for two main reasons. First of all, we want to make sure any future troubleshooters who are not intimately familiar with our system will have all the data they could ever want on how we set it up the first time. Again, think of this document as the as-built for the automation software. The other main reason for recording this information is for a monthly or yearly inspection. Depending on the results of your RA, you will want to check the function and location of your limits every so often. This will usually end up being monthly or yearly. Having all this information recorded will take the guess work out of deciding whether the behavior you witness during those inspections is correct or not.

Conclusion

The point of all this paperwork is to document all your hard work to this point. It is to help your future self remember all the vagaries of the decisions and choices you made to get the show open. It will help you in the future in diagnosing problems. Possibly most importantly, it will help future people in your role continue to operate the system as safely as it was operated on Day 1. Equally, and separately from this specific production, documenting your decisions this well will come in handy in the future. When, years down the road, you remember you did something really great on this show but you can't remember the specifics, you will be able to refer to all this amazing documentation you have on file.

Takeaways: Beginners

- We must have and use inspection sheets regardless of the size or length of our production.
- Documentation is not a waste of time; rather, it is a great way for our present selves to help our future selves.

Takeaways: Professionals

- We should take the time and extra effort to make our paperwork functional for the end user. Functional paperwork is more likely to be used correctly each time.
- Longer-running productions should have written training plans and cue sheets.
- Investing time in as-builts and exit information recording is a key characteristic that separates the pros from the amateurs on medium-term and long-running productions.

Part 2

It's All About Deceleration

It's time for some math homework! Designing and executing a working system is a feat in and of itself. But to do so without considering the forces your rig will put through the building and the performer is at best negligent and at worst fatal. In this part we will discuss how to think about mitigating the forces our code-compliant system will exert and how those forces are absorbed by the people and objects that come into contact with them.

4   Reducing Forces on the Body and the Building

When Dale Earnhardt Sr. tragically died at the Daytona 500 in 2001 it was not because his car hit the wall traveling at an enormous speed; it was because his organs, most notably his brain, hit his skeletal system at an enormous speed. The stop he came to was too abrupt, resulting in fatal injuries. He, as a mass, did not have enough time or distance to decelerate safely. This is the same set of issues we must constantly be aware of when designing and executing performer flying rigs. It can be all too easy, while being completely incorrect, to say and believe something like, "If something goes wrong, I want the rig to stop immediately." Broadly, we can all agree with the sentiment but in practice doing exactly that can result in very dangerous situations.

First, let's review Isaac Newton's Second Law of Motion, which states that force equals mass times acceleration. $F=m \star a$. First published in 1687. (Take a moment to marvel at *that* fact. Think about the world as it existed at that time when Newton pulled these laws out of thin air. Math is an amazing thing.) From this simple equation we can see that there are only two ways to reduce force. We can either have less mass to accelerate, or we can accelerate that mass slower. An important concept to understand here: as far as force is concerned, deceleration is a form of acceleration. The math is the same. Don't waste your time Googling "force from deceleration formula" and being aggravated when you can only find formulas showing acceleration. It's the same thing!

Now that we've established that the only two variables that control force are the mass of the object we're arresting and the acceleration at which we arrest that mass, the next logical question would be: What is the maximum force a human body can endure? Fortunately, this answer is well qualified from scholarly research; it is 12 kilonewtons, or roughly 2,700 pounds. "How did we derive that number?" the more curious among you might be asking yourself right now. There are many stories out there claiming to extol the true story of who first discovered this value and how. There's the one about the French wanting to best size their paratrooper's parachutes, and so they threw prisoners out of planes with various sizes of parachutes, stumbling upon the answer with 'chutes that were too big. You can imagine the mess these experiments caused, if this story is true. (Gross.) Then there's the one about the Germans, trying to size thrusters for ejector seats for their pilots, experimenting with cadaver spines to determine their breaking strength. All the stories though, regardless of nationality, revolve around military research during World War II relating to advancements in air combat. Following all this, we also have the work of J.P. Stapp in the 1950s, who greatly helped NASA understand the maximum forces the body can withstand by strapping himself to rocket sleds that would rapidly accelerate and then similarly rapidly decelerate. Emphasis needed on *rapidly*. Some of the videos of his tests can be found on YouTube if you're looking for a good time.

For those of you with strong fall protection backgrounds, *2,700 pounds* may be setting off your Spidey Sense. This is more than the 1,800-pound maximum arresting force OSHA (the Occupational Safety and Health Administration) mandates a fall protection system may exert on a body. It is understandable OSHA would cap the maximum force these systems can exert on a body at a value below the absolute maximum before serious injuries occur. Aside from the fact that we wouldn't want someone to experience the maximum force they possibly could, it is also important to remember that most of the testing on this topic has occurred with people in the military or others who are particularly physically fit. As a result, some padding has been added by OSHA to the 2,700-pound maximum number, and understandably so.

So now we know the maximum force the body can take, and we know what OSHA says on the topic. Are there any other organizations' opinions worth being aware of? The ESTA E1.43–2016 Performer Flying Systems standard, which has since been adopted by ANSI (the American National Standards Institute), says that a performer shall not be exposed to more than 2.8Gs for longer than 0.2 seconds without regard for direction of force. What do we mean by "without regard for direction of force"? This means higher values *could* be acceptable for specific situations, but given the variability of performances, it is best to use this value as a governing philosophy. To put that differently, very few performer flying rigs involve restraints and repeatability like those found on a roller coaster. As such, erring on the side of caution is always a good idea. But now we've introduced a new variable to the conversation: duration. It is not enough for us only to know how much force the performer will endure; we must also figure out how long that force will be endured for.

Stopping Force versus Speed

A common misconception in the world, let alone in our industry, is that one way to reduce stopping force is to reduce the maximum speed the object is traveling at. This is in fact untrue. As we covered earlier, F=m*a. You will notice there are only three variables in that equation, and none of them are speed. "But surely," some will say, "when I run full speed into a wall it hurts more than if I walk slowly into the same wall." Yes, but this is not an apt comparison. Also, this person should probably address why they have such experience with running into walls, but that is a topic for a different book. There is a fourth variable hidden in F=m*a, which is also not speed. It is time. Acceleration is a change in speed over time.

A more apt analogy here for our friend who walks into walls would be the use of two different-sized parachutes. Fail-safe brakes on a winch are very much like parachutes in that they are simple machines that always exert the same amount of force. A parachute, just like a fail-safe brake, limits the amount of force the object connected to it will experience in a stop, but (and this is the critical point to understand) it will always exert its maximum force. They are both a bit double-edged in that way.

Let's deep dive this analogy more. If we take a 100-pound person and connect them to a parachute of a given size, the force they will experience when decelerating will always be the same. Let us take two examples: first, that person is still accelerating towards terminal velocity; and second, that person has reached terminal velocity. In each case, the force on their body will always be the same as long as the size of the parachute doesn't change. What will change, however, is the length of time they experience that same force. Think about the way the acceleration is calculated. It is the change in velocity (over) the time it takes to achieve that change (Figure 4.1).

Because the parachute is not changing size between our two examples, in both cases we are decelerating to the same slower speed to gently land back on terra firma. The only variable that is changing is the starting speed when the parachute engages.

"Ah ha!" our distinguished wall-slammer-into will say. "You see! Speed does change the force."

"Nooooooope," you will now be armed to say.

The result of the equation will remain the same. This is because the starting speed is not the only variable in the equation that will change. The time it takes to achieve the deceleration will also change proportionally with the starting speed. This is because the parachute, being a fixed size, cannot slow down any more abruptly than its size allows. Therefore, the force on the performer strapped to the parachute will remain unchanged. However, and to drive this point home again, the length of time the performer experiences that same force will be different based on the speed at the initiation of the stopping event. This is an important variable to pay attention to when thinking about stopping forces. As we have previously discussed, the longer the length of time this force is experienced could push you over the barrier of ESTA's 2.8Gs for 0.2 seconds. Most of Dr. Stapp's research for NASA revolved around

$$\text{ACCELERATION} = \frac{\text{CHANGE IN VELOCITY}}{\text{TIME TAKEN}}$$

Figure 4.1 Acceleration Formula

discovering how much force the human body can absorb. Over very short periods of time (periods significantly shorter than 0.2 seconds) the human body can absorb far more than 2.8G, but this requires the force to be exerted in a specific orientation to the body. Given that we cannot guarantee the body's orientation and that our stopping events take longer than the periods enumerated by Dr. Stapp, we need to avoid having offensively high G forces for long periods of time. So, what mitigations exist if the forces are too high, or too long?

If the speed at which we initiate the stopping event truly is irrelevant to the stopping force exerted, then is there no way to change the stopping force? Are we doomed to experience these forces no matter what? Let's unpack that. There are a series of variables here we cannot control but there are still a few that we can, most notably the size of the parachute. If we make the parachute smaller, we will experience less force over a longer period of time to slow to the same decelerated speed as our original parachute with the same 100-pound performer. If we make the parachute bigger, we will experience more force over a shorter period to achieve the same results.

Now replace the word "parachute" above with the word "brake", and you should be well on your way to understanding the effect of a brake on stopping a load. The oft-used wall analogy breaks down quickly when you begin to understand the true behavior of a brake. Because we use our brakes in a performer flying situation to come to a complete stop, running into a wall can, on its surface, seem like a fitting analogy. But in reality this is not how brakes behave. Instead, think of the brakes like you would a shock pack on a fall protection lanyard. The point of a shock absorber in fall protection is to limit the amount of force the body will experience by lengthening the stopping event. Regardless of the force initially exerted on the shock pack, once the shock pack begins to deploy the body experiences a significantly lower maximum force until it decelerates to a stop. A brake works similarly. Regardless of how fast you are going when the brake engages, it will stop with same amount of force because it will always exert the same stopping force. What will change, however, is how long the built-up speed, or inertia, will be able to drive through the brake until it comes to a complete stop, just like the fall protection shock pack, and similarly to the parachute.

It's All About Deceleration Distance

When you are driving your car and you see a stop sign in the distance do you (a) continue driving at the same speed until you are even with the stop sign and stomp on your brakes, or do you (b) begin gingerly applying the brake to slowly come to a stop at the stop sign? If you chose (a), you are very strange person indeed, and you probably live in Maryland. Most people would cite (b) as the correct, if not the more comfortable, choice. It is more comfortable because we have a long deceleration distance and as such we do not experience a large increase in force on our bodies in the car during the stop. In (a) we would experience a larger force, as we are thrown forward into our seatbelts because we have a very short time to go from the coasting speed of the car to a full stop. This is, on a much smaller scale, what killed Dale Earnhardt Sr. and this is what we have to be worried about with any abrupt stop our system can cause. While a fall from a great height can cause too abrupt a stop, so too can brakes that are inappropriately sized and therefore too strong. As previously alluded to in this chapter, it can be easy to think that in the event something goes wrong we want to stop as quickly as possible, but as our stop sign example shows, that can be a dangerous line of thinking. What we actually want is to balance the concern of affecting a prompt stop with the concern of exerting so much force on the performer that they sustain an injury. To put it differently: What good would it have been to stop Mr. Earnhardt's car before it hit the wall by means of some emergency stop, if that emergency stop would have caused the same result by stopping too fast and causing the same injuries?

EXAMPLE 1:

A 90-pound performer is attached to a 1/8 inch, 7x19, cable with 3 feet of slack. The performer walks off an edge and free falls those 3 feet to a dead stop.

EXAMPLE 2:

Two performers weighing a total of 300 pounds are attached to 200% stretch bungee with 20 feet of slack. Those performers walk off an edge and free fall those 20 feet into the bungee.

Take these two examples. Which one do you think exerts more force on the performer?

Hopefully by now the answer is obvious to you, but you might still be surprised by how different they are. The correct answer is that Example 2, the one with the 200% stretch bungee, exerts significantly less force than Example 1. This is because of the length of time and deceleration distances difference between the two examples. In Example 2, because the bungee stretches to twice its starting length, the performers will not experience much more than their own weight in terms of stopping force. There will only be about 350 pounds exerted on either anchor of the bungee. On the other hand, in Example 1, in just 3 feet of acceleration, because of the extremely short stopping distance, the system will experience about 1,800 pounds of abrupt stopping force, or shock load. This should be setting off your Spidey Sense for two distinct reasons: (1) 1,800 pounds is the most force OSHA says a body can safely experience in a fall arrest scenario, and (2) the example states that this performer is on 1/8 inch, 7x19 cable, the breaking strength of which is about 2,000 pounds depending on your specific supplier. Hopefully we can all agree 1,800 pounds is dangerously close to 2,000 pounds in a performer flying scenario. If this cable wasn't flawlessly swaged, or has even the slightest wear to it, it could easily break, causing an even bigger problem. You may be thinking to yourself, "But why would I ever slack my system like that?" You would be right that you would never intentionally cause this situation. But also think to yourself how small 3 feet is and how quickly that slack could be generated by mistake. These are the kinds of scenarios you should always keep in mind when spec-ing out your system.

Calculating these forces still comes down to simply using F=m*a. There are also plenty of apps that can be purchased which will do these computations for you. It can be very beneficial, however, to create your own spreadsheet with these formulas instead of relying on the internet for the answers. The creation and testing of your own spreadsheet will help you understand how the variables in the formulas for acceleration and force affect each other. You should create one for calculating stopping force based on distance, and another one based on time as these are the two variables we are usually after. You will always need to know one of these variables to run the equation. Writing your spreadsheet to solve for either scenario will save you time in the long run. In both versions you will need to know your speed at the beginning of the stopping event and your speed at the end. (In our case the speed at the end will almost always be 0.) Then you will be able to determine the force your system is exerting either by getting the exact stopping distance off of a graph from your automation system, or by deriving the exact time of the stopping event. While some will be quick to use the stopwatch function of

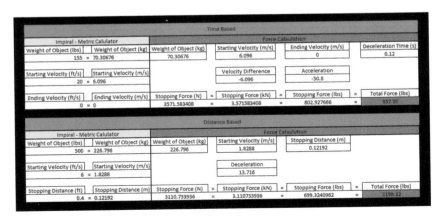

Figure 4.2   Formulas Spreadsheet

their smartphone, it is better to get the precise time from your automation software. With the length of time normal to our stopping events, that being less than 1 second, very small fluctuations in time can result in wildly different results at the end of the formula. As such you will want to be as precise as possible. Your spreadsheet will end up looking something like Figure 4.2.

The way this sheet has been set up, you need to know all the fields highlighted in yellow to compute your stopping force. But how do we go about gathering the data to fill in those fields? Clearly we want to test our system with our most resilient subject first, that of course being our old friend Sandy the sandbag. This will allow us to test the stopping forces of our rig without putting a living, breathing human in any danger. After we run the system with Sandy we will be able to pull out of our automation software the data we need to compute how much force a performer on the rig will experience in the stopping event. But what do we do if we discover that our system will in fact exert far too much force on our performers?

The number-one avoidable cause of stopping forces in performer flying being too high is by underutilizing a winch. While a machine rated for 500 pounds will easily fly a 90-pound performer, the unfortunate reality is that the winch still has brakes designed to stop 500 pounds. The brakes, sadly, don't know they are flying a small load. As discussed earlier in this chapter, the fail-safe brakes will always apply the same force, and that force will always be their maximum. And don't forget, those brakes are redundant. They don't stop 500 pounds together; rather they each stop 500 pounds. And on top of that, each brake is designed to stop even more than the rated value of the winch, usually at least 125% of the rated capacity. (The exact value will vary based on which code you are trying to be compliant with. A detailed discussion on this topic can be found in Chapter 10.) You can imagine how abrupt the stop would be then if we have two brakes, each rated for 125% of 500 pounds, both simultaneously stopping a 90-pound load. The reality is the 90-pound performer will be brought to a violently abrupt stop because he or she will not have enough inertia to pull through the closing brakes as the intended 500-pound load would. So what options are available to us? Do we have to start over and build a new winch? Swap the brakes, perhaps? Both of those are viable options, but usually more drastic than needed. The first question might be "Is this the right winch for the job?" Or, put differently, "Do we have, or can we get, another winch with a more appropriate capacity for this use case?" If the answer is no, as it so frequently will be, then what else could we do? Remember, the machine, the system, the rigging, and the building were designed and engineered to handle all this force. (Hopefully, if we did all our proper prior planning!) We are now only concerned about the force at the performer. As such, we do not *have to* solve this problem at the winch. All we have to do is find a way to elongate the stopping event for the performer. If we lean on our knowledge of industrial fall protection, we know that shock packs do just that! Instead of clipping the performer directly to the winch line, simply add a shock absorber inline. This is a great Get Out of Jail Free card, but it still requires planning and detailed thinking to validate. You will need to do fair amount of math to ensure the normal forces you are going to exert, like accelerating to your max speed, will not trigger the shock pack. You will also want to make sure that your shock pack has sufficient deployment distance to absorb all the force it will need to without bottoming out. All that being said, it is a great solution to an otherwise huge, although oft-overlooked, problem.

Measuring Stopping Forces in Real Life

Some more advanced readers may be wondering why we have been talking all about deriving stopping force with math when there is a perfectly good component out there that can do all the hard work for us. These people are thinking of something called load cells and they are a fantastic tool. Load cells are covered in more depth in Chapter 6, but to speak broadly about them here, they are a component that measures force by transmitting milliamps back to the automation system, which has been scaled to turn those milliamp readings into load values. Basically, they are a fancy electricity-based scale. When used correctly and with intention they are a great tool. However, all too often they are used without a full understanding of their complexities, options, and fundamentally how they work. The first concept that is not paid attention to, or not understood at all, is sampling rate. The sampling rate of a load cell is how many times per second the load cell is sending readings out. Depending on which specific load cell you use, the sampling rate will vary wildly. If you are sampling too slow you might miss the peak of the stopping event. If you are sampling too fast you might be seeing a spike higher than any force that we need to take into account.

In Figure 4.3 we see a stopping event taking place over 1 second. Our load cell in this case only measures twice a second, as noted by the two vertical lines at .5 and 1. As you can see from this graph, in this example we miss almost all of the force of the stopping event. Our load cell system would only report to us the load at the two moments our vertical lines intersect with our stopping event. Not good!

In Figure 4.4 we see the same stopping event, except now we are measuring 20 times per second, as noted by all the vertical lines. Now, unlike the previous example, we will get data back on every moment of the stopping event. While this is objectively better than less data, it can also produce scary values if you do not fully understand what you are looking at. The tighter your sampling window, the higher your peak value will be. It is important to not only stare at the peak value, but to also understand how long that peak value is exerted on the system. You may see a value so high you do not understand how your system hasn't fallen out of the sky! If you've gone out and bought a load cell meant for measuring loads in military rocketry (don't laugh, it's happened),

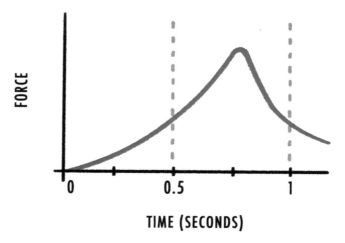

Figure 4.3 Low-Sample Graph

your sampling rate could be so high that you end up seeing loads that only existed for an insignificant amount of time for our purposes. For example, if that scary value you see as the peak is only exerted for 0.2 milliseconds, you might be wise to zoom out a little on your graph and elect to view the loads on your system over a slightly longer period of time. Each situation should be evaluated with your team for what should be considered significant time for this particular application, but in general if you are zooming in tighter than 50 milliseconds, or one-quarter of ESTA's 0.2 seconds, you are probably looking at your event too closely; certainly so for how this data relates to the safety of our performers.

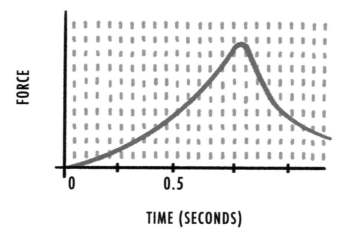

Figure 4.4 High-Sample Graph

Another fact missed about load cells is that most are not designed for measuring dynamic loads. Much like your bathroom scale, they are designed to measure static loads. As such, if you try to measure a dynamic event like an acrobat's movements, or shock loads like an e-stop, with them they will read as inaccurately as your bathroom scale will if you jump on it and watch the dial go crazy. If you are going to measure dynamic events, make sure you have a load cell designed for that purpose so that your results are accurate!

The third feature that is often forgotten is to check the load cell's accuracy. All load cells come with a rating of how precise they can report back on the load they are measuring. For example, if your load cell is rated for 5,000 pounds and has an accuracy rating of ±10%, then your findings could be 500 pounds off in either direction. Depending on your specific system this could either be well within the margin of error or a terrifying overage. As with anything else in performer flying, make sure you fully understand the features, design intent, and use case of the particular load cell you are using. Given all these considerations, you can see why double-checking your findings with good old-fashioned math can be a wise decision!

Conclusion

Thank god for Isaac Newton and his simplifying of this very complicated topic down to $F=m \star a$! But even this can be overcomplicating the things we need to worry about. Long story short: we want the stopping event to be as long as can be accommodated. The eternal battle here is balancing that concern against the desire to be able to stop promptly in the event of an emergency.

Takeaways: Beginners

- Stopping immediately, while the right idea, can be very dangerous.
- We want to exert as little extra force on the performer in a stopping event as possible.
- Underutilizing a winch is the most common way to have stopping forces too high.

Takeaways: Professionals

- Our goal should always be to elongate the stopping event as much as can be reasonably achieved.
- Make a spreadsheet to calculate stopping force based on stopping distance and time elapsed.
- If using a load cell, be sure to check that it is designed for dynamic loads, and has a sufficient and reasonable sampling rate and a worthwhile accuracy.
- ESTA E1.43–2016 states that 2.8G for 0.2 seconds is the maximum force a performer may be exposed to without regard for body position.
- Reducing speed does not reduce stopping force; it reduces the duration that force is experienced for.

5 Flavors of Stops

There are many ways to bring our automated flying machines to a stop. In Chapter 4 we focused on only one kind of stopping, that being the worst-case scenario, also known as Category 0 (Cat-0) stopping. In fact, there are several categories of stops that we can affect depending on the situation. In the entertainment industry, which of the three categories of stop is actuated is tied to the input that triggers the stop. Stopping a cue with the Stop button on the console is considered a Cat-2, while Cat-1 and Cat-0 stops can be initiated by the "big red button", aka the E-Stop button, or by striking a limit switch depending on exactly how your software is set up. We will deep-dive limit switches' purpose and placement in a performer flying machine, needed quantities of them, and how to correctly set them up in the next chapter. For now, just know that they are fail-safe mechanical switches that are tied to the drivetrain of the machine and, if struck, indicate we have traveled beyond the safe operating range of the equipment. Understanding the difference between the three categories is paramount to designing a safe system.

Cat-0 Stops

A Cat-0 stop is the most abrupt stop a machine can generate. Simply put, this is what happens if you were to kick the plug powering your machine out of the wall. In a Cat-0 stop the power is cut to the big-power part of the machine while 24v control signals may remain active. Industrial machines, like the electrical cabinets that power them, have high-voltage, or "big power", parts and low-voltage, or "little power", parts. The immediate removal of power affects stopping because the brakes of our performer flying machine need power to remain open. If power is suddenly removed while the machine is moving the brakes will close completely, immediately, and with their full force, bringing the machine to a very abrupt stop. You may be thinking, "But how often does the power go out while the show is going on?" Here are a couple of important points on that:

1. It goes out more often than you would think.
2. Is the show the only time the machine is moving? What about pre-set? What about load-in? What about during system-testing periods?
3. While the behavior of a Cat-0 stop above is described as "kicking the plug out of the wall", that is not the only way to cause this kind of stop. Many emergency-stop systems, particularly older ones, use this as their default stopping method if an E-Stop button is pressed.

For these reasons and many more, like the ones we discussed in Chapter 4, it is crucial that you know and prepare for whatever type of stop your system *can* actuate, not only the ones you think are most likely. There are countless stories of people planning for a stop generating significantly less force than a Cat-0 while spec-ing components, only to see their creations bend, yield, or break when the true worst-case scenario occurred.

Figure 5.1 is showing position and velocity versus time. The red curved line is the position of the winch, while cyan is the velocity commanded. You can see how abrupt the commanded Cat-0 stop is. There is very little time between when the velocity is commanded to 0 (in this case because power has been removed from the drive) and when the red line flatlines.

As mentioned above, many older systems still use a Cat-0 e-stop as the default mode of stopping. When these systems were first designed, the machines were so rudimentary that flying a person on one would never have crossed anyone's mind. While a deck track stopping hard might be visually displeasing, it was rare that anything worse than the aesthetics of the moment were ruined in the stop. Now that we are flying people, forces must be kept in check and be kept on our minds at all times. Some of the first automated performer flying systems also had Cat-0 stops as defaults; mercifully though, the most responsible designers

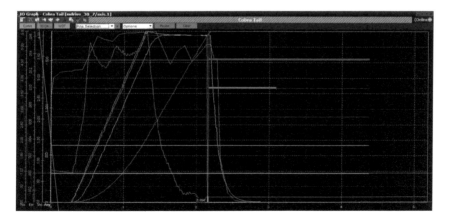

Figure 5.1 Cat-0 Graph

in those days had the foresight to spec brakes that had appropriate stopping force to arrest the system, but were weak enough to allow the inertia of the system to pull through those brakes enough that the Cat-0 stop did not peak forces into dangerous ranges. Even with that mitigation, and certainly in the cases without that forethought, this abrupt style of stopping in the up direction can cause the payload to continue traveling up even though the machine has completely stopped. This means that the abruptness of the brakes allows the performer to slack the system as their inertia pushes them above the lifting media holding them up. When gravity finally wins, as it always does eventually (thanks, Newton), the payload falls until the line gets back to tension, causing a shock load to the system. In the most extreme of cases this can cause an undersized, or otherwise weakened, component of the system to break.

So why then would we ever want a Cat-0 stop? As noted above, they are unavoidable in the event of a loss of power, so we must always plan for the forces they can exert on our system. But other than that, why? Cat-0 stops are the style of stop that will arrest the system with the least distance covered. As such, they are the correct stopping format when you are dangerously close to your end of travel. Modern automation systems can be set up to only allow these stops to happen when certain switches are triggered, and as such are usually only set up on the last switch before a collision happens. These stops, also known as e-stops, should only be actuated when the "e", which stands for "emergency", describes the situation. Since we have classified the event as an emergency, we want the big-power electricity to be removed from the machine. This means the machine will not be able to be commanded to move again immediately after the stop without digital acknowledgement of the incident. This acknowledgement usually comes in the form of a reset button. This extra step to re-energize the machine means the user has noticed something atypical has occurred. This removal of power, and the subsequent dropping of the brakes, is what causes the abruptness of a Cat-0 stop.

What if the machine is moving, we want to stop promptly, and the situation is just shy of an emergency?

Cat-1 Stops

The clear advantage of a Cat-0 stop, despite its shortcomings, is that the machine will come to a stop in the shortest distance possible. Any other form of stop will require more distance to stop, but such is the tradeoff for reducing stopping forces. As discussed in Chapter 4, it's all about declaration distance! A Cat-1 stop involves using electric power to stop the machine with its variable frequency drive (VFD) and then cutting the big power, thereby closing the brakes. Now, that may sound like every other stop, but there are crucial differences. First of all, although the classic definition of a Cat-1 stop means the machine has come to a complete stop before the power is removed, this is not always the case. Most often in high-speed performer flying the system is arranged to keep the brakes open for one full second. In that available second the safety system then decelerates the winch as fast as it possibly can, usually at twice the normal deceleration rate. This has the effect, assuming the machine is being used within the limits it was set up to work with, of coming to a complete stop at the same moment the brakes set. If, however, the machine has been over-sped or over-weighted, it is possible that the brakes will set while the machine is still moving. This would cause the same behavior as a Cat-0, although for a much-reduced amount of time. In this scenario the machine will have slowed significantly from its top speed, thereby reducing the time over which the hard stop will be exerted on the system. For all the same reasons as with a Cat-0 stop, the user must acknowledge the stopping event via a reset button to allow the machine to be re-energized in a Cat-1 stop as well.

In Figure 5.2 we have all the same variables as in our Cat-0 Graph above but now we can see how much more distance, and therefore time, is covered during our stopping event. As such, this Cat-1 stop will produce significantly lower forces than its Cat-0 brother.

This form of stopping (Cat-1) is the preferred type of stop for modern systems with the exception of the e-stop limit switches being struck. It balances many concerns about bringing a payload to a controlled and quick stop in both directions of travel. Even though the system above is stopping at twice the programmable deceleration rate, it is slow enough to not cause the payload to shock-load the system, but the stopping event is still very much a dynamic event. This is achieved by increasing the distance it takes the machine

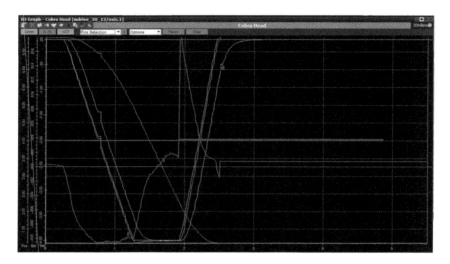

Figure 5.2 Cat-1 Graph

to stop. The additional stopping distance will cut into your available area to fly in and should be planned for in advance. (This concept is covered in great detail in the next chapter.) As an added benefit, when executed appropriately, performers do not usually notice these e-stops as being out of the ordinary. As such, we want to make sure all stops triggered by our system are Cat-1s. Cat-0s should only be caused by power outages, e-stop limit switches, and any other scenario your RA/RR have identified.

Cat-2 Stops

Cat-2 stops, simply, are normal stops. They are not actuated by an over-travel switch and do not occur in emergency situations only. When Cat-2 stops are completed the machine can immediately move again as no power, big or small, has been removed from the machine. These are the same stops you can write any cue with. To be more pragmatic about it, these are the stops that occur when you press the Stop button on your console, instead of the big red button (see Figure 5.3).

These stops do not look like, nor do they feel like, emergencies, and that's because they are not used for emergencies. For the comfort and confidence of the performer we should endeavor to only ever have the system stop in a Cat-2 style. This of course is also the type of stop that takes the longest to complete from full speed. While we always want the performer to be comfortable, stopping abruptly before the performer strikes an object will always be better than slowly coasting the performer into the offending object. Even though Cat-1s can be gentle enough as to not be felt as emergencies by the performer, we should still endeavor to not need the big red button when we have a performer on the line. As such, we should hope to only ever need our Stop button on the console, and not the E-Stop button. That said, we should not be afraid to hit the big red button if we ever think we need to!

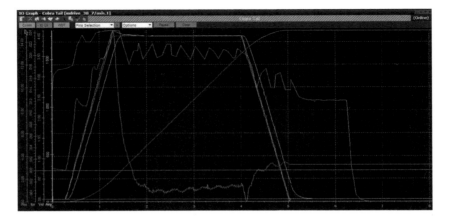

Figure 5.3   Cat-2 Graph

Conclusion

The difference in the stopping modes can be best thought about in terms of the different ways we stop cars. Cat-2 stops are equatable to normal use of the brakes in your car. You see a stop sign in the distance and you begin to slowly apply the brakes to bring the car to a stop without causing a huge increase in force to be felt by the passengers. Cat-1 stops are equatable to our Maryland driver from the last chapter. We've noticed the stop sign too late and jam on the brakes. We stop in less distance, but the passengers experience a noticeable increase in force, their seatbelts holding them in their seats. Cat-0 stops are equitable to the airbag going off. The passenger feels a huge increase in force. The passenger is alive, but possibly not unharmed. It is critical that we understand the consequences, in terms of force applied, of these different stopping modes in each unique system we work on. It is similarly critical that we make sure all three stopping modes have been engineered for and the facility impact of each has been considered. If it is at all possible for your system to generate a force, we must plan for it to be exerted no matter how rare the instance might be. Fully understanding these stopping modes will help you better risk assess your system if you are in the planning phase, and better operate the rig if you are in the show–execution phase.

Takeaways: Beginners

- There are three categories of stop that an automated system can actuate.
- Cat-0 is the most abrupt stop.
- The Cat-0 forces and physical outcomes must be known and planned for.

Takeaways: Professionals

- Cat-0 and Cat-1 stops are for emergencies while Cat-2 stops are for more normal stops.
- In Cat-0 and Cat-1 stops big power is removed from the machine as part of the stop *because* they are emergency stops.
  - This means an extra step is required to acknowledge the stop and re-energize the machine.
- Don't forget to consider the possible ability of our payload to outrun gravity in a Cat-0 stop, causing a shock load to the system when gravity ends up winning.

Part 3

Types of Rigs

We are finally ready to start talking about types of performer flying rigs! It can be easy to jump ahead to the topics and challenges in the pages ahead without considering the pages that came before. While this can work out from time to time, it is always better to think all the way through your system early and often. Both halves of solving the problem are equally important. Picking a type of rig without thinking about how to fabricate it is just as unproductive as making inspection sheets for a rig that doesn't exist yet. In this part we will review the most common types of performing flying rigs as well as concerns that cover all rigs, such as rescue, and selection of the right lifting media.

6 Making a Safe Sandbox

You may remember visiting playgrounds as a kid, or you may still now to blow off some steam. In those playgrounds of yesteryear you may have found a sandbox in which to play. This area was likely well defined with some wood edging or some other unmovable object to keep the pile of sand in place and defined. Remembering these sandboxes is a great way to think about the limitations of your fly rig. In this thought exercise the full available space your show takes place in is analogous to the playground. Once you have put limits on your rig so no collisions are possible, you have laid down the wooden beams that define the sandbox, an area inside of which you are safe no matter where you go. Now, with our limits correctly placed, anywhere you can get your rig inside the sandbox will be covered in "sand"; special safety sand. If you were to roll a winch into a venue, rig the line to the roof, and start running it, you would not be appropriately or completely protected from incident. This exercise would be equivalent to running around the playground with a blindfold on. While it might be fun for a while, you are bound to run face-first into a pole eventually. By defining a safe space and only playing inside it you have removed many variables that would otherwise need to be constantly monitored. It allows you to focus on the performer and the performance.

Sandbox Components

Component #1: Appropriate Hardware

To build your sandbox, you're going to want appropriate hardware. What exactly does that mean? First, to be clear, at the moment we are talking about connecting hardware. Carabiners, quick links, and quick-release clips. The simple goal here is "Do Not Become the Manufacturer." It can be upsetting to think about creating flying effects this way, but your primary thought when selecting hardware should be: What would happen in a court of law if this piece of hardware were to fail and cause an injury? If you approach hardware selection with this in mind, the choices become obvious. Clearly then, we want every piece to have identifying information on it. As a minimum it should include the manufacturer's name, a working load limit (WLL), or ultimate/ minimum breaking strength, and a lot/batch number. In an ideal world a unique identifying number would also be included (Figures 6.1 and 6.2).

Clearly then this rules out most hardware that can be purchased at the local hardware store. In recent years these "Home Depot Special" pieces of hardware have started to have load ratings stamped on them, which gives some less informed people comfort in using them. This comfort is ill-founded in reality, though. If a company were unwilling to put its name on its product, what would make you believe the load rating? Without all this information

Figure 6.1   Quick Link Comparison

Figure 6.2   Carabiner Comparison

included, the hardware simply has too questionable an origin to trust it with someone's life, or your reputation. If the goal is to not become the manufacturer yourself then you want to know the true manufacturer of the hardware will stand behind its product in the event of an accident.

Many of the same principles apply to construction hardware (i.e. nuts and bolts), if not the same hard rules. There is no hard rule about Grade 5 versus Grade 8, for example, or a particular hardness rating required. What is important is that the hardware shows appropriate and common markings as to its origins and strength.

As you can see in Figure 6.3, some bolts purchased from your local hardware store, while perfectly acceptable for small projects around the house, do not comply with industry-standard minimum-build-quality ratings. As such we do not want to see them in our flying systems. Make sure you or your mechanical designer understand the differences in the various grades of bolts. There are no fundamentally wrong decisions when it comes to what grade of bolt. But making these decisions without intention is a common mistake.

We have succeeded in not becoming the manufacturer of the hardware. How do we avoid becoming the manufacturer of the system as a result of the hardware selections we made? As always, and as discussed in Chapter 2, it is crucial that these decisions be approved by an engineer familiar with the dynamic forces the system will see.

Component #2: Appropriate Machines

Machines to fly people can come in many shapes, sizes, actuation methods, and levels of user friendliness. That said, most take on the form factor of a

Figure 6.3   Bolt Head Comparison

winch. Given some of the functions and features we are about to discuss, that will not seem like a coincidence. However, any machine having the following components is worthy of flying people.

Broadly speaking, what does every machine need? At its most fundamental level every machine needs a way to cause movement and a way to hold position. This means we need a method of actuation. In the case of a performer flying winch the actuation comes in the form of an electric servomotor. Why a servomotor? We want precise, repeatable control of the motor. In recent years the prices of both servomotors and the variable frequency drives (VFDs) that control them have come down to the point where such fine control is not out of reach to our industry. A generation ago the cost of such technology was simply out of reach for many staged productions. Various simpler and cheaper motors were used for rudimentary stage machinery. Without deep diving the differences in the different kinds of electric motors, the topic of whole books all by itself, just know that other kinds of motors were acceptable for simpler machines with less risk. Think of effects like deck tracks, or even flying inanimate objects. In a modern and safe performer flying machine, however, nothing less than a servomotor is acceptable (Figure 6.4).

Now that we have a way to move, we will need a way to stop. That means we will need brakes. All performer flying winches must have two independent brakes. The goal of two independent brakes is redundancy. If one entire brake were to fail, we would still have a whole other brake to arrest the load. As the need for two brakes comes from the desire for redundancy, each brake must be able to stop the whole load by itself (Figure 6.5).

Since we are designing the machine so that each brake by itself could arrest the load, each brake needs to be sized to do exactly that. Depending on where

Figure 6.4 A Servomotor

Figure 6.5   A Brake

your system is to be used, local codes also insist that each brake not only be rated for the WLL of the machine, but also have some headroom on that value. The exact value varies from code to code, which is discussed in detail in Chapter 13, but generally speaking each brake must be rated for somewhere between 110–150% of the WLL of the winch. If you're thinking all the way through the system, you might be saying to yourself "Does that mean if both brakes hit at the same time that we have up to 300% of the stopping force we need?" The answer to that is yes. That is why we have different stopping modes, Cat-0 versus Cat-1 versus Cat-2, which we discussed in Chapter 5. Clearly we want to avoid 300% arresting force on our system, and also on the performer experiencing such loads. Both brakes slamming shut simultaneously should only be a feature of a Cat-0 stop, and we should work to limit the scenarios in which a Cat-0 stop is triggered by the automation system. This is a product of good software design and a well-thought-out risk assessment.

Both brakes must also be fail-safe. We will discuss this further below when talking about limit switches, but to be succinct, this means that in the absence of electricity the brakes will be fully closed. To put it differently, the safe state of the brakes (closed) will be the passive state (no power). This means the only way to cause the brakes to open is to make the choice of supplying them with power.

Now we have a way to cause motion (our servomotor) and a means to stop (our brakes) we will need a way of managing our lifting media. *Lifting media* is really just a fancy way of saying "rope" but using the term "lifting media" indicates that we are talking about all forms, materials, and construction methods of rope. In this section specifically the term "rope" is used to loosely to cover steel cable, 12-strand synthetic fibers ropes, and other types. Again, these machines can take many forms so there are many ways to solve the problems of managing the rope. In the most common machines (winches) the answer is easy: it's a grooved drum (Figure 6.6).

One of the few things all the existing codes agree on is that the drum must be grooved to capture the rope. This thoroughly rules out another common drum style, the pile drum. In a pile drum the individual wraps do exactly as the name suggests; they pile on top of each other. While this can be a perfectly good solution for some kinds of scenic effects (and is certainly acceptable for pulling your Jeep out of a ditch) it is unacceptable for performer flying. The main reason for this is positional accuracy and repeatability. Neither is accurate enough to know the system will be reliably repeatable when a life is connected to it. Other concerns with pile drums relate to how the lifting media can become damaged as it piles on top of itself, often with varying degrees of tension in the line. Fabric rope in particular is very susceptible to damage as it rubs past other wraps on a pile drum. A grooved drum by comparison causes each wrap of the lifting media to have its own contact to the drum, not touching any other wrap of rope. Having enough real estate to lay all your rope so cleanly is why performer flying winches tend to be long, fat, or both. You need a drum large enough to house all the rope you're going

Figure 6.6 A Grooved Drum

to use! The further you want your available travel to be, the more drum you will need to manage the rope in this manner.

Now we have a way to move our machine (servomotor), a way to stop (brakes), and a way to store our lifting media (grooved drum), we need a way to know where the machine is. A GPS unit, if you will allow the comparison. For this purpose, our machine will need encoders (Figure 6.7). In the example of our machine being a winch, we will need rotary encoders. An encoder is an electromechanical addition to our winch that feeds back to our automation system a signal that increases or decreases at regular intervals. A "count" is the unit of measurement encoders send down the line. Encoders do not feed back units of measurements to the automation system. There are not different encoders for feet and inches versus millimeters. Encoders only feed back counts at regular intervals. Once this data reaches the automation software, we then scale those counts in our system so that it displays to us a unit of measurement we recognize instead of the encoder's raw value. For a broad understanding of encoders, the interval between counts does not matter, just that they are regular. From a more precise machine design perspective the frequency of counts does matter; this is called the resolution of the encoder. We want a lot of counts in a small distance. This will give us very fine control of the machine and high repeatability of position. Think back to the point made above about scaling; it is better to tell your automation software that 100 counts equals 1 inch than to tell it that one count equals 1 inch. The more counts the encoder reports back to the automation system over a reasonable physical distance the better your resolution, and therefore your positional accuracy.

Figure 6.7   An Encoder

Encoders fall into two main categories: incremental and absolute. Incremental encoders require power to remember where they are in their counts. This means every time you lose power with an incremental encoder you have to re-zero your machine. (To "zero" a machine is to tell it where it is in space. This is normally achieved by driving to a known position that has been spiked and then telling the automation software that is where you are.) Some incremental encoders have small watch batteries on board to help prevent this, but none of them feed back when that battery is low. The problem with this might seem obvious to you. Invariably the one time you need that battery to work you will discover it went dead during the last presidential administration. Quite oppositely and conveniently absolute encoders do not lose their position when they are powered down, and do not need a battery to remember their position. As a result, they are the preferred style of encoder for performer flying. They are also the preferred encoder for not ending up in an argument with an inanimate object.

As with everything in performer flying, we want to build redundancy into our machine. As such, two encoders are required on any performer flying machine. The encoders must be driven directly off the main drive train, and at least one should be an absolute encoder. With two encoders your automation software can now compare the counts from the two separate devices to make sure they are both working. If the difference between the two values becomes too great, the machine should come to a stop. This would indicate that one or both encoders are not functioning properly and should be inspected. Encoders tend to be fragile as most of the ones used in entertainment are optical encoders, which work by shining light through glass plates. If your machine takes a tumble it is not uncommon to have a busted encoder as a result. You can add this to the long list of reasons to not let your performer flying machines take unwarranted tumbles!

Now that we have a way to move (servomotor), a way to stop (brakes), somewhere to put our rope (grooved drum), and a way to accurately and repeatedly position the machine (encoders), we need a safety mechanism to prevent us from destroying our machine. These devices are called limits switches (Figure 6.8). The broadest of goals for the limit switches is to prevent us from driving our lifting media off either end of our drum. As we think more precisely about our system the goals for our limit switches also become more precise. Since our machine hopefully has far more capacity for lifting media than we need, we will need the limits to prevent us from physically running our performer into an obstacle. Because redundancy is one of our goals in the design of this machine, there will always be at least four limits switches on each machine, two at each end of travel. Limit switches are physical switches that are tied to the movement of the machine itself via a connection to the drivetrain, just like our encoders. Unlike our encoders, they do not require any software to know where they are. Since they are driven directly off the drivetrain of the machine, they will always strike in the same place relative to the machine's movement, eliminating any

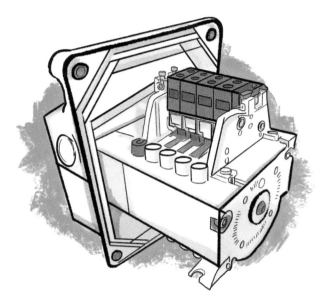

Figure 6.8 A Limit Switch

confusion on the software side of where "zero" is. These then protect you even if the automation software ends up thinking you have hundreds of feet of clear room to run when you are in fact near the end of your available travel on the machine. In that scenario one of the limit switches will get struck, triggering the automation system to immediately stop the machine.

Limit switches, like our brakes, are always wired to be fail-safe. However, unlike the brakes, which require electricity to get out of their passive (closed) state, our limits are normally closed switches which require a constant circuit of electricity to indicate they are in their passive (safe) state. When the switch is struck this circuit opens, cutting power to the bit in our automation system watching this switch, which causes the machine to stop. This provides an additional redundancy in that if the switch wears out or malfunctions, or wiring to it becomes damaged, the switch will behave as if it is struck, indicating a problem. As a result, a failure of any part of the switch or its electrical system will cause the automation system to default to a safe state. We are, as we always should be, monitoring the safe state of the machine.

To sum up the last several paragraphs, performer flying machines *must* have:

- Means of actuation (servomotor)
- Brakes
- Means of managing lifting media (grooved drum)
- Limits
- Encoders

There are also a host of add-ons that a performer flying machine might have. In certain jurisdictions some or all of these are required (for more information on code compliance see Chapter 13):

- Cross-groove detection
- Slack line detection
- Load monitoring
- Additional limit switches

Cross-groove detection is a means of knowing that your lifting media is laying correctly on the drum. There are many ways to achieve this monitoring but most of them follow the same idea. A bar is installed touching, or nearly touching, the rope as it spools on the drum. If the bar is designed to physically touch the rope on the drum then it is also serving another function and is called a pinch roller. In the case of the pinch roller scenario a switch of some kind, usually a proximity switch, is mounted into the end of the roller. If the cable spools incorrectly it will push the spring-mounted pinch roller away from the drum, triggering the proximity switch. This would then cause the automation software to stop the machine. If the cross-groove bar is mounted only near, but not touching, the rope then the monitoring is achieved in one of two ways. The bar can be designed to have a tall side and be knocked over by the rope not spooling correctly, and therefore piling on itself poorly and taller than it would otherwise. This in turn would strike a limit switch, again causing the machine to stop. Another method would be to have a small charge (usually 24v or less) running through an all-metal bar. If the rope is conductive and comes into contact with the bar the circuit becomes shorted and this state change causes the automation system to stop the machine. This, of course, relies on your rope being conductive and unobstructed to the bar. As previously discussed regarding limits, all these monitoring techniques must also be designed to be fail-safe.

Slack line detection is a means of knowing if your machine suddenly has a line that has gone slack, or suddenly has no load on it. This may seem like something that should really be noticed by technicians watching the machine or effect during regular use, but this monitoring can come in handy in certain situations. For example, if your flying system has to lower a person between obstructions in a tight spot and the person were to get hung up on something on the way down, you might want the system to be monitoring a slack state for you as it would be able to react faster to stop the machine. If the cue were to continue in that scenario without the operator noticing said slack, you would be exposing the performer to a potentially fatal fall. As helpful as slack line detection can be in that scenario it can be equally unhelpful if your effect involves sudden changes in the load on the winch. Many circus acts, and all bungee routines, should spring to mind (pun intended) as examples of easily causing this issue. That is why this feature is an option, and not a must-have, in most jurisdictions. Much like cross-groove detection there are countless ways to monitor for slack line conditions and all are acceptable as long as they are fail-safe.

Load cells (Figure 6.9) are the equivalent of having an in-line scale on your lifting media. They let you know exactly how much load is on your machine at any time. They can provide not only the obvious over-load monitoring but also under-load monitoring. In that way, load cells are starting to make stand-alone slack line detectors yesterday's news. They can be anywhere in the system of a machine's build, although building them into the winch, or at least a fixed part of the system, tends to make the cable management to the load cell easier. Two common locations are replacing the center axel of a sheave within the winch with a load cell pin, or designing your winch to have a load cell be the connecting hardware between the drum and the frame of the winch.

Load cells are built to measure force in one direction or axis. It is important to be sure if you are trying to measure compressive force that you have an appropriate load cell for that task. The same goes for tension and shear. Load cells usually feed back to the system an analog signal of milliamps. Just like encoders do not feed back feet or millimeters to the automation system, load cells do not feed back pounds or kilograms. Load cells are calibrated by hanging a series of known weights on your lifting media and recording the milliamp value the load cell reads back. From that information you can graph the curve between your known values so that the software can convert the milliamp feedback from the load cell into a more recognizable and palatable unit. A common mistake is to use the load cell to automatically stop the winch if the max lifting capacity of the winch is exceeded. While this sounds great at first, remember from our review of forces in Chapter 4 that if our

Figure 6.9 A Load Cell

winch is rated for 500 pounds, and we accelerate at full speed, the winch will see more than 500 pounds for a few moments. If we have our automation software stopping the winch if we exceed 500 pounds, this would cause the winch to stop while it was being operated under acceptable conditions. A calculated window must be left for acceleration and deceleration forces if such a safety feature is to be implemented. Another form of mitigation requires very advanced automation software but is becoming common. This would be to have an algorithm increasing and decreasing the acceptable load window live based on the acceleration, speed, and deceleration of the winch in real time. It is very difficult to set up, but is very impressive when it works!

Additional limit switches can be added to any machine if the need for such is identified early enough in the design or purchasing process. Why would you ever need more than four limit switches? Isn't that safe enough? Simply put, yes, it is. But through the process of RA/RR you may uncover a variable that needs to be accounted for. Examples here might be the need for a slow zone, which will be discussed in detail shortly, or an interlock. Some touring systems, which have to work every night despite surprises individual venues might throw at them, will have eight switches on them to account for a high-/low-trim situation. Clearly these are not features one would want to add in the field under duress. File this under more reasons for proper prior planning.

Component #3: Appropriately Set Limits

The number-one mistake that gets made when drawing automated systems as they interact with buildings is showing the payload attached to the machines coming within millimeters of the nearest obstruction. While this may seem logical to the casual observer, this is rarely achievable. We must allow additional travel distance for the machine to come to a complete stop before colliding with said obstruction. Thinking back to our sandbox analogy, you don't want to sprint around the sandbox right near the wooden beams defining the edge. What if you fall down and slam your head on the surrounding framing holding all the sand in? It would be much safer to move your adventures in from the edges to make sure that if you fall you still land in nice comfy safety sand (Figure 6.10).

As noted above, a winch correctly built for performer flying has two physical limit switches at each end of travel, an Ultimate Limit (or Emergency Limit) and an Initial Limit (or Hard Limit). Depending on which end of the machine each limit is at, they are referred to as the "+" or "-" limit. So, you might say to your coworker, "I'm going to go set the E+." This would mean you are about to work on the Emergency Limit on the "plus" end of the machine. When these limits are correctly set they can be run into at full speed and come to a complete stop without striking the next limit (in the case of the Initial/Hard Limit) or the first obstruction (in the case of the Ultimate/Emergency Limit). So how do we get the information we need to correctly space the limits for this necessary over-travel?

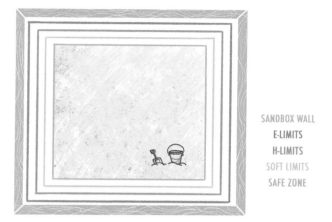

SANDBOX WALL
E-LIMITS
H-LIMITS
SOFT LIMITS
SAFE ZONE

Figure 6.10   Limited Sandbox

While theoretical numbers can (and should) be generated by computing the latency time of your switches, brake set timing, and inertia of the winch, when it comes time to actually set the limits empirical testing should be performed to get actual observed numbers. With the winch fully loaded to its rated capacity you want to intentionally run into the limits at full speed to record the required stopping distance. Does that mean we need to start off by guessing and hope we don't run into anything? Of course not! We can temporarily set the limits anywhere we want, like in the middle of the available travel, for example. Even easier, the limit switch can be manually triggered at any time. You will need to be graphing several data points as they come in for this to be successful.

Stop Starting Position – Fully Stopped Position = Stopping Distance

At minimum you will need Position and Velocity. Ideally you will also have the state of the switch shown in the same graph. All these variables should be graphed against Time. You need position so that you can measure the distance covered in the time between the stop being initiated and being completed. Velocity is needed to make sure you are actually at top speed before you initiate the stop. The state of the limit switch is ideal to have so you can be as precise as possible with your calculation of the distance covered during the stop. It will be pretty obvious on a graph when the stop was initiated, but without the state of switch you might discount about 300 milliseconds of time between when the stop was actually triggered and when the system started to react. This might seem negligible, and often it is, but depending on how fast your system moves at top speed this could add a significant distance

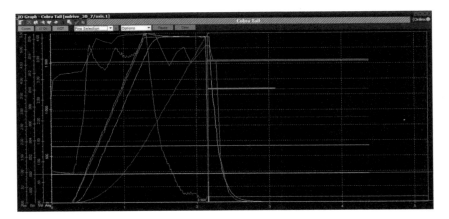

Figure 6.11   E-Stop Graph

to your stopping distance. If you can see the moment the switch is struck in your graph, the machine's position at that moment will be your "Stop Starting Position" in the above equation. Without that input on your graph you would have to take the position of the machine where the velocity clearly starts to nosedive as the "Stop Starting Position" (Figure 6.11).

This testing must be done for each limit at least once. It never hurts to do it more than once to make sure your data is correct and repeatable. That said, Cat-0 e-stops at full load and full speed are the worst-case engineering the machine and system has been designed for and as such should not be intentionally caused over and over again just for fun. It is also critically important to make sure you are triggering the correct flavor of e-stop (Cat-0, Cat-1) while performing this testing. As discussed in Chapter 5, these two flavors have very different stopping distances which we intentionally leverage to reduce forces on the system and our performers. The goal here though is to make sure we can hit our limit switch at full speed and still come to a complete stop before triggering the next switch or hitting the first obstruction. Clearly then it is important that our testing of the factual stopping distance use the correct flavor of e-stop.

The limits must always be set for your worst-case scenario. Worst-case, in this instance, means the longest distance it will take to come to a complete stop. For example, while testing your Initial Limit's stopping distance, if you were triggering a Cat-0 e-stop when in fact the system will be set up for a Cat-1, you will end up with a significantly shorter stopping distance than will exist factually. What could the outcome of this be? As the winch flew past the Initial/Hard Limit it would then hit the Ultimate/Emergency Limit because you didn't allow for enough over-travel. If your Ultimate/Emergency Limit were set up correctly there would be no damage to the system since this switch was set up to be hit at full speed and still stop before a collision. In this

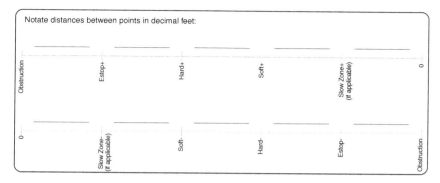

Figure 6.12 Limits Timeline View

situation you would, by the definition of a Cat-1 stop, hit the Ultimate Limit at less than full speed, and so you would stop well before hitting your first obstruction. While your machine will have safely stopped you would now be stuck on your Ultimate/Emergency Limit, which cannot be bypassed by your software. This would require a rescue of any performer on the winch, or if this were to occur during testing, a technician to get to the offending machine to physically bypass or move the limit. This is why the spacing of limits is so important! Once you have your safe sandbox you know you can do anything the machine says it can do and you are still protected not only from collisions, but also a constantly recoverable automation system. You then have the freedom to focus on creating not worry about these unpleasantries!

Now that we have measured what our stopping distances are, how do we use that information to correctly space the limits on the winch (Figure 6.12)?

- Part 1: Setting the Ultimate/Emergency +

  1. Slowly drive the machine to just before the collision with its first obstruction.
  2. Move the machine away from the first obstruction the stopping distance calculated plus a small safety factor of your choosing.
  3. Set the Ultimate+ Limit
  4. Physically bypass the limit at the winch.
  5. Drive the winch away from the limit in the opposite direction.
  6. Remove the physical bypass of the Ultimate+ limit.
  7. Reversing direction from Step 5, slowly drive into the limit.
  8. Once the limit is struck, determine if its location is adequate to come to a complete stop before striking the first obstruction.
  9. If yes, move on to *Part 2: Setting the Initial/Hard +*. If no, repeat Steps 3–8 until the location of the limit is acceptable.

- Part 2: Setting the Initial/Hard +

1. Move the machine to away from the Ultimate+ Limit location the stopping distance recorded from the Initial Limit testing, plus a small factor of safety of your choosing.
2. Set the Initial+ Limit.
3. Drive the machine away from the limit.
4. Reversing direction, slowly drive into the limit.
5. Once the limit is struck, determine if its location is adequate to come to a complete stop before striking the Ultimate+ Limit.
6. If yes, success! If no, repeat Steps 2–5 until the location of the limit is acceptable.

Lastly, we must set our Soft+ Limit. This limit is the innermost edge of the wall of our sandbox. It is digital only, meaning its position is based only on a position in your automation software. The stopping distance when striking the Soft at full speed is not as much of a concern as the Ultimate and Initial limits. The purpose of the Soft is really for your software to keep you from running into your Initial Limit all the time, which would cause a fault in your software. All that being said, the Soft Limit is set a distance far enough away from the Initial so that the Initial Limit is not triggered by mistake. This distance will depend upon your max speed, but it is commonly set 2–6 inches from the Initial Limit.

These steps should then be repeated for the Ultimate Minus (U-) and Initial Minus (I-) limits.

Once all these steps are complete, we have successfully and correctly set our physical limits to protect us! We now know that we protected ourselves from most, but certainly not all, catastrophic events that could come out of a mistake in programming. This point cannot be stressed enough, and this is why limits must be set before any person gets clipped onto a machine. These limit switches are what keep us from running into, at full speed, the edges of our sandbox. Once we have them set, everywhere inside our Soft Limits is our safe sandbox in which we can play freely. We have achieved the promise of Figure 6.10!

Not Enough Remaining Travel

We now have our limits set correctly and because we did all our pre-planning correctly we have enough travel to get everywhere we want to. But what if we didn't plan so well? What if now that we are safe we cannot fly out high enough because of our needed stopping distances? Or what if during our planning we realized that we wouldn't be able to get close enough to one of the extents of travel? Let's focus on the things we can control to improve our situation.

What determines our stopping distance? It is the relationship between the top speed of our machine and how fast the system arrests that speed. As you likely appreciate, since the machine is already installed and mostly tested in this scenario, now is not the time to go redesign the machine and buy new brakes. So that leaves only one variable to play with: our max speed. The first question we have to ask ourselves is: Do we need to go as fast as the machine says it can go? If the answer to that question is no, then you've got a readily available and easily executable solution at your disposal. Simply re-test your stopping distance with your newly selected top speed. If those values get your stopping distances short enough then all that is left to do is to reset all your limits. But is that enough to ensure we're safe? We just decided not to go as fast as the machine can go. But what happens if someone, being very tired, inadvertently commands the machine to go faster than we all just agreed to? In that scenario our newly reset limits would be insufficient to stop before colliding with our first obstruction. One cannot simply decide never to program the machine to go faster than X when the machine has the physical ability to go faster. For the system to be safe in using a top speed less than the full capacity of the machine, the VFD for the machine must have its parameters adjusted to not allow the machine to draw enough power to exceed the decided-upon speed. Only then can you be sure, even in a situation where the control software loses control of the machine, that it will not exceed the parameters you set your limits to.

Slow Zones

Let's say your limits encroach too much on your flight space, but you also need the full speed of the machine for the effect. What then? Well, as discussed above, the two factors are your top speed and the stopping force of the brakes of the machine. If we need the top speed for our effect, it seems like the only option remaining is the brakes. But what if we could guarantee that we would only be going a fraction of the top speed when we were near our limits? This idea is called a "slow zone" and it is the most common method to get around this problem. This will allow you to drastically shorten the stopping distance of your Initial/Hard Limit. Sadly we cannot shorten the Ultimate, or E, Limit. We always want that limit to be set for full speed, as that limit is our last line of defense in the event of a runaway machine.

As we talked about earlier in this chapter, every performer flying machine will have at least four limit switches and they will be driven directly off the main drivetrain of the machine. To achieve our slow zone we will need one additional switch for each slow zone we want to create. So, if you are only worried about the over-travel for your plus limits, you will only need one additional limit switch, making a total of five on your machine. If you need a slow zone at both ends of travel, you will need two additional switches, making a total of six on your machine. It is becoming increasingly common for newly built machines to be designed with six limit switches as standard for this exact issue. It is way easier to not program those switches to anything in your control system than it is to add them later, in a hurry, when you realize you *need* them.

There are seemingly easier ways to achieve this. However, they range from not being safe enough to not being safe at all. The most obvious other possible solution is by far the least safe. Why, you might ask, don't we just use the position of the winch and tell our control system to slow down when we reach a particular point from zero? If everything worked perfectly all the time this could work, but as we all know that's not the world we live in. Let's break that one down in two ways:

1.   What would happen if someone made a mistake zeroing the machine? Since your slow zone was based on a distance from zero and not a distance from your first obstruction, your slow zone would start somewhere you are not intending. One impact of this would be your slow zone starting inside your sandbox, which would negatively impact your cues, which were all programmed inside your sandbox walls. That is not the worst case, however; the opposite case is. Imagine your slow zone starting closer to your extent of travel than you thought. In this case you would be flying into your Initial/Hard Limit faster than your slow zone speed, which would mean it would take longer to stop once you hit that limit. Depending on the exact values involved in your specific scenario this would be very bad indeed. At best, you will end up stranded on your Ultimate/Emergency Limit. At worst you may collide with your first obstruction.

2.   We could strike out this concept in Example 1 before we even started down its path if we thought through some fundamentals first. Anything that is going to be for life safety should be driven off the drivetrain of the machine. Doing so gives us a similar safety backup as our other limit switches. We should not be relying on anything digital to pay attention to the position of the machine. We want everything this critical to be a physical switch unaware of where it is in space. Clearly then the best way to monitor the starting point of a slow zone is with a switch driven off the drivetrain of the machine.

You might now be asking yourself "But if my machine has an absolute encoder – can't I use the position off of that to activate my slow zone?" While this is the best way to trigger a slow zone if you absolutely must and you don't have extra switches, it is not 100% safe. First of all, powering down equipment can affect your drive's reading of the absolute encoder value. It's rare, but it can happen. Similarly, when you re-spool the winch, if you do not put the exact same amount of lifting media on the machine your slow zone will again be in the wrong place. The danger is that you are no longer protected and you wouldn't know until you needed the protective service of your slow zone to save you. This is because you are monitoring the unsafe state. Pushing into the unsafe area of travel triggers a behavior instead of the preferred opposite. To put it another way, your sandbox wall has broken and you have no way of knowing until you are past the wall.

To properly set a slow zone we first need to decide what we want our slow zone speed to be. The easiest way to do this is very similar to how we figured out what the stopping distance for our limits were. Remember: the goal of this is to reduce the needed stopping distance if/when we run into our limits. So, the first step in the process is to open a graph in your software that is showing at least position, speed, and time. Now you will run the machine at various controlled speeds. Depending on your situation, starting in increments of 1 foot per second will yield good data. So first you will move your machine at 1ft/sec and then strike the Initial Limit switch. In your graph you can then determine what the stopping distance was. You would then repeat that process at 2ft/sec, then 3ft/sec, and so on until you observe the stopping distance you are after. Now you know what your new limit distance should be for your Initial Limit, but how do we know where to start our slow zone?

To properly set a slow zone we will want to know how long it takes for the machine to go from full speed to our desired slow zone speed. Our desired slow zone speed is equal to whatever speed we discovered in the test we just did. By limiting the speed of our winch to a value that allows us to stop in the space we have available to us we can put our Initial/Hard limit much closer to the Ultimate/Emergency limit than we otherwise could. First, we will make sure our additional switch is mapped in our software to cause the machine to be limited to a particular speed; for this example we will say 1 foot per second, commonly abbreviated as 1ft/sec. Open a graph in your software showing Speed, Position, and Time. Next, run a cue that will take the winch up to full speed. When full speed is observed on your graph, physically trip the slow zone switch. Once your winch has slowed down to the slow zone speed you would then stop the cue. Now on your graph you can calculate how much distance is required to go from full speed to your slow zone speed.

Lastly, we need to reset our limit stack. Our Ultimate/Emergency Limit remains unchanged. We set it to be the stopping distance we measured for a Cat-0 stop from our first obstruction. Nothing about this process has changed any of the variables involved in that stop. As such we leave that limit where it was. Our Initial/Hard Limit will now be based off the newly measured stopping distance of our slow zone speed. Just as before, we will drive our winch to a position that is our slow zone speed stopping distance from the spot our Ultimate/Emergency Limit is triggered. Once the winch is at that position we will reposition the Initial/Hard Limit switch here and test that it triggers where we are expecting it to. Once our Initial/Hard Limit is in the correct position we will set the location of our slow zone switch. We will take the distance we measured for how long the winch takes to slow from full speed to slow zone speed and set the switch that distance from the spot the Initial/Hard Limit is triggered. Then we will test that this switch is being triggered at the correct position, just as explained earlier in this chapter. The only step left at this point is to adjust our Soft Limit. We still want that to be just a touch from the spot our Initial Limit is triggered. This may seem incorrect at a quick glance, but the slow zone area is still useable travel space; we have only restricted the speed at which we can travel in that zone. The Soft Limit is designed to make sure we do not run into our two limits at the end of travel, but we want to be able to use the slow zone area as useable travel. Our Soft Limit will end up near the end of the normally useable slow zone area, just before the Initial/Hard Limit. Our slow zone then is analogous to a baseball-style warning track near the walls of our sandbox.

Conclusion

It takes great time and care to successfully and correctly build a safe sandbox in which to play. This process starts by understanding early where the walls of your sandbox will be and making sure those walls are far enough outside where you need to travel during the performance that you have enough room left to stop. This is the downfall of so many rigs that we allow ourselves to believe are "basic" or "easy" or "just …" To be clear: nothing in performer flying is "just" anything. Each situation is unique and should be approached as such. That said, there are basic fundamentals that must always be adhered to. Most notably from this chapter are the basic building blocks of a safe performer flying machine. Regardless of the specific scenario we are in we will always need those parts listed above to be in our system to allow ourselves to fly a person. They are just as important to the creation of our safe sandbox as our limits stacking up. While this process can be time consuming, both from a proper prior planning standpoint and an execution one, successfully building a safe sandbox in which to play gives you the peace of mind of knowing you've removed a number of otherwise catastrophic risks from your day-to-day life.

Takeaways: Beginners

- Building a safe sandbox is critical to protecting yourself and your team from accidents.
- The safe sandbox doesn't prevent all accidents.
- All performer flying winches must have a servomotor, a grooved drum, fail-safe redundant brakes, two encoders (preferably with at least one being an absolute encoder), and a means of safely making sure the machine cannot run into anything or eat itself (limits).
- The setting of limits for a performer flying machine requires testing, precision, and time.
    - Plan accordingly.

Takeaways: Professionals

- The sandbox analogy can seem rudimentary, but it can be a great tool in explaining your process to others who may not be as experienced as you in the field.
- Understanding whether your machine has the basic components to be a performer flying machine is paramount.
- Make sure you fully understand the stopping distances of your machine before you lead the process of setting limits.
  - This is one of, if not *the*, most important safety steps in the process.
- If your system involves a complication you are not familiar with (load cells, slack line detection, etc.) ask for help! Don't pretend to know something you don't!

7 Single-Axis Rigs

Having only a single axis of motion can seem, on its surface, as easy as it gets. Depending on what you're doing with it this can be true, but it's often an incorrect assumption. For example, some are quick to think a single-axis rig means we can't use any harnesses requiring a connection at each hip. This is not at all true! The "single axis" refers to the number of lifting axes, not the number of lines you've connected to the performer. With a single-axis rig you can fly with a single line from the winch to a performer wearing a Jerk Vest (covered more thoroughly in Chapter 11), or have that single line off the winch be connected to a spreader bar above the performer with two lines going down to the performer to pick up on their Bungee Harness, or even have two lines coming off your winch directly to the performer's hips. If the gag is something simple like an angel going straight up and straight down, your single-axis rig could in fact be an easy day. However, if you are trying to do a Cirque du Soleil-style pendulum flight, your single axis can quickly become one of the more challenging tricks in the performer flying canon. Never, ever, let yourself fall into the trap of thinking a performer flying effect is "just" anything. Even things that appear simple on the surface can become very complicated very quickly, and possibly result in serious injury. The discussion that follows assumes we have already considered and done everything in Chapter 6, so we know we have a safe sandbox in which to play.

At its simplest design a single-axis rig could be a machine in the roof to lift and lower a performer with the line coming straight off the drum. This means we have no rigging beyond that which is keeping our machine in the air. The line comes straight off the machine and connects directly to our performer. Complicating the rigging slightly would see the introduction of a single sheave so that the machine could be on the ground with a line coming off it, up through the aforementioned sheave, and back down to the performer. This can work great in non-traditional settings where the sight of the machine in the performance space is not a problem. However, for most productions there will be a strong desire to not have the big ugly performer flying machine out in view of the paying public. To solve this issue we get to a frequently used configuration: the two-sheave, single-axis rig (Figure 7.1).

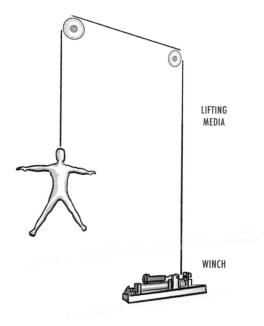

Figure 7.1   Two-Sheave, Single-Point Rig

In this configuration, the machine is placed on the ground off in a wing (of a proscenium space) with at least one line coming off it, running up to the first sheave, traversing laterally through the second sheave, and then down to a performer. We now have our machine hidden from the audience and the line dropping exactly where we want it on stage. If our machine is a zero-fleet winch, or is a manual system, then the placing of the first sheave (or "loft block" if in a theatre) immediately above the system is easy. Simply place it precisely and immediately above the system; structural analysis allowing, of course. Hopefully you have done your homework with your site survey and your third-party engineering before this moment so you have already finished hemming and hawing over where the load can be transmitted into the building while also not leaving the system in a wholly inconvenient location. If, however, your winch is not a zero-fleet machine you will need to ensure that your first sheave is far enough away from the winch so as not to be operating outside of an acceptable fleet angle. What exactly is acceptable fleet will depend on a variety of factors, such as the type of rope you are using and if your sheaves have donuts on them (more on that later), but keeping it under 1.5 degrees of fleet angle is always recommended. For a more detailed discussion of the concept of fleet angle please see Chapter 1.

To this point we have been discussing these sheaves as rigidly mounted to a roof structure of sufficient strength. But what if bolting your sheaves to the grid (like those of a common counterweight system) is not an option? You can in certain instances choke an industrial sling (or similar) to a structural member and flag your sheave off the end of it. This has its benefits and drawbacks. For example, introducing this flexible connection can help you in a difficult fleet situation. The sheave will now be able to pivot about its connection to the building as the lifting media needs it to move about the drum. If we are to rely on this to help us out in a less-than-ideal fleeting situation we must also consider more regular inspections on both the sheave and the lifting media, a necessity that should have been called out in our RA/RR paperwork. Another drawback of this plan is the positional inaccuracy it can add to the system. Only when loaded substantially will the sheaves flag consistently to the point they will remain rigid in space. At any other load the sheaves will not be able to stay in the same place. Instead they will pivot down about their connection to the building as load is removed from the line. (Yay gravity!) This can result in challenges to precise programming repeatability. That said, this same behavior can also have a positive shock-absorbing effect on the system. As with any other design choice it's crucial to think all the way through your system to decide if this idea is suitable for the particular effect you are trying to realize.

The two-sheave, single-axis rig scheme is great for the simplest of gags. The performer comes out on stage and is raised and lowered straight up and down. This plan, of course, relies on the performer to hit his or her spike perfectly every performance. If they don't, they will begin to pendulum around. This will in turn cause the cable to enter the sheave poorly or in extreme cases possibly jump out of the sheave altogether. This is the same problem we just went to great lengths to avoid by calculating the fleet between the machine and the sheave above it! Why then would we not take the same care for the other end of the rope and its first sheave? How can we prepare for a performer to be off their spike by mistake? The same way we would prepare the same style of rig for a performer to swing intentionally in one axis, or even make a conic flight.

Donuts

While often critical to the start of the day in the entertainment industry, we are not talking about the pastry kind of donut here. Instead we are talking about an additional assembly that helps to ensure the rope always hits the sheave or drum of the winch correctly. The pivot point for a swing will be the first object the rope rests on. Without mitigation this will be the exit point of the sheave immediately above the performer. If we instead add an additional object to act as the pivot point, we have created a donut. This addition allows us the peace of mind of knowing the rope will always be hitting the sheave correctly, regardless of what is happening below the sheave. Sometimes these devices are placed right at the exit point of the sheave, but they don't have to be. They can be as far away from the sheave as need be as long as they line up within acceptable fleet limits of the sheave they are protecting. Why would you want the donut far from the sheave? Well, consider if your grid is 80 feet above the stage, but to get the swing pattern you are after you need the pivot point to be 40 feet off the deck. You can still mount your sheave to the grid 80 feet away, and then add a sufficiently sturdy donut in space directly below the exit point of that sheave at your desired pivot point. Now you have created a pivot where you needed it and you also know the rope will always hit the sheave just the way you want it to. A good day's work!

So how do we make one of these "donuts"? They can be made in all shapes and sizes, depending on your particular use case. The important thing, as always, is to think through the whole problem and make sure you considered all your use cases before deciding which style donut, if any, is right for this particular effect. The most basic of donuts is best described as a "sacrificial donut". In this case the material of the donut is selected because it is intentionally softer than the rope material, but still strong enough to withstand the forces it will be exposed to. Delrin, Nylatron, or similar plastics are great examples when used with steel wire ropes. With appropriate engineering sign-off that the chosen plastic can withstand the moment forces it will be exposed to, there is nothing wrong with choosing such a material that you know will wear over time. In many ways, knowing the lifting media is stronger than the donut, and will therefore always win the wear battle, can be a great choice.

Of course, there are many additional considerations to keep in mind when making this decision. As we see in Figure 7.2, frequent inspection will be

Figure 7.2   Sacrificial Donut

required. Knowing that the donut is significantly softer than the lifting media lets you relax in the knowledge that the donut will not degrade the rope, but on the flip side we *know* the rope will degrade the donut. As a result, we will want to have frequent inspections, and if the production is at all long-running, it would be advisable to have replacements on standby. After the lifting media has worn a gouge in the donut material it will need to be monitored closely regarding losing too much of its material for its structural integrity, or increasing the fleet angle too much. However, the performer on the end of the line will likely complain of feeling the rope jump in and out of said groove long before either of those become the real issue.

If, through your design process, you discover that a sacrificial donut won't do, then the next step up would be to have a donut with moving parts. In this design concept the donut is made of rollers, allowing the lifting media to pass through it without rubbing. This allows us to use the donut concept even on the most fragile of fabric ropes. Material selection of the rollers is still crucial and needs to be made on a case-by-case basis to ensure that the roller will not damage the lifting media. Do not forget to take into consideration the effects the spinning donut parts will have on the lifting media if they suddenly seize up between inspections. These edge-case scenarios are particularly important on single-point rigs, where you are, by definition, in a single-point-of-failure condition. These are the kinds of scenarios that need to be addressed and mitigated in your RA/RR paperwork.

In Figure 7.3 we have a donut composed of four rollers in two pairs, offset 90 degrees from each other, known as a quad roller donut. This captures the rope within a tolerance close to the overall diameter of said rope. This means you will always hit the sheave with near-perfect alignment. This design also means that regardless of which direction you bend the rope it will be in contact with at least one, and often two, rollers. Astute readers might question the D:d relationship of the roller to the rope. Good job! This all depends on how far around the roller

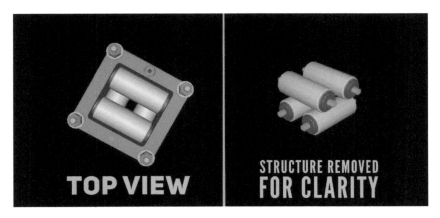

Figure 7.3 Quad Roller Donut

you will be bending the rope, under what load, and how often it happens. Every donut must be thought through for its unique use case. If you were planning on coming out of this donut at a 45-degree angle with a lot of load, the conceptual design here could likely be recycled to something with larger-diameter rollers that would better respect the D:d ratio of your lifting media.

Donuts' Effect on Limits

A common weak spot in RA/RR paperwork on rigs involving donuts is the taking into account of how the donut will affect the needed placement of limits, and in turn how that will affect the overall system. If you are using a donut as shown in Figure 7.3, clearly the rope termination running into the donut would be your first obstruction, and not the sheave above it as is so often assumed. This means all your normal travel-limiting consequences of limits will exist below the donut. This is a common, and needless, source of frustrations and arguments at rehearsals. Make sure you take this into account before it's staring you in the face! Another difficult scenario for RA/RR that comes from donuts is a common workaround for the limits issue. As seen in Figure 7.2 with the sacrificial donut, you can make the center big enough for the rope termination to pass through the center of the donut. Then, so the faulty line of thinking goes, we can set the limits just as we would if the donut weren't there at all. While this design concept does allow for the rope termination, and possibly even a prop attached to the line, to pass unharmed, it does not allow a human to pass through the center of the donut at all. While one function of the limits is to protect the equipment, their main purpose is to protect the performer on the line. As such, the limits must still be set to prevent the possibility of pulling said performer through the donut. This is a particularly common mistake in acrobatic effects, especially those with long drape-y apparatus, like tissue. "But we have to be able to fly the tissue out of view," someone will say. This is an understandable expectation, but not reason enough to justify the risk. There are two ways to solve this, neither of which involve putting the performer in harm's way by having the limits set above the donut. One is to simply fly the apparatus out until the winch hits its Soft+ Limit, and then manually pull the line the rest of the way out of view, through the donut. This way, the performer is protected by the limits and the director still gets his or her wish of not having the tissue hang there all night. The other is a complicated design task to take on, both mechanically and on the controls side, but is not insurmountable. That would be a removable donut.

There are a number of reasons why you might want to be able to remove the lifting media from the donut after you have terminated it. As previously mentioned, allowing the automated control of the winch above the donut before and after the donut's use is a common reason for this feature to be included. Also consider, in a touring application, if the donut is located in a different part of the rig from the winch. You will need to be able to remove

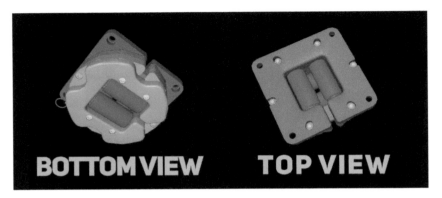

Figure 7.4   Quad Roller Opening Donut

the rope from the donut in order to coil it back to the winch for transport. In the latter example, the opening mechanism need only be secure enough to pass engineering and the eye test. In the former example, however, where life safety is at stake, this will also require the addition of a powered switch to tell the automation system when the donut is there and when it is not. The specifics of this setup will of course depend, and vary wildly, on the vagaries of your particular control platform.

In Figure 7.4 we see our old friend the quad roller donut but now with the ability to remove the line from the capture of the donut. This is achieved, in this example, by using a simple spring plunger to hold the donut in its closed position when in use. As this feature on this particular donut was designed to aid in the load in/out of the equipment, there is no control input/output device to report the donut's status back to the automation system.

Spreader Bars

As previously discussed in the opening paragraphs of this chapter, a "one-point rig" does not limit you to having only one point connected to the performer. To split our one actuation line into two, or more, connection points to the performer we will need a spreader bar. These will vary in shape and size based on their intended use. The most basic form connects a single line from a winch on its top and has two, often thinner, lines coming off the other side to connect to a performer's hips (Figure 7.5).

While this basic shape and function will cover 90% of the rigs involving spreader bars, it is important to not get complacent on checking the original engineering for the bar against what you are next planning to do with it. It is not hard to imagine the outcome of using a spreader bar off the shelf for a load or an e-stop force it was never designed/engineered for.

When designing a spreader bar from scratch, we also have the opportunity to remove several pieces of single-point-of-failure hardware from the system.

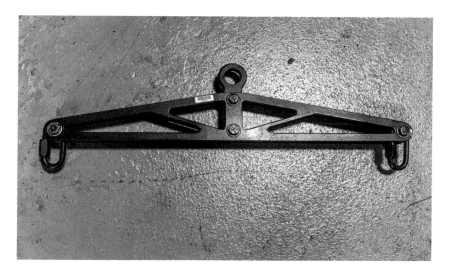

Figure 7.5 Basic Spreader Bar

With single-point rigs, controlling the direction the performer is facing is always a challenge. As we will discuss later in Chapter 10, many common lifting media have a rotation bias to them. This means that simply loading the rope will cause the load at the end of the line to spin. To combat this, most one-line rigs will have a swivel between the rope termination and the performer. When a swivel is added to a system as an afterthought, it will require a piece of connecting hardware on either side of it as most swivels are solid rings on either side of a bearing. A spreader bar designed in a vacuum will come out of the shop with solid rings, or holes in a plate, to connect to the rest of the system. This is great if you are planning on swaging or splicing the lifting media directly to the bar. But if you're going to use a swivel, why not design the spreader bar to accept the swivel somehow (Figure 7.6), allowing the removal of the otherwise-needed connecting hardware to the swivel?

As with any other part of a performer flying system, the whole effect should be thought all the way through when deciding to design a spreader bar. The above swivel integration is just one example of a feature that can be built into a custom-made piece of gear. A more detailed discussion of swivels' effects on wire rope can be also be found in Chapter 10.

Think about the end user and the script. Is there a prop the performer will have to hold? Does it need to be safetied? An additional feature of the spreader bar could help with that. How much extra weight will be needed for the system to run safely without the performer on the line? The spreader bar could be made intentionally heavier than need be to perform the task of being your needed line weight, while always, of course, considering the overall visual impact of your bar on the scene it will be used in.

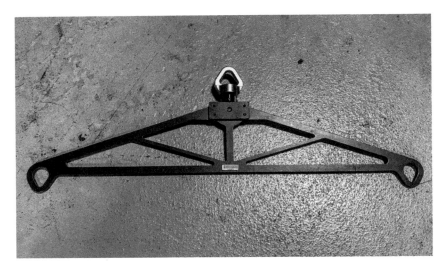

Figure 7.6 Spreader Bar with Swivel

Line Weights

An oft-forgotten feature of performer flying rigs is that they need weight on them to run safely when the performer is not on the line. This is another area that can result in arguments with the artistic staff if not considered and talked about early in the process. The exact amount of weight you need will vary, as so many features do, based on your needs for this particular effect. The most obvious factors are how much rope is off the drum that you need to move, and the weight per foot of that rope. The location of the winch and the spacing between sheaves will also have a huge impact on how much your line weight will need to weigh. This is an area of client management where under-promising and over-delivering is the way to go. Promising a director or other artistic person the line weight will be impossibly small, only to show up with a 50-pound sandbag, will always result in difficult conversations. The opposite, however, will make you a hero.

At its most basic, your line weight can be a sandbag or steel plate with a single connection point (Figure 7.7). This will allow you to remove the performer, spreader bar, prop, or other pretty thing from the line and replace it with your weight to fly the system out of view. This is most ideal when a technician is able to do this out of view. This is also fairly common in circus at the end of an aerial routine. The acrobat performs the apparatus-for-weight switch after taking their bow. Wouldn't it be great though if we didn't have to take the weight off the line in the first place?

Enter the inline weight (Figure 7.8). Here we have basically the same concept as above. It can be something soft, like a sandbag, or a solid steel

Figure 7.7   Sandbag with Ring

Figure 7.8   Inline Weight

construction. The only difference is that we have a connection point on either end of the weight. This allows us to put it between the winch line and the performer, apparatus, or prop and leave it there always! This can be viewed as less-than-ideal by the artistic people in the room because of its visual impact. That said, you get to control the line weight's aspect ratio as you design it. You can make it short and fat or long and thin, and still have it weigh the same. Don't forget to consider that in this configuration the line weight is part of the load path of the system and as such will need engineering approval. If only there were some way to have the weight always on the line but not be part of the load path …

Enter the clamshell weight (Figure 7.9). Here we have taken our inline weight, removed the eyes, and sliced it in half down the middle. After machining out a hole slightly smaller than our rope diameter and drilling and tapping a few other holes, we now can clamp the weight around the lifting media above our termination. Drilling the hole slightly *smaller* than the rope diameter is a crucial design feature; this allows the clamshell weight to grip to the rope. That said, we don't want to make it so small that the clamshell weight can damage the rope. This tolerance takes some prototyping with your particular lifting media. All the same artistic concerns will exist with this line weight as with the inline weights. But, as with those, you can control its aspect ratio while you design it.

As the use of the clamshell puts the weight above the termination, do not sleep on how this effects your limit placement. Your first obstruction is no longer

Figure 7.9   Clamshell Weight

the end of the rope termination, but instead the top of the clamshell weight. This will require resetting your limits accordingly. Yet another reason to think your system all the way through in the beginning and not make it up as you go!

Clamshell weights are rarely used on fabric ropes as shown above as the metal of the weight will likely cause damage. For fabric ropes you can use a sandbag that has been sewn to have a hole down the middle. With this you will retain the ability to have the inline weight above your rope termination, but you will lose the clamshell's feature of being able to be removed without cutting off the rope termination. There are countless other creative solutions for getting winches to run without their human load on. (Powered diverters come to mind; an electromechanical device that holds constant tension on the line.) That said, the solution isn't always another machine, or a more complicated control system. The best solutions often come from a mix of proper prior planning and situational awareness as the show comes together.

Pendulum Flights: Where to Begin

Our artistic team have now said that they don't want the flight to be as easy as straight up and down. It needs to be a flight in one plane, swinging from one part of the stage to another à la Peter Pan, or it needs to be a big conic flight so our acrobatic straps performer can swing all over the stage. Many people get very intimidated when inertia is injected into their flying schemes because they don't know where to begin. A simple dissection of what we're trying to achieve though reveals how easy this can be.

We will start with the Peter Pan example. With a single point we want Peter to enter stage right, take off, swing, and land stage left. A common mistake is to start this programming effort by putting a technician on the line and letting the programmer guess-and-check until it looks okay. This puts the technician in a lot of undue danger. As we will discuss later in Chapter 14, we never put a human on the line before we test with a sandbag. But where do we even begin with a sandbag in this scenario? First of all, it is crucial the sandbag weigh the same as the performer who will be riding the winch. Now is not the time for vanity, and it's not the time for round numbers. We need to know exactly what the performer weighs, and we want to get the sandbag very close to that number. Don't forget to include the weight of the costume and any props they will have on them!

Once that is achieved, we will take the sandbag and connect it to our single line coming off the winch. We will raise the sandbag with our winch until the bottom of the sandbag is a few inches off the stage. Now we know when we swing the bag it won't hit the stage. Next we will have the automation operator open the stopwatch function on his or her phone. We will then back up with the sandbag, better referred to as Sandy, to the desired takeoff point. When we release Sandy and let gravity do its thing, we have our operator friend time how long it takes for the bag to get from the desired takeoff spot to the desired landing spot. Now we know how long the up and down cues to fly Peter can take to have him land safely! Once that test is complete, we need to establish what our takeoff and landing heights will be. To do this we will land Sandy on the ground and connect the spreader bar or other attachment device to the winch line. We then hold tension on the system while our programmer pays out the line until it is in a sufficient spot to take off/land. With this information, the programmer can work on a first draft of an up cue and a first draft of a down cue. The goal here is to have the time to execute both those moves complete in the time we recorded with the swing test.

Now we can test these cues with Sandy so that if anyone gets hurt due to an errant number being typed into a field in our control software it's our dear inanimate friend Sandy. It is strongly recommended to protect your stage surface with a crash mat of some kind during these tests. Barring an error from your programmer, you will be shocked how close to perfect this first draft will look. Of course, the cue will need refinement to make it look clean, but these steps will get you very close very quickly. What happens next is a judgment call on your part as the Flying Director. If you or someone on your staff is a competent and qualified flyer you may want to dial in the cuing with your technical staff so when the performers show up you are teaching them how to ride a finished product of a cue. If, however, you are not staffed in this manner or you have very experienced performers, you may want to simply get the cuing to a safe place and wait to do the final dialing in of the cues until you have your performers on the line. In any case crash mats should always be used during training to protect anyone flying, as well as a liberal use of Sandy to be the first to test any cuing changes. It only takes one errant number in your control software to cause an event that can end in a serious injury, even after you've made your safe sandbox.

Yo-Yo Flights

Often in performer flying there is a desire for someone to yo-yo up and down over and over again. Writing a series of standalone up-and-down cues and running them over and over again can easily enough achieve this goal. However, this approach will almost always look rather disjointed and mechanical. To this point we have only spoken about single-axis rigs in terms of design, math, and hard skills. This is where we begin to transition into needing to be interested in the art of it all. Creating a performer flying rig can be a huge technical achievement, but these systems only serve to embellish an otherwise worthy artistic endeavor. As such, we need to view our programming with an artistic eye. Just because one way to program is the fastest line to being done, that does not mean it is the best way to make the effect look the most convincing.

In Figure 7.10 we can clearly see the difference between writing a series of trapezoid moves versus combining them into one long motion, referred to as a "profile". In the trapezoid moves, each up or down must completed and brought to a complete stop before the next can begin. When we also take into account the amount of time the automation system takes to acknowledge the first move has stopped and the next one can begin, we being to see a very

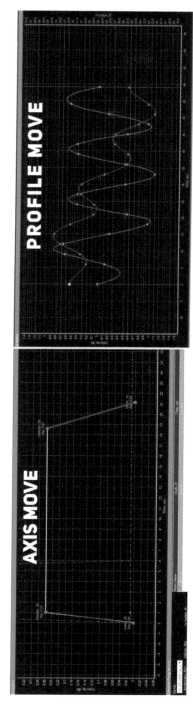

Figure 7.10   Axis Move versus Profile

disjointed series of moves on the end of the line. Instead, if we write this as a profile we can smooth the deceleration of one move directly into the acceleration of the next. This, while slightly more difficult to program, will result in a much cleaner and more natural-looking up-and-down sequence. It can take a fair amount of trial and error to get it just right, but when you do it will always have been worth the time invested. This smoothing is quite often the difference between making it look like the performer is controlling or commanding their motions in the air instead of just being along for the ride.

While this is an advanced feature of modern automation platforms, this happens nearly automatically with manual systems. The human on the operating line will smooth the various accelerations and decelerations into each other. While this makes the flights more quickly look like a beautiful aerial dance, a manual system still cannot guarantee the positional repeatability of an automated one.

Conclusion

While single-axis rigs can seem to be very easy when taken at face value, they are in fact just as complicated as other rigs. Do not be lulled into complacency by thinking a single-axis rig is "just" this or that. Single-axis rigs have all the dangers and pitfalls of more complicated rigs, while also having a few booby traps unique unto themselves. Do not make the mistake of under-thinking, under-planning, or under-scheduling a single-axis rig just because it's "only" a single axis. Whether you have one person or 20 in the air, the rig deserves your same attention and efforts.

Takeaways: Beginners

- Single-axis rigs are for more than just simple up-and-down flights.
- Thinking through your system early and often needs to include things like spreader bars, line weights, and donuts.
- Programming can be complicated. Make sure you allow for appropriate time.

Takeaways: Professionals

- If your flying machine is going to be on the ground and routed through sheaves above, make sure you have appropriately addressed any fleet angle concerns in your design.
- Make sure to take into account the effect of your various system add-ons (like donuts) on setting appropriate limits.
- Programming pendulum and conic flights need not be intimidating.

8   Two-Axes Rigs

A single-axis rig can be very versatile, but it has its limitations. While it can be used to transport a performer from one end of the stage to the other, that will always be a dynamic move. There is simply no way to use a single axis to slowly lift and travel a performer a great distance. Similarly, if we have a series of simple up-and-down lifts in our show but they need to happen in various positions over the stage, we have no good way of doing that with a single axis, or we might need several machines, only using each one once in our show. Enter the two-axes rig. These can manifest themselves in many different configurations, which we will discuss in the pages that follow, but there is a theme that connects them all: separating the lifting action from the travel action. By being able to independently control each axis of motion we are able to create flight paths that are simply unachievable with a single axis.

Lift/Travel Rigs

Lift/travel rigs are aptly named, as they do just that. They have two axes of motion, one for lift and one for travel. In a single-axis rig we can only really control the lift of the performer. If the axis were a horizontal one, you could control motion in that direction but not up and down. As such the horizontal only performer flying rig is rare. By utilizing a pendulum effect we can *initiate* travel with a single lifting axis, but we can't really *control* it. By separating the travel axis from the lift, we can create repeatable motion. Lift/travel rigs are usually achieved by slapping a set of tracks on a run of truss to support the movement of a trolley back and forth. This traveling motion is one of our two axes. At its simplest design, we then attach a lifting axis (like a winch) to these tracks and drive the whole lifting machine back and forth across the truss. While this is the least complex lift/travel rig from a rigging design standpoint, it gets fairly complicated as we drill down on the machine design details. For example, the traversing axis is usually achieved with some sort of rack-and-pinion design. The vagaries of this style of machine may be outside the expertise of your designers. This plan also clearly mandates the need for automation. To be clear, lift/travel rigs need not be automated. There are countless ways to reeve a lift/travel system to be run manually or automated. For example, instead of tracking the whole lifting machine back and forth across a truss or track, what if we instead ran just a sheave back and forth on a skate? Now we have the ability to move the sheave immediately above the performer anywhere along the track we want, simply by running our lifting axis rope through that moving sheave. As such, one of the first decisions we need to make for our lift/travel rig should be what reeving scheme will work best for this production. While there are variants and filigrees that can be added to any system, the reeving of this kind of system breaks down into two main groups: mechanical compensation and electrical compensation. What do we mean by *compensation*? In this case, *compensation* is referring to how we are decoupling the lift axis from the travel, and how that decoupling effects how we control the lifting axis. We will start by showing E-comp in practice to explain this concept.

Electrical Compensation

As we can see in Figure 8.1, we have a lifting line running through a trolley on a set of skates on a truss. Done and done, right? What else is there to talk about? Well, we need to discuss what happens when one axis moves without the other. Remember, these axes of motion are being controlled by separate machines. What happens if we move the travel axis but not the lift axis?

As we see in Figure 8.2, if we move the travel axis 1 foot without moving the lifting axis, the performer will rise 1 foot. If we were to travel in the opposite direction the performer would lower by 1 foot. So then, to achieve level flight while traveling we need to also move the lifting axis a proportional

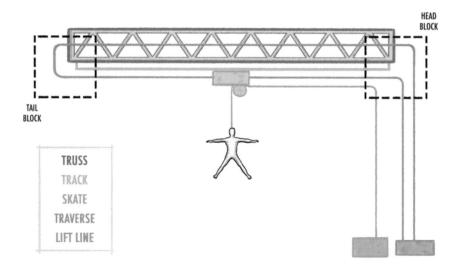

Figure 8.1 E-Comp Rig

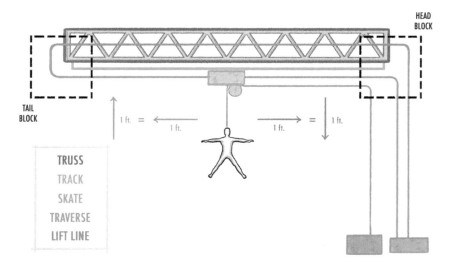

Figure 8.2   E-Comp Rig Annotated

amount. This is what we mean by *electrical compensation*. The compensation is how we are achieving level flight while traveling. We consider this to be compensation to be "electrical" because you are most likely using your control software to achieve level flight. "But wait," you may be saying, "I thought you said this can be done manually." Lift/travel rigs can, and frequently are, done manually; however, very rarely is this reeving scheme used. As such, this is referred to as "electrical". Most manual rigs are achieved with mechanical compensation, which we will cover later in this chapter.

Various softwares handle electrical compensation differently, but to speak broadly enough to be talking about no one piece of software specifically, these two axes need to be grouped so that they are always looking at, and listening to, each other. This may seem like the easiest way to achieve a lift/travel, and from an ease-to-rig standpoint you would be correct. Generally speaking, this style has fewer sheaves than a mechanically compensated one. In a touring application, this can be a big design asset. One less sheave in the system is one less opportunity for someone to reeve it wrong on the day. However, there are several design downsides to keep in mind when choosing an E-comp system.

Given the way the system is reeved, our lift axis will need the ability to store more rope than just the distance we need to travel up and down. Since we need to pay out rope just to stay level as the trolley travels farther from our lifting axis, we need to be able to store enough rope to run all the way down the track, and then reach to the floor at that far end.

In Figure 8.3 the track is 100 feet long and trims 50 feet off the deck. As a result, we will need our lifting machine to be able to store 150 feet of rope. This is an important feature to be thinking about when making the decision to use

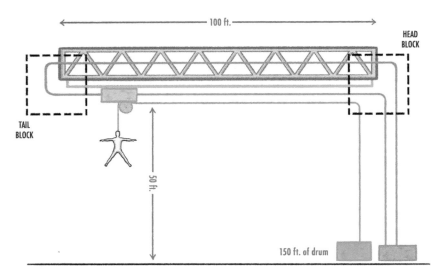

Figure 8.3   E-Comp Lift Needed

an E-comp system. Making sure your lifting winch has enough drum to hold all the rope you need is a detail that is overlooked frequently in the planning stages and can really ruin your day when it is later discovered all too late.

There is a similar issue here to think about in relationship to speed. To achieve level flight as the traverse axis runs, we will need to pay out or reel in lifting line at the same speed the traverse axis is running. This means if we want to be able to move up or down while also traversing, we need our lift axis to be able to go that much faster than our traverse axis. To have the full range of motion we will want available to us in an E-comp rig we need our winch to not only hold much more rope than we might assume at first, but also go much faster than we would have thought too.

The next feature to be aware of, and design around, is the double-edge of the how-easy-it-is-to-rig sword. We are all well aware of the consequences if the one line we are flying the performer on breaks, but in this reeving scheme what happens if the travel line breaks?

Because of the resultant forces the reeving of the lift line puts on the trolley, the travel line becomes as important a part of the system as the lift line. If one side of the travel system breaks (and, depending exactly how your system is reeved, if either side breaks) the performer load on the trolley will cause it to uncontrollably run until that load is no longer on the trolley. In this case that would be the moment the performer hits the ground. This has the potential to result in serious injury and as such must be mitigated. This is usually achieved as part of the trolley design. A simple solution would be to design a brake that uses the tension of the travel system to stay disengaged. You will have therefore created a fail-safe brake! The tension in a travel system will

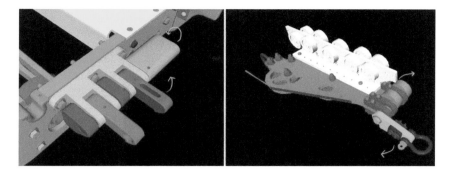

Figure 8.4   E-Comp Break

vary from system to system but is often in the neighborhood of 400 pounds. This is more than enough force to defeat a brake feature that then springs into action if there is suddenly slack in the travel lines. The brake can then interact with the track from which the trolley is hanging, the truss on which the track is hanging, or any other perfectly repeatable idea you can validate through rigorous testing. It's okay if this brake system ends up deforming itself, the track, the truss, or whatever piece of the system it comes into contact with. It only has to work once, and the show doesn't need to continue immediately after its use. As such, don't overcomplicate the design by trying to make it reusable. If parts of the system need to be replaced after such an event due to this kind of deformation, that's okay. The important thing is that everyone involved got to go home at the end of the day, *not* that we could continue Act 2 after such a near-miss event.

The last things to consider when choosing an E-comp system are the complications added to your control system. As previously mentioned, you will need a system advanced enough to create a relationship between these two axes. You want to make sure that neither axis is able to move without the other axis being alive and able to move. This will help prevent the classic mistake with an E-comp lift/travel rig, which is running the trolley away from the lift axis without moving said lift axis until the lift termination deads into the sheave on the trolley. Depending on the relative strengths of various components of your system this can result in something as dramatic as the lifting axis rope breaking, or as benign, but embarrassing, as the travel axis having a position error fault and stopping. In either case, this event should be avoided by making sure you've tested your sandbox and proven it safe by making sure you cannot do this in the first place. You should also have good long think, and additional run through your RA/RR, about how the limits on each axis will work in this reeving scheme. If we were not compensating for the travel of the system by paying out additional lift line, then setting the plus limits on the lift axis would be the same as any single-axis rig. However, because of the reeving of this system, the plus limits will only be able to protect you in one spot, that being at the top of the end of travel closest to the lift axis. There are a variety of ways to mitigate this risk. Now that safety-rated encoders, and safety-rated input/output cards to read them, are available, simply installing those on your winch can solve the problem. That said, at the time of this book's publication, these items are new-ish and as such are expensive and will almost certainly require an update to your control software of choice. Another possible way to deal with this risk would be to steal a page from some old chain motors and put an input switch on your trolley that something connected to your lifting media strikes when the rope termination gets too close to the trolley. The needed over-travel of your system will need to be considered when designing such a feature, but this can be a great way to make sure you have a safe sandbox to play in.

Mechanical Compensation

Don't get too intimidated right off the bat by Figure 8.5. A quick glance can make this look like we're trying to make a sweater out of our rig, but once you understand how we got here it's quite simple and brilliant. Let's break each complication down to show how we got here. The first, and most important, concept is to understand how the reeving negates the need to run the lift axis whenever the travel axis is moving.

In Figure 8.6 we see the performer line runs down to the end of the track just like in an E-comp rig. But then it turns 180 degrees around a sheave and runs down to the other end of the track, to then be terminated back to the

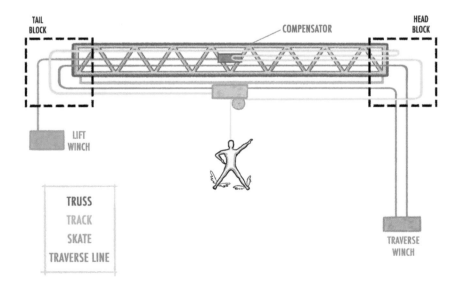

Figure 8.5　Mech Comp Rig

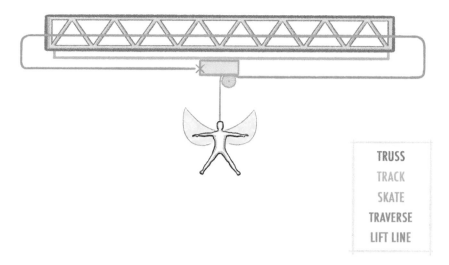

TRUSS
TRACK
SKATE
TRAVERSE
LIFT LINE

Figure 8.6   Mech Comp Skate Reeving

trolley. Now imagine what happens if we drag the trolley 1 foot in either direction. If you said, "The performer stays in the same place vertically", or anything like that, you win! This is because we have created a system in which there is a finite amount of rope. If we pull the skate in the direction that in an E–comp rig would result in the performer going up, the movement of the skate gives us the 1 foot of rope we need to stay level. The equal and opposite thing happens if we go in the other direction. How cool this is cannot be understated once you get it. If you're not blown away by how cool this is, keep staring at it until you get it.

Great! We've eliminated the need to use our winch to achieve level flight, but it would seem we've also eliminated our ability to move the performer up and down. Good point. Let's take that cool factor up a notch.

In Figure 8.7 we've added a deviation to the performer line and connected our lift axis to it. The block through which the performer line runs that is connected to the lifting axis is called the compensator block. By moving the compensator block with our lifting axis, be it electromechanical or manual, we can lengthen or shorten the lift line while leaving the other end connected to trolley. As a result, we don't need to move the lift axis to stay in level flight (the reeving does that for us) but if we want to go up or down we can now independently cause that to happen. Astute readers may have noticed that this reeving through the compensator block also causes the performer line to be on a 1:2 as it relates to the winch. Very good! This means in this configuration you can only load the performer side of the rig to half of what the lifting axis' nameplate says it can lift, but the performer will be able to achieve twice the speed the machine's nameplate says it can. Such is the burden of mechanical advantage.

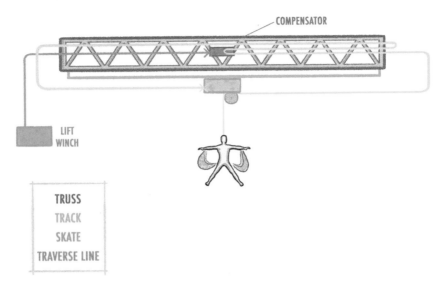

COMPENSATOR

LIFT
WINCH

TRUSS

TRACK

SKATE

TRAVERSE LINE

Figure 8.7   Mech Comp Skate Reeve with Lift

This reeving scheme solves a lot of potential problems previously enumerated about an E-comp rig. Since we've decoupled the need for level flight from the lift axis moving, we can set our plus limits once, anywhere on the track, and they will work everywhere on the track. This is because we are only using the lift axis to lift, just like in a single-axis rig. Similarly, we do not need to consider the length of the track when deciding how much drum we need on our lift winch. We need only consider how much vertical lift we need! We also do not *need* to have a control system that links these two axes. While it might still be a good idea depending on our RA/RR, it is not a requirement like it would be with an E-comp rig. We also don't need to worry about the travel line breaking, at least as it relates to the performer falling to the ground. Thanks to the lift line being a loop that connects back to the skate, the resultant forces in the line cancel each other out. This means we are not relying on the travel line to keep the performer in the air. Through the reeving scheme we eliminate a single point of failure!

Why not always use mechanical compensation then? There are some other factors to consider before deciding to go down this path. As you can see from the above diagrams, there is a lot more rope in the system. This means you will need a larger sandbag or line weight than you would need with a similar E-comp rig. There is so much more reeving in a mechanically compensated system that this can be an un-ideal choice for a touring application. Since it must come apart for every move, it will likely need to be un-reeved to go in the truck, although there are design solutions for this problem too. Should it need to un-reeved for each move, this means the touring staff will need to spend more time than they would with an E-comp rig reeving the system at each new venue. They will also need to really understand how the rig works to make sure they reeve it conceptually correctly every time. Even if they get the concept right every time, they will also need to successfully run the rope through each one of those sheaves correctly at each stop, not running over a single keeper pin or twisting any ropes together. There is simply more opportunity to do it wrong with a mechanically compensated rig that comes apart every day.

So, are all mechanically compensated rigs this complicated? Is there no easier version of this concept? Excellent question! There is another reeving concept called "floating pulley" that accomplishes many of the same benefits with a substantially easier reeving scheme.

This reeving scheme is best thought of like a clothesline. As you can see in Figure 8.8, there is no change to the travel system. It is simply connected at either end of the skate. The lift line though runs through the skate on its way to terminating at the other end of the track. A loop of lift line is then left hanging below the skate with a pulley as our connection point to the system; hence the name "floating pulley". Now, with sufficient weight on the pulley, as the skate is driven back and forth along the track the load below traverses with it. The lift winch does not need to be moved to achieve level flight back and forth, just as in our previous mechanical compensation example. Some more astute readers may have noticed that this reeving scheme causes a 2:1 mechanical advantage for the lift winch. Good eye! This means that you will be able to lift twice as much as the lift winch says it can lift, but only at half the speed. Always remember to consider the load limits of every part of

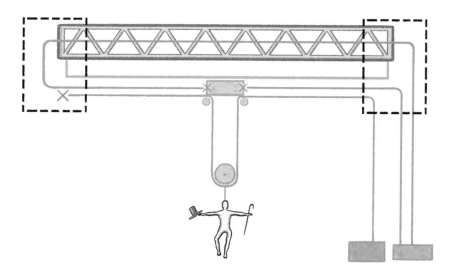

Figure 8.8 Floating Pulley

your system before taking advantage of this increase in lifting capacity. Also, do not forget to account for the fact that your lift winch will need to have capacity for twice as much rope than you would otherwise need for this rig. Because we have caused a 2:1 mechanical advantage we will need to store twice as much rope. Such is another burden of mechanical advantage (thanks, Archimedes).

Machine Up Rigs

The first example cited in this chapter of strapping our lifting axis itself to the track and tracking the whole machine back and forth is also a form of mechanical compensation. Both of the previous examples shown assume your axes, or operators, are stationary, which is to say the machine, or person, stays in one place and we route the lines around our rig. Especially with big, heavy machines it can be easiest to plop them in one spot and leave them there, then run their cable to them in their one spot, cleanly. But what if we decided to do something obtuse like moving the whole lift winch across our track instead of reeving its rope through the system?

We've now created a situation where we have a lot of benefits from each of the previous two scenarios (Figure 8.9). We can have a smaller sandbag or line weight as with the E-comp rig, our plus limits will work anywhere along the track, and the lift axis is decoupled from the travel axis. We've put our lifting winch on a trolley and decided to drag the whole machine back and forth on the track. So, what's not to like? Well, for starters, this rig is substantially

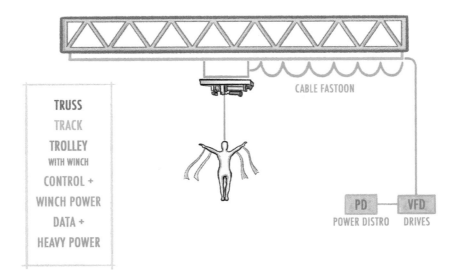

Figure 8.9   Winch Trolley Rig

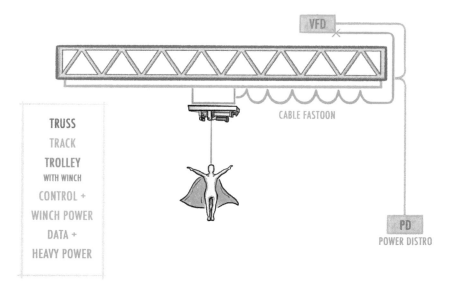

Figure 8.10 Winch Trolley with Drives

heavier than the last two scenarios. While this is not insurmountable, it does need to be thoroughly studied. Now that we've taken that large and heavy lifting machine and put it on our track, we will be stressing the truss and the roof more than we would have otherwise. We can easily add more lifting capacity in the form of stronger, more, or both chain motors but the facility impact to every venue you are going to must also be considered. It doesn't matter that you have 20 tons of lifting capacity if the venue can only hold 10! Having the lifting axis up in the air can also complicate some rescue plans. In the case of a brake release rescue (which we will cover more in Chapter 12) having to climb up onto the track and scurry down to the winch will always be more involved than simply walking over to winch in the backstage. Lastly, but also important to consider, is the fact that if the electromechanical machine is to move back and forth across the track, you will need a way to get the electro to the mechanical. Figure 8.9 shows one way to achieve this, that being simply festooning cable behind the trolley on the track. You could alternatively design a busbar system into your track to deliver the power and control signals to your machine. This solution is not recommended for touring applications however, and it can really complicate the mechanical design of your trolley if you are unfamiliar with this concept's common parts.

This also raises the concern of making sure you are not exceeding the maximum cable length of any of your components by putting the machine a variable distance away from that which it plugs into. Most control protocols have a maximum cable length of 150–300 feet before needing to be repeated.

Depending on the length of your track and/or the location of your drives in the building this can result in you needing to fly the drives on the truss. This not only increases the weight of your flown system further by adding the weight of the drives, but also that of your cable pick as you now need to run heavy power up to the rig too. Don't forget that your automation technician will now need to climb to troubleshoot drive issues as well.

As with anything in life, all these scenarios all have their pluses and minuses. The important thing, as always, is to think your system all the way through early and often to make sure you've correctly balanced the concerns of this production's needs.

Swing Cancellation

Now that we are able to lift and travel a performer without their inertia from a swing being a necessary ingredient, we've created a new hurdle to overcome. That, simply put, is not wanting to see the performer swinging around at all. Nothing kills the illusion of a performer controlling and commanding their own flight quite as quickly as seeing them pendulum back and forth, like a grandfather clock, after traversing across the stage. It immediately reminds the audience that this is all fake and takes them out of the moment. So how can we try to prevent this? Well, the first rule of swing cancellation is to not get objects swinging in the first place! Seems obvious, but this can be achieved in one of two ways using our machines. Either we always have a long ramp into and out of each traversing move, or we more actively program our traverse move to counter the forthcoming swing.

The quickest way to get rid of 80% of the eyesore that is uncontrolled swinging is to extend your acceleration and deceleration into and out of your travel moves. Put differently: elongate the amount of time you spend accelerating and decelerating. This has the effect of keeping the load under the trolley for most of the move. The cause of the kind of swing you don't want to see is either the trolley getting ahead of the load, or the load getting ahead of the trolley. Once that happens you have created a pendulum that will slowly deteriorate over time. By extending the amount of time we accelerate to speed and then decelerate from that speed we can better control the load's position as it relates to the trolley. It's not perfect, as the trolley will still start traversing before the performer below it catches up, and equally and oppositely at the other end of the move, the trolley will stop before the performer does. But by stretching the time spent accelerating and decelerating you can remove around 80 percent of what would otherwise look very unnatural. As said above: don't let the object start swinging in the first place!

The above-mentioned technique requires you to have enough time to stretch out the acceleration and deceleration long enough to kill as much of the swing as possible. But what if we don't have that time, or if we need to move so fast that this scheme just isn't an option with our available travel?

Then we must actively kill the swing. Instead of trying to prevent the trolley from getting ahead or behind the inertia of the performer, we will instead intentionally cause this scenario to get moving and then rapidly do the opposite to fight the swing. If this isn't making sense, go tie a small weight on the end of a string, something like a fender washer on a piece of twine. Now hold the end of the twine in your right hand with the washer hanging below your hand. With your left hand create a swing with the washer in one plane. Now move your right hand back and forth to kill the swing of the washer. You will find the best way to do this is to move your right hand in the opposite direction of the swing of the washer. If the washer is swinging away from you, you will pull your hand closer to you, then as it reaches the apex of its swing, you will rapidly move your hand away from you to get directly over the washer. This will kill its swing. Once you master this game, then try moving your right hand away from you rapidly while keeping the washer hanging plumb. If we were to graph how you do this with your hand, it would look something like Figure 8.11.

As you can see here, the trolley is doing a lot more work than simply moving in our normal trapezoidal move. What we see here is the trolley moves forward quickly to get ahead of the performer. It then slows down substantially to let the swing of the performer catch up to its position along the track. Once that happens it immediately speeds up, so that both the performer and the trolley are moving in unison across the track. Then, to come to a stop the trolley does just the opposite. It slows down substantially, short of its final resting place, letting the performer swing out ahead of it. Then, as the

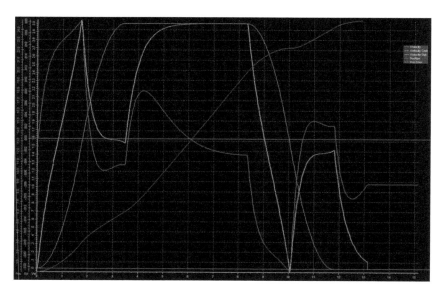

Figure 8.11 Swing Cancellation Graph

performer reaches the apex of that pendulum, the trolley speeds up to meet the performer out at that apex, which also happens to be where we wanted the travel move to come to a stop. When done correctly, the performer will not be swinging at all after this fast and dynamic move.

"How on earth do we program this?" you might rightly be asking yourself. The answer, sadly, is guess-and-check, and a lot of it. Important note on that point: while there are many times where knowing the actual weight of the performer with all their costume and props is crucial, this is not one of those times. Being close will be sufficient since we are trying to cancel a swing instead of cause one. The only variable that matters to us is the length of the pendulum. So, since we are going to guess-and-check our way through this, we want to have a good idea that this is the final height at which this flight will take place. Every time this height (but really the distance from our pivot point) changes, we will have to tweak our swing cancellation profile. Now, all that said, some of the more advanced automation software can now do swing cancellation internally. Some require an angle sensor be mounted to the spot on the trolley where the lift line(s) exits the sheave above the performer, while others can do it predictively after you correctly enter information about the length of the pendulum. The future looks bright for not needing to spend late nights beating your head against a wall guess-and-checking until you can't take it anymore!

Having a good idea of how violent you will need change direction to achieve your swing cancellation goals is an important tidbit early on in your planning. A common mistake is to think, "They want to go 10ft/sec, so I got winches that will do 10ft/sec. I'm all set!" If you want to have the performer traveling at 10ft/sec, and you know you will at some point need to shoot the travel axis out ahead of it, you had better make sure your machine can do just that. The sad outcome of the incorrect thought in quotation marks above is that you have to slow down the show speed to allow you to swing cancel at 10ft/sec. This is an unfortunate and preventable outcome with some simple proper prior planning.

V-Rigs

There is one more popular way to achieve a lift/travel kind of motion with two axes. All the aforementioned rigs need a structure to mount tracks and trolleys to, usually in the form of a truss of sufficient size and strength. But what if you can't hang a truss where you need to fly? You could be trying to fly over the house in an ornate historic building that will absolutely not let you punch a hole in the ceiling to drop your chain motor point. You could be in an open-air stadium where there simply is no roof. Enter the V-rig (Figure 8.12).

In this case we've taken two lift axes, put them on opposite sides of the building from each other and then connected them into a bridle. The length of

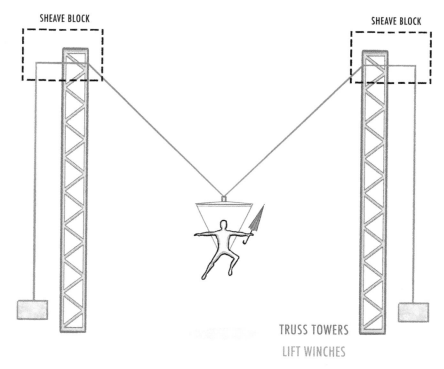

SHEAVE BLOCK

SHEAVE BLOCK

TRUSS TOWERS

LIFT WINCHES

Figure 8.12   Basic V-Rig

each leg of the bridle can be controlled with machines or manually. Now we can lift and travel by adjusting the length of the legs of the bridle independent from each other. It is crucial that we do a lot of basic bridle math to make sure we are not overstressing the rope, the building, or the winches (or the manual operators), and whatever we have decided is the connection of the two lines. A common error in the planning phases of V-rigs is to overestimate the available flight envelope of this system. "Flight envelope" is a term used to describe the space that a rig can cover, taking into account winch limits, maximum allowable forces, and the physical realities of a given room.

It would be easy to think that we can get anywhere in the shaded rectangle of Figure 8.13 with our V-rig, but this would be incorrect. There are many forces in play here that will prevent us from achieving all these locations. If we flippantly delivered this flight envelope to the artistic team, we would be hard pressed to make good on our under-thought promises when it comes time to deliver. The first common mistake is that you cannot get directly under either point of the rig when running a V-rig.

In Figure 8.14 we are now seeing something more realistic. You cannot get direct under either point of a V-rig because of the weight per foot of the long leg of the bridle. You will not be able to pay it out enough to be able

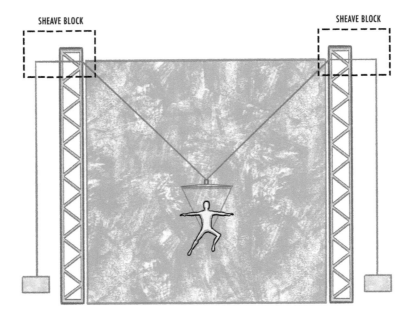

Figure 8.13   Incorrect V-Rig Flight Envelope

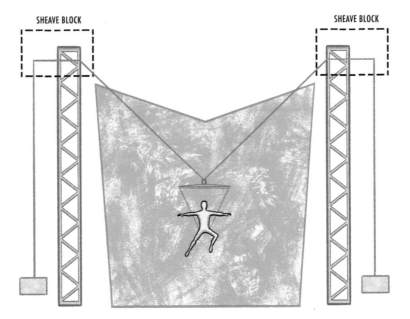

Figure 8.14   Correct V-Rig Flight Envelope

to swing directly under the near point. You can get close, but eventually you will reach a point of diminishing returns where you are introducing more weight into the system, pulling you away from your target, by further paying out the long leg of the bridle. This can seem counterintuitive, but it is a fact. The exact proportion of this problem will depend on a particular rig's aspect ratio. That is to say, how tall the rig is compared to how wide it is. The shorter and wider a rig's aspect ratio, the worse off you will be in both your ability to get near either point and in your maximum achievable height. The more like a letterbox your aspect ratio looks, the more you should cheat the sides of your flight envelope away from being directly under your points. Do not forget to take into account that you will want to keep your long line off the ground, or, in the case of over-the-audience flights, out of the crowd. This will further inhibit you from paying out more line into the system, which will in turn further prevent you from getting all the way under the near point.

Max height is the other common area of over-promising with V-rigs. Don't let the fact that you're flying a person complicate this for you. At the end of the day, this is simply a bridle between two points. This means the worst-case loading scenario will be in the center of your two points, as high as you calculate you can go. For some reason many do this math one-quarter of the way away from either tower and think they have found their worst case. They have a rude awakening when they can't get anywhere near that high in the center of their rig. As you get closer to one point or the other you will be able to fly higher and higher, as the load becomes closer and closer to being able to affect only its own weight on the short line, and that load is increasingly only on one winch, or operator. The selection of winch capacity in such a rig is often determined more by the aspect ratio of the rig than the load of the performer being flown. Similarly, how high a V-rig can go when being flown manually will be a limitation dictated by your operators. As such, it's important to fully understand how bridle math works. Although many, *many*, bridle calculators are readily available online or in apps, the act of creating your own bridle math spreadsheet or app will help you intrinsically understand what you are looking at in real life. Harry Donovan's *Entertainment Rigging* is a fantastic resource on the topic of rigging math. Also, please note, it is spelled b-r-i-d-*l*-e, not b-r-i-d-*a*-*l*. Unless someone is wearing an impossibly expensive white dress while they are rigging, there's simply nothing *a-l* about this!

In a V-rig, swing cancellation isn't nearly as big of a concern as it is in a true lift/travel rig. This is because the rig never causes a pendulum, assuming you are connecting your performer or prop directly to your connection point between your two lines. If you are lucky enough to have such a generous flight envelope that you are substantially tailing down from that point, then all the same processes we spoke about earlier apply. The concept of making sure your system can accelerate and decelerate as quickly as you think you will need to achieve your swing cancellation goals cannot be overstated. It is the most common feature of two-axes rigs that is missed in the planning phase. Unfortunately for those involved in such episodes, unnatural swinging is the easiest thing for even an uninitiated audience member to notice, making all your hard work look cheap and poorly executed.

Conclusion

Two-axes rigs open up the doors to many more options for our creative team. Being able to initiate and control horizontal motion can often be much more appealing than big pendulum flights from a single-axis rig. There are many different common ways to use two axes to control lift and travel in one plane. E-comp, mechanical compensation, and V-rigs each have their pros and cons both from a system-level viewpoint and an end-user viewpoint. It is important to consider all these rigs and all their pros and cons when selecting the correct one for your effect. After choosing a rig be sure you understand whether or not swing cancellation will be required artistically, and if so, make sure you are mechanically ready for it. Be sure to plan for the additional programming time associated with swing cancellation. Two-axes rigs are some of the most versatile rigs out there, allowing for a great many options in the field.

Takeaways: Beginners

- Two-axes rigs introduce many new concerns to be thought about during your RA/RR phase.
- Make sure you understand why you have selected a particular reeving scheme.
- "Because we've always done it this way" is not a good enough reason!
- If you are going to want to cancel swings as part of your effect, make sure you plan for it.

Takeaways: Professionals

- Understanding the precise differences between electrical and mechanical compensation is paramount to being able to correctly choose between them situationally.
    - Make sure you understand the different risks between the two layouts and correctly plan for each.
- If you decide to put the flying machine in the air, be sure to consider the electrical cabling and facility-impact changes to your system.
- Practice makes perfect when it comes to swing cancellation. Don't feel like you have to wait to have a gig to practice this programming. There's nothing stopping you from setting up a small rig in your shop and practicing!

9 3D Rigs

Most performer flying rigs out in the wild are single-axis rigs, two-axes rigs, or a variant thereof. There are two main reasons for this: (1) they are extremely versatile systems that can perform a variety of tasks, and (2) they can both be performed manually or automated. This means that both solutions are open to anyone with the will to fly a performer as there is (nearly) no barrier of entry as far as cost is concerned. 3D rigs, on the other hand, tend in the modern era to be automated and as such have a high floor on their cost. While there are tales of people running these complicated systems manually, this is highly ill-advised. 3D rigs require the flawless synchronization of at least three axes of motion, and often times many more. This level of precision is best left to automation professionals, which has a barrier of entry in terms of price and technical skill. The good news is it's a rare occasion that a 3D rig is really *needed* for a production. It is almost always a "because we can" kind of decision. As a result, you will rarely need to take out a loan as a small production company for this kind of effect.

So why go 3D at all? In reality, there are few situations that back you into the corner of really *needing* a 3D rig. For example, what if your effect is to take place in a stadium with no roof above it? Clearly hanging a free-spanning truss from one end of the 400-section to the other is highly impractical. This can lead you to a V-rig if you only need to travel in one plane, or to a 3D rig if your performer flying train needs to arrive at multiple stations. Stadiums, though, are a bit unique in their need for 3D rigs. So why would you use one in an arena or other venue that has a roof? Weirdly enough, the answer often comes down to practicality. If your performer wants to get out over the crowd at his or her arena show and do the "parade float" routine around the arena, you are presented with two options. You could make a tracking system to ride around a curved truss system that needs to be supported every so-many feet, or you could rig three points in strategic spots in the roof and be done with it. From a touring perspective, the choice is obvious: less gear, fewer trucks, less time. The flip side of the same coin, however, is that you need a technical team that can handle the day-to-day challenges that come with touring such an effect, where almost any touring technician could handle hammering some truss together and hanging motors. Still, the cost of trucks and time normally outweigh the need to pay higher-skilled individuals than you might otherwise hire.

But both of these examples are very touring-centric, and large-scale. What if your show is small and in one place, or maybe even a one-off? Why bother? Well, this is a fair question. As with so many things we do in the entertainment industry, it comes down to the desires of the artistic team. Sometimes, as stated above, it is wanted because there is a perception that this is the next step. Sometimes an entire marketing campaign has been built around seeing a performer fly over the audience. (At least one prominent, shockingly expensive, former Broadway show comes to mind here.) There can also be structural reasons to go with a 3D rig in theatres though. If your intent is to fly someone all over the building but the venue has an ancient roof, or even more problematically if it has a ceiling that is an historical monument of some kind, they will simply not allow you to reinforce or perforate their building. A 3D rig can minimize your impact to the building (only needing to reinforce about three spots) and still have the same effect as demanded by Team Artistic.

Flight Envelope

When planning a 3D rig it is crucial to think early and often about the flight envelope. As mentioned in Chapter 8, this is the 3D space which you have promised the artistic team the rig will be able to get their performer to. All too often this is glanced over and not really thought about. Much like the example given in the previous chapter about V-rigs, it is all too easy to over-promise and under-deliver. The name of the game with 3D rigs is to do exactly the opposite: under-promise and over-deliver. No one ever got yelled at or not hired again because the rig turned out able to do *more* than everyone thought it would be able to do. Plenty have seen their client list shrink after doing the opposite.

In Figure 9.1 we see the first classic mistake. We've got three points, we draw a line connecting those three points, and that's our flight envelope. Wrong! For many of the same reasons discussed in the last chapter on V-rigs, you will not actually be able to ride the line between any two points. The weight of the line you are trying to slack to get all the way to the edge of the envelope will in fact start to pull you away from your goal the more you slack it off. Additionally, most automation software, being designed to keep a reasonable tension in each line, will not let you pay out that much line, even if you could get there. So, our first correction to this flight envelope is to trim in from the edges of the envelope by about five degrees. There is no hard-and-fast rule to how much to cut back, but remember: the goal here is to under-promise and over-deliver. When in doubt, cut more in!

The envelope in Figure 9.2 is looking way better. Let's send it to Artistic! *Wait!* We're not there yet. The next mistake we have here is that we are showing the area immediately under our points as accessible. This is almost

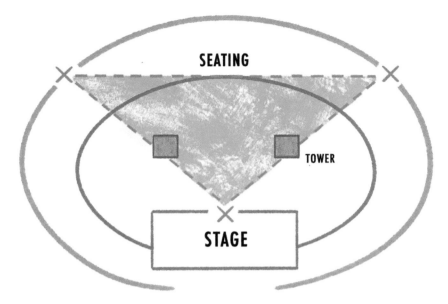

Figure 9.1   Bad 3D Envelope

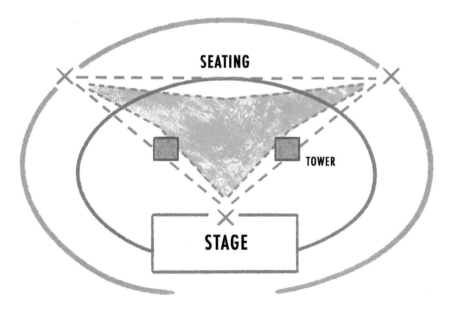

Figure 9.2   3D Envelope 2

never the case. On a small scale this is because of all the same reasons listed above as to why you can't get all the way to the edge of the envelope. That said, in this particular scenario, if there were nothing in the way, you would be able to get close. But, and it's a big *but*, there is always something in the way. Most notably in most cases, seats! The point of these effects is most often to get the performer or prop out over the audience. That being the case, you will end up putting your points as far into the corners of the room as you can possibly get. This means you will likely have mezzanines or nosebleed seats in the way long before you get right up to your sheave. This is where we need to start understanding how high we can be in different areas of the flight envelope, something we will cover more later in this chapter, so that we can accurately represent how much of the raised tiers of our venue, if any, we can get over safely.

The envelope in Figure 9.3 is great! Now we got it. Ship it!

Wait! We're very close, but not there yet. In a wide-open field, with nothing else in the way, this envelope would be good to go. However, that is not what we're dealing with in this scenario. Note the tower in the middle of what we've shown as accessible air space.

We have to take into account that this will be in the way of our flight path (Figure 9.4). Remember, the three lines are always connected. That means that for any point in this space you are going to say the rig can get to, all three lines have to be able to get there too. For simplicity's sake, let's assume this

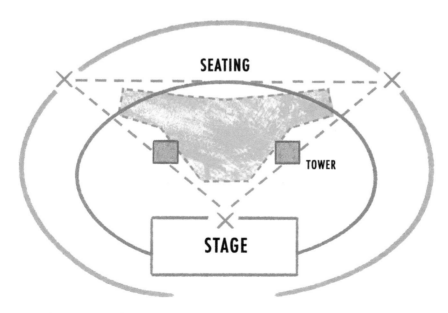

Figure 9.3   3D Envelope 3

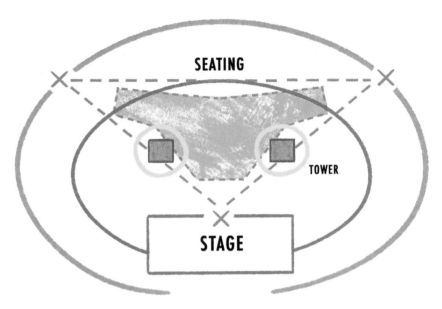

Figure 9.4   3D Envelope Tower Highlight

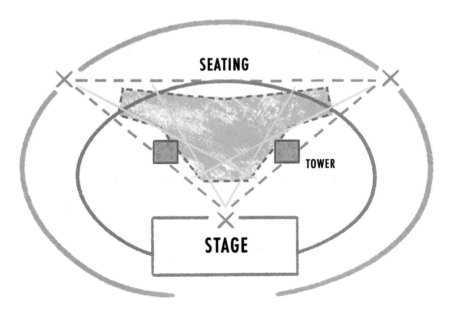

Figure 9.5   3D Envelope Tower Lines

tower is taller than we can get our rig, meaning we can't overfly it. Taking that constraint into consideration, let's draw lines starting at our three points showing how the ropes will interact with the offending tower (Figure 9.5).

Now we're starting to see where we can actually get to and how that tower is limiting us. Now, if we draw a line connecting all the rays coming from our points, and not forgetting about the other cut-ins we've made, we get our true flight envelope (Figure 9.6).

This takes into account everything we know about the space to this moment. We've cut away from the edges of the flight envelope, we've cut away from our points and the rising seating, and we've accounted for obstacles in the way. This is a respectable, achievable, and promise-worthy flight envelope.

Hopefully this exercise underscores to you how important a thorough site survey is. From time to time someone will suggest that a site visit isn't really necessary or isn't in the budget. This suggestion should be shot down hard and quickly. The less information you have about the venue you are trying to install this into, the less you will be able to promise. To be sure you can do all the things your artistic team is asking for, you should visit the venue in question and take your time while there.

So, are we then to believe that 3D rigs on arena touring shows are developed after a careful and lengthy visit to each venue on the tour? The answer, interestingly, is both yes and no. The no answer is exactly what you think. No, the designers and developers of these rigs do not in advance of every show visit each venue and plan excruciatingly for each one. Similarly,

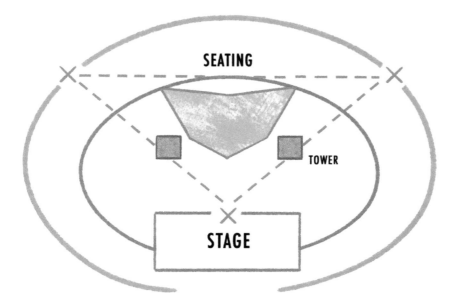

Figure 9.6   Correct 3D Flight Envelope

the touring productions do not have an advance team that goes in a week before and dials in the gag while waiting for the rest of the show and the star to arrive. Instead, the rig has been planned to be as pliable as possible, relying on highly skilled and seasoned (usually with salt) veteran touring technicians to figure it out on the day, every day. This also means that less can be promised outright, as the realities from day to day are unknown. The yes answer involves the people selected to work on such extravagances. This is not the kind of project someone does as their first performer flying rig. Everyone involved, from the designers to the end users, has done these things before and as a result has the requisite experience to not make the same mistakes again. Experience, in this case, is the most valuable asset to the team and the production.

Flight Envelope Shape

Now we've dialed in the (x,y) limitations of our flight envelope, but understanding the three-dimensional shape of the flight envelope is also critical to success. In all simpler rigs discussed in previous chapters you can pretty well understand where you will be able to get the performer with a single, plan-view drawing. This, however, is not the case with a 3D rig. While the exercise we went through earlier in this chapter is important, it's only half the story. Thanks to that exercise we know where we can get in plan view, but what about in section view? Can we get to the same height everywhere in the envelope we've drawn? The answer, as you may have guessed, is "No, we cannot." As a thought exercise, where do you think is the worst-case loading situation in a 3D rig with four points forming a square in plan view? Spend a few minutes. Think about it (Figure 9.7).

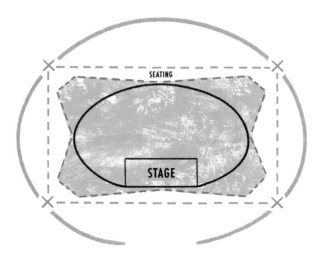

Figure 9.7   Four-Point 3D Rig Plan View

Done? What did you come up with? A common first answer is "In the middle of the square, as high as you can go." This, however, is incorrect. In fact, this is the opposite of the worst case; it is the best case! The middle of the square, with all four lines loaded equally, will be the highest point you can get to in your 3D rig. You are spreading the bridle load across four lines evenly. As a result, you can get the highest and tightest of anywhere in the rig before overloading any one axis. So now that we've established that fact, what is your second guess for the worst-case loading scenario?

In Figure 9.8 we have an isometric sketch of the 3D shape of the flight envelope for the above scenario. Did you get it right? The correct answer is "In the middle of any two points, as far over to that side as you can get." In Figure 9.9 it is circled in plan view, in case that description is insufficiently unclear.

Sometimes the answer is simply to not over-complicate the problem. When you get over by the edge of the envelope, in the middle of two points, you are nearly in a two-point bridle. When you then try to get as high as you can, you are splitting that load between nearly only two axes. As a result, this is the lowest high point you will have.

The 3D shape of our flight envelope is best described as a dome with spikes at the ends near our points. This of course is because as the load gets closer and closer to a single point more and more of the payload is shifted to that point, and the bridle begins to lose its ability to magnify the forces. As a result, we could theoretically get all the way to the sheave in any given corner of the rig. But, as discussed above, there are almost always seats or some other obstructions

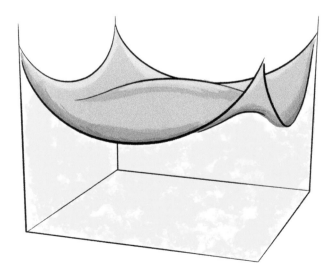

Figure 9.8 3D Flight Envelope Shape in 3D

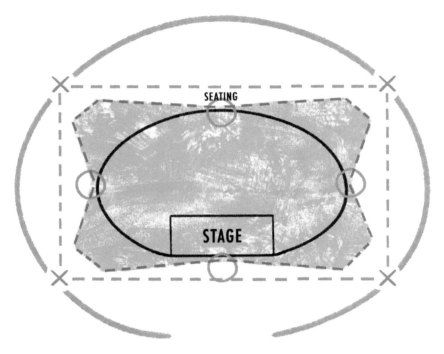

Figure 9.9   Worst-Case Loading

in the way of this happening. This is a great example of why both of these shapes need to be understood to be able to draw a reliable and accurate flight envelope.

Programming

Taking a wild guess at a figure, you probably have a 50/50 shot at having an artistic team that has worked with a 3D rig in the past, and honestly those are pretty generous odds. As a result, it is often difficult to get people to accurately describe what they are artistically after from the rig. The correct approach will vary depending on how the specific person you are dealing with processes information and how your automation software of choice operates. One of the best ways is to print out sheets of your flight envelope in plan view, and sheets of the venue in section view. Then you can ask your artistic person to draw what they are after. Now you will have a rough shape, both in plan and in height, of their desires. This is a great starting point to have conversations with them about achievable heights, speeds, and locations. The next thing you can have them do is to draw points along the path they are after with times between them. This will seem unachievably daunting to them at first.

Simply point out to them that they can use iTunes as they listen to the music involved to describe the time they want things to take. Do not be surprised when, on their first pass, they request moves that would require winches to move at 100ft/sec or more! This is a great opportunity to work together to solve the problem.

All the other rules of performer flying enumerated in earlier chapters apply here too. Most importantly: always use a sandbag first, and always use a sandbag after making a change to a known-good, tested profile. You are relying more on your software and less on physical switches than with any other style of rig. Recognize the system you've strung together with three or more axes has the power to really, *really*, hurt someone. Take those factors into serious consideration when someone asks if you *really* need to sandbag such a small change.

At the end of the day, very few people, including those who work on these rigs all the time, have the ability to clearly explain what they want one of these systems to do. This is definitely one of those times when it is way easier to be an editor than a creator, and that's okay too! There is nothing wrong with suggesting to an artistic person that you and your team will program some boilerplate stuff to facilitate a conversation about what looks good. If that is the shortest line between A and B, don't be shy to suggest it! Equally and oppositely, it is important to make sure the artistic team understand that 3D programming takes longer than they may be used to with simpler performer flying they may have done in the past. It is up to you and them to manage the time you have to make sure you are getting the most out of your programming time and not spinning wheels. Almost invariably, there will be a request to change something after you no longer have access to test the flight because the audience has begun to file in, or some other department has the space until that time. This must be met with a forceful, but polite, "No." You will not have the opportunity to test the new programming with a sandbag, to say nothing of the performer who will never get to ride it before show time. This is both unsafe and unacceptable and should be explained as such.

Three-Point Rigs versus Four-Point Rigs versus More-Point Rigs

Previously in this chapter we have covered both three-point and four-point rigs without really explaining why you might want one or the other. Simply put, you want as few axes as possible to achieve the artistic goals of the effect. This should seem reasonable, as the fewer axes there are, the less there is go wrong. This does not mean every rig should be a three-point; it just means extraneous axes should be avoided. It does mean, however, that we should start with three axes of motion and evaluate if that will cover the artistic intent. As we can see above, though, it rarely does. The available flight envelope of a three-point rig is (nearly) a triangle. While this is a huge effect and can be very impactful, most end up wanting a four-point rig, as you can get much more of a flight envelope for a (usually) insignificant increase in price and complexity. Four-point rigs are the most common 3D rig, but the fun doesn't stop there. What is stopping us from making a five-point rig? Or a six-point rig? Or more? The only things limiting you are your imagination and the ability of your control software. Don't make the mistake of promising a solution that may take a year of R&D from your software team to deliver on! If you don't work for the company that owns the software don't promise something that you will have to pay the company who owns the software to R&D for you either, unless of course you have that kind of time and money. Then by all means push the envelope and challenge your vendor to do something new and extraordinary! All that said though, given how this paragraph started, what would ever compel you to go to five, six, or more points?!

Consider the flight envelope in Figure 9.10. You submit this to the artistic team and they report they are thrilled with how much of the field you can cover, but wish they could get out over more of the downstage seating. Thanks to the shape of the stadium, simply moving the DS (downstage) two points around won't get you there. You seem to be stuck

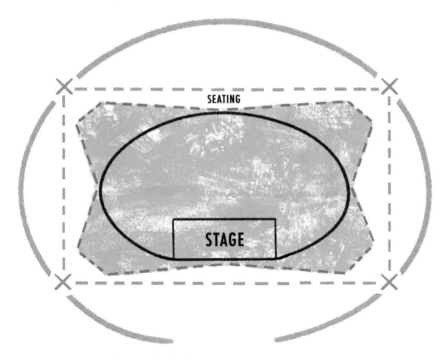

Figure 9.10 Four-Point with Audience

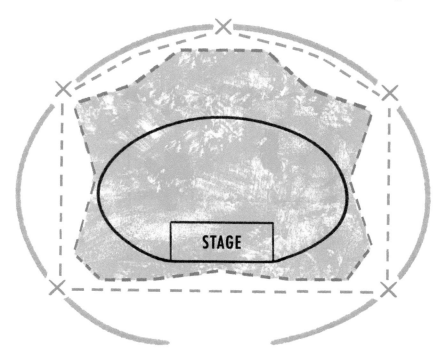

Figure 9.11 Five-Point with Audience

and will have to have a difficult conversation about how it simply can't be done. But what if we add a fifth point to the system downstage center (Figure 9.11)?

Now all of a sudden we can accommodate Artistic's wishes! As you can see, the addition of fifth, sixth, or more points is very situational. It's another tool to have on your belt when you need it, but remember: always use the fewest possible axes to achieve the artistic goals.

Center-Bound versus Non-Center-Bound

All of the 3D rigs we've discussed so far are "center-bound rigs". This means the points all come together at as near the same point as possible. This point is usually a piece of custom hardware of some kind designed to handle not only the load of the performer, but also all the bridle forces trying to rip it apart. The performer is then hung underneath the aforementioned block, always hanging plumb.

This is a key feature of the center-bound rig (Figure 9.12). As the rig moves around the flight envelope the block will tilt to and fro as individual lines connected to it have more or less tension. The performer, being suspended

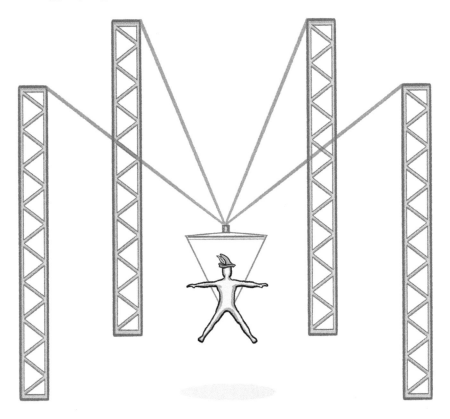

Figure 9.12   Center-Bound Rig

underneath this block, never experiences this tilting because the block is acting as a pivot or bogey bar for the performer. This pivoting feature, though, is a double-edged sword. Since the performer can free-pivot, sudden changes in speed will result in the performer swinging back and forth just like in a lift/travel rig. As a result, we need to swing cancel just the same as we would in a lift/travel. We can cheat and just use long accelerations and decelerations to mask the free pivoting or we can plan ahead and make sure our axes can go faster than we want the performer to be flying so we can still swing cancel at that full speed. For a more detailed discussion of swing cancellation please see Chapter 8.

The other option is to not have all the points come together at a single point; instead, the points are connected to a larger frame. This is called, quite creatively, a "non–center-bound rig". The most well-known version of a non–center-bound rig is the Twisty Belt effect popularized by P!NK. Instead of her four lines coming together above her, they come to either side of a metal ring,

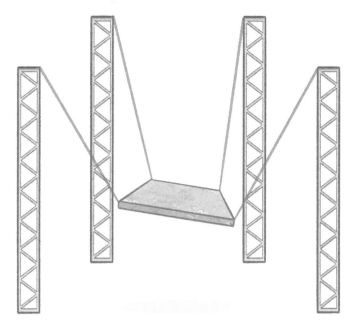

Figure 9.13   Non-Center-Bound Rig

in which she is harnessed. This makes her the center of a non-center-bound rig (Figure 9.13).

As a result, there is no pendulum created by her sudden changes of motion; good thing, as she has many of them! On the flip side, however, as she approaches the edges of her flight envelope, the belt cocks in different angles as the tension in the four lines changes in relationship to each other. P!NK, being a seasoned veteran of this effect, handles this with deftness and grace, but such a pro is a rare occurrence out in the field. This inflicted angle can often be the difference between a performer achieving a full flip and not making it all the way around. The solution is simple enough in those cases. You simply shrink your flight envelope until the belt cocks only to the point that the performer can still achieve their routine. This reveals the true drawback of a non-center-bound rig. The larger the frame, and therefore the further from the center of the rig the lines connect to said frame, the more exacerbated this tilting is and the smaller your flight envelope will be while remaining plumb (enough). This does not rule out non-center-bound rigs from use; clearly, as P!NK's Twisty Belt routine is one of the more well-known examples of 3D flying out there today. It is simply another behavior of the rig that is important to take into consideration when in the planning phase of your project.

Conclusion

3D rigs are complicated performer flying effects that are best left to automated systems. They are rarely really needed by a production; rather, they are often chosen for the spectacle they provide. For all the complexity spoken about in design and execution, it is critical to make sure the people you have hired to achieve this effect know what they are doing and have requisite experience under their belts. This experience will help make sure you are making safe and sane decisions throughout the production process.

Takeaways: Beginners

- 3D rigs are complicated and not for first-time technicians.
- Make sure your organization has sufficient experience, or has hired a vendor who does, to make sure everyone stays safe.
- 3D programming takes longer than 2D flying. Plan accordingly.

Takeaways: Professionals

- Make sure you believe in your flight envelope in both plan and section.
- Make sure your decision between center-bound and non-center-bound is made with intention.
- Do not attempt to create or lead a 3D rig without having been a more junior member of a successful team on another 3D rig.

Part 4

It Depends

Armed with our new-found knowledge of the various common forms flying rigs take, we now have a series of further, more specific decisions to make and plan for. The information and decisions outlined in this part apply to all rigs. While your specific selection of a particular style of rig may make some decisions that follow easier, most of what follows is situational. In this part we will go over the pros and cons of various types of lifting media, harnesses, and rescue plans, and code compliance. Great care has been taken in these chapters to *not* promote any one option as the catch-all solution. This is by design. Every rig is a special snowflake of unique circumstances. As such, the information that follows is designed to help guide you in your answering of all these "It Depends" issues.

10 Lifting Media

What is considered an acceptable material for lifting a human being? While there is no succinct answer to this, there are some generally accepted guidelines to help you in your search. Many will say that the lifting media should be a domestic product or made in the US. This is a good jumping-off point, but ultimately is an oversimplification of what is actually important. You want two main things out of your lifting media:

1. You want to know where it came from. This means you should know the name of the company who made the rope.
2. You want the rope manufacturer to be located in a country in which there are consequences for not meeting published minimums. You need to know the manufacturer stands behind its product to the point that it has tested the product well enough to sell it to you for your purpose, and that the manufacturer will stand behind its product in a court of law.

Unfortunately, these two criteria rule out nearly all ropes made in China as many are sold simply as a "Product of China". The simple fact is that companies in China cannot reliably be held accountable in a court of law for their actions. As such, the quality of their goods cannot be trusted, particularly when we are talking about single-point-of-failure life-safety items. Do not be fooled by suppliers who claim to have an "in" or a "contact" in China as a sign of quality assurance. Often they will make sure the first few spools you receive are of their best work, and slowly but surely after that the quality will degrade to what we have come to expect of these manufacturers.

All that being said, these criteria do not rule out products of a huge chunk of the rest of the world. Japan, England, and South Korea immediately spring to mind as countries which manufacture lifting media that meet our two criteria above. This also should not be seen as ruling out reputable manufactures not based in China who have some or all of their manufacturing done in China. Although the work may be getting done in the same factory in many cases, the difference is the reputable manufacturer has taken on the liability of quality assurance with the product coming out of China. So again, while "domestic only" is an easy policy to put on paper, and simplifies some of your worries in this arena, it can also limit you from buying perfectly wonderful products from perfectly reputable manufacturers.

Steel Cable versus 12-strand Rope

The first choice to make when selecting your lifting media is a broad, categorical one: steel or fabric. We will deep-dive different kinds of each later in this chapter, but for now let's go over each category's characteristics, generalizing broadly about each. Both styles of rope have their pros and cons. As with so many other parts of a performer flying rig, the devil is in the details. Taking the time to think all the way through your effect to select the right one for your current application is paramount.

Steel cable is a great candidate for performer flying. It is very strong for its diameter, allowing for thin cables to lift a person. With the help of a good lighting designer the cable can even be made to disappear into the background. It is very resilient, and excellent at withstanding both heat and abrasion. It is also great at dealing with ultraviolet light (UV) and chemical damage, neither being a big concern in normal use. It is readily available all over the country and the world in diameters common for our industry's applications. It is easy to terminate with minimal training and is quick to cut and re-terminate. To put it succinctly: steel is robust and gives you a lot of room for error.

That said, it does have its drawbacks. Steel, without intervention, is silver. Galvanized aircraft cable, or GAC, is common in the entertainment industry and is a slightly duller silver, but still silver nonetheless. Many manufacturers offer this cable blackened by various methods, but all these methods come with additional cons. A common blacking method from around 10 years ago is to powder-coat the cable after it has been woven. The finished product looks beautiful on a spool but flakes off quickly when run over sheaves or around a drum. This not only has the effect of the cable being silver again, but the flaked-off powder coat also gums up any moving component it comes into contact with. The process can also increase the diameter of the rope enough to see the coating catch the walls of a grooved drum, further exacerbating the flaking problem. As such, this method of blacking is becoming harder and harder to find as it has fallen out of favor with nearly everyone who has ever worked with it. Another common blacking technique is to black-oxide the rope. This is a process that sees the rope put into baths of various chemicals which have a reaction with the surface of the cable. The final product is impressively black, doesn't flake off, and barely increases the diameter of rope. Also, unlike powder-coating, which only blacks the outside area of the cable, black-oxide completely blacks the outside of every strand of the cable. However, this blackening method can only be applied to certain materials. Most notably for us, any galvanization on the rope must be removed before the black-oxide process can begin. This means your final product does not have any more rust protection than a raw piece of steel. In black-oxide's real-world applications, it is bathed in oil as a final step to achieve rust-proofing, but this can be problematic in the entertainment industry where everyone is wearing fancy costumes. As a result, black-oxide steel wire rope can be acceptable in some applications but should be flagged as needing constant inspection to spot rust at its immediate onset. While not proven in any scientific manner, black-oxidized rope has also been observed to be more brittle than its non-oxidized brethren. This can increase the number of broken strands found in systems where the D:d ratio has been pushed low, or can result in lower-than-expected breaking strengths in particularly violent and dynamic stopping events. This can lead you to discover stainless steel cable that has been black-oxidized. All the magic of black-oxide but with the rust protection of stainless! This is true; however, duly note that stainless steel cable has lower breaking strengths than its raw steel brother. This fact should not remove stainless cable as an option for your system; it's just another critical piece of information to be aware of while making your decisions.

The other main category of lifting media is fabric, most notably 12-strand rope. The term "12-strand" refers to the rope's construction, which is a weave that is the same as that used in a Chinese finger trap. Twelve-strand ropes are the strongest lifting media in the world when compared to the rope's weight. Also of note: these ropes are significantly lighter than similar diameters in steel. This strength-to-weight ratio makes them an ideal selection for rigs involving large bridles, like V-rigs and 3D rigs. The improvement in strength at a given diameter over steel is wonderful enough by itself but on top of that, since the rope is so very much lighter per foot than its comparable diameter of steel, we have significantly less catenary sag out in the system when using these ropes (Figure 10.1).

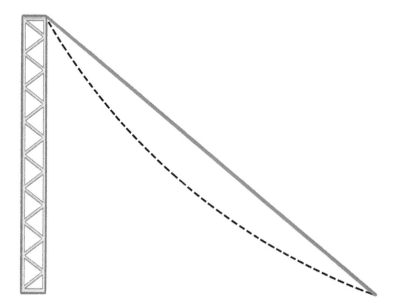

Figure 10.1 Catenary Sag

Generally speaking, and to be clear it depends on the specific rope and specific steel construction, 12-strand ropes are as strong as steel cable at diameters in the less-than-3/16-inch range, and stronger than steel at any diameter above that. The difference in strength is close at 3/16-inch to quarter-inch, depending on the exact rope, but the difference becomes exponential as you get thicker from there. Twelve-strand rope can be stored very easily, often simply being flaked into a bag. There is also zero corrosion concern with fabric ropes as there are no metals in their construction. These fabrics are tan-ish naturally but can easily be painted or dyed by the manufacturer during, or after, the weaving process. While the color does fade over time, it takes a long time and can actually be a great wear/age indicator.

Twelve-strand rope, like steel cable, also has its shortcomings. While this family of ropes is great at dealing with heat and abrasion for rope, it pales in comparison to steel. Certain varieties when put in front of common lighting units will melt into oblivion or get too near to their critical temperature. (This is covered in greater detail later in this chapter.) If reeved incorrectly through a system, being run over a keeper pin for example, they can and will degrade far faster than steel. These ropes are also very susceptible to damage from UV and chemicals. If being used outdoors, in addition to being concerned about UV you should think about animals wanting to take some of your rope as a souvenir. Birds in particular like to peck strands out of the rope, presumably for use in their nests (Figure 10.2).

Figure 10.2 Bird Eating Rope

Tying knots is not the correct way to form an eye in 12-strand ropes. Knots grossly negatively affect the breaking strength of these ropes, far more than other common entertainment ropes. Terminating 12-strand requires precise training in splicing, the process of taking apart a rope and weaving it back together to form an eye, end, or joint. This process can be time consuming if not practiced often.

Terminations: Swaging Steel Cable

Precise instructions on the swaging techniques for a given tool/swage combination should always be received from the manufacturer and will not be explicitly laid out here. Instead we will discuss the concept of swaging, how it works, and some common misconceptions. To speak broadly, swaging works with compression and surface area. The steel cable is inserted into soft metal sleeve, which is then crimped by a tool to compress the sleeve around the cable (Figure 10.3). The number of crimps for a given diameter of cable will vary from manufacturer to manufacturer. This is because, of course, each company patents its tool. The width and depth of the crimp is critical to achieving enough friction and surface area between the sleeve and the cable to hold in tension. The two most popular manufacturers of such tools in the US are Nicopress (owned by the National Telephone Supply Company) and Loos and Co. "Loos" is pronounced "loose", which you may (correctly) be thinking is a weird name for a company that makes swaging tools given the above explanation of how they work.

Figure 10.3   Swaged Eye

Since no two companies have the same depth and width of crimp between them, each one needs a different number of crimps for a given diameter of cable. It is critical that you are sure you are looking at the right chart, for the right tool, from the right manufacturer when you are terminating steel cables.

These tools also come with go/no-go gauges, often called simply "go gauges" (Figure 10.4), which are intended to check that your tool is crimping to the correct depth. As such, each tool comes with its own gauge. A gauge for a 3/16-inch oval swage from one company is not suitable for checking the crimp from another company. In the case of Nicopress, some of its gauges are even specific to the tool they came with, meaning the go-gauge for a given oval sleeve with *this* tool might be different than the one for *that* tool. Be sure you have the right go-gauge for the sleeve and tool you are using! These should be used on every crimp, of every swage, every time.

Some will argue that you only have to check every *XX* number of swages. As long as you think the tool will always pass the gauge, this can be a fine strategy. However, the first time a crimp doesn't pass, it immediately calls into question every crimp you've made with that tool since the last time you checked. For the amount of time it takes to use the gauge every time, which is to say it is a highly insignificant amount of time, you should use it on every crimp, of every swage, every time.

There is an oft-repeated myth that the tool, after making a crimp, must remain closed for 10 seconds for the crimp to be correct. This is sometimes attributed to the idea that the act of crimping the swage causes the swage

Figure 10.4 Go/No-Go Gauge

material to liquefy from heat. The 10 seconds is therefore intended to allow the melted swage material to seep into the weave of the cable, solidifying the swage's hold. While the process of swaging does get the sleeve material to behave plastically, it does not cause the material to melt and wick into the air gaps in the construction of the wire rope. Some will say that the tool must remain closed for three seconds instead of 10. All these time-based tool-closure rules come from wanting to make sure the tool has completely closed. There is no discernable amount of time a swaging tool must remain closed for a swage to be crimped properly. That said, you also don't want to be swaging cables in a manner that you might use to operate manual hedge trimmers. The bottom line here is to make sure you've closed the tool the entire way so that your crimp will pass your go-gauge.

As we've covered earlier, swages work through compression and surface area. There is no melting of the swage in the process of crimping it, as can be seen in Figure 10.5. If there were this would call into question the structural integrity of any cable left in a truck in the summer when it arrives at the next venue. What is actually happening during a crimp is that the sleeve material is being cold-formed into the cable. The sleeve does reach its plastic deformation point, but at no point does it melt. All this being said, the idea of holding the tool closed for 10 seconds can be a good one, if not a little exaggerated. When crimping a swage you want to make sure that you completely close the tool each time. While you don't want to crimp cable like you would trim a hedge, keeping the tool closed for 10 whole seconds seems equally silly. Just be a responsible adult while swaging and it will turn out correctly every time.

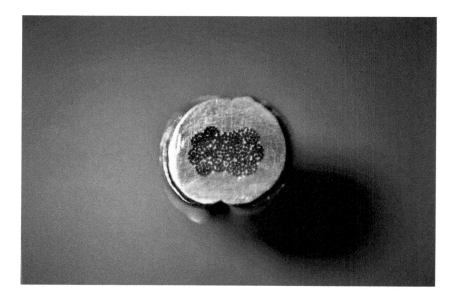

Figure 10.5   Swage Cross-Section

There is also often a debate about whether or not you have to buy your swages from the same company that made your tool. Nicopress is the only company that insists on such a thing, but it's important to better understand what we are talking about here. All swaging sleeves made by reputable manufacturers conform to a MilSpec, which is short for "Military Specification". For copper swaging sleeves, a very common material for sleeves to be made from, the MilSpec in question is MS51844. It is important when purchasing swages that you are buying ones that conform to this standard, as all swaging tools work with these. So then, what makes Nicopress' swages special? The company takes a conforming batch of swages and stamps "Nicopress" down the side of them. Some may see Nicopress' insistence on using its sleeves only as a way to draw more business from its customers, and there is likely some truth to that; however, in this day and age of counterfeit goods it could never hurt to have an additional layer of security when buying your materials. Other manufacturers, like Loos and Co., simply insist that you buy sleeves that are known to meet MS51844.

A correctly swaged cable is rated for 95–99% of the breaking strength of the cable. The exact value should be referenced from the manufacturer of your specific tool. Please note that 95–99% is not 100%. This slight strength reduction should not be forgotten when thinking about the breaking strength of the cable in your system.

Terminations: Splicing 12-Strand Ropes

Splicing, like swaging, should be done under the express instruction of a manual from the rope manufacturer, or a manual that it has recommended. Many default to the *Samson Splicing Manual*, which is a fantastic instructional splicing book for both beginners and pros. Very few have actually read that full publication, opting instead to jump to the instructions for whatever splice they need to perform. Sadly for them, they miss out on a wealth of information on spliceable ropes. If teaching yourself from one of these books, or even if being taught by a professional, it is strongly recommended to send off some samples of your completed splices to the rope manufacturer for break testing. Almost every manufacturer offers this service for a minimal fee. In return, you get the knowledge that you are doing everything correctly and that your splices are of a sufficient quality to be used for human flying. A correctly spliced rope will break at 100% of the rope's published minimum breaking strength.

The tools used for splicing are known as "fids". Pictured above is the most common set found in the entertainment industry: the Samson Selma Splicing Kit – Set of 5 (Figure 10.6). They come packaged in a tube, the fids nesting inside each other like Russian Matryoshka dolls. A fid is both a tool and a unit of measurement in splicing. A fid as a unit of measurement is used to determine how much rope must be tucked back down the center of the rope to achieve a 100% termination. A fid is approximately 22 times the diameter of the rope and so the tool known as a fid is made to be this length for a given diameter of rope. This means when you are making a splice the tool you need to weave the rope is also your measuring tape! (That said, the Selma fids in particular are longer than this value.) You will use this tool to "tuck" the rope back into itself, utilizing the Chinese-finger-trap feature of the rope to achieve the same thing swaging does: a termination based on surface area and compression. As such, you should fight the urge to grab your fid with any tool, and especially ones with teeth like needle-nose pliers. This will mar the fid, making it more difficult in the future to slide the fid through the center of the rope.

Remember that the rope is fragile and time should be taken to not unduly destroy the rope while performing the splice. Keeping your fids smooth will help with this. Always make sure to get a hold of the strand, the whole strand, and nothing but the strand you're aiming for. Leaving individual threads behind or grabbing extra individual threads from your strand's neighbors are some of the quickest ways to have to cut your work off the line and start over.

Depending on exactly which splice you are performing you may also need to lock-stitch the section of rope you've tucked back into the center of the rope. This requires special needles and thin, strong splicing twine. This is one of the more Zen activities in rigging and should be given adequate time to be done right. This stitching works to make sure shock loads and/or uneven

Figure 10.6 Selma Fids

loading on the eye of the splice doesn't pull the tuck back out of the rope the way it came. Put differently: this stitching holds the two ropes together so that the outer rope has time to Chinese-finger-trap the rope running inside it, thereby holding the load. Just like with swaging we are relying on surface area and friction to maintain our eye. In a large-scale show with multiple splicers working on a system, different color threads can be used as an indicator of who spliced a given line.

Always make sure the splicing guide you are following is appropriate for the rope you are currently splicing. This may seem obvious, but complacency can easily lead to splicing a new rope "the same way we always splice 12-strand" out of laziness. Consult the rope manufacturer and send it some samples to break test when you first work with its product. Just because you've gotten one 12-strand sample of someone else's rope break-tested in the past does not necessarily mean you will see the same results with someone else's rope. The most common finding in these break tests is an insufficient tapering of the tuck, which the lab will tell you if that's the issue with your sample. Remember: the goal is to smooth out that transition from two diameters of rope back to one as much as possible. The smoother that transition, the higher your breaking strength will be! (Assuming you've done the rest of the splice correctly, of course.)

Common Steel Cable Types

Let's begin with how wire rope is built to inform our understanding of why it is classified the way it is.

Wire rope is made up of wires, which are twisted together into strands, which are then twisted together into wire rope (Figure 10.7). The direction of said weaving is referred to as the "lay" of a cable. Fun fact: a "lay" is both a direction of the twist holding the rope together, and a unit of measurement. The distance along the wire rope it takes for a strand to wrap all the way around the circumference of the rope once is also referred to as one "lay" of the cable. Wire rope is classified and purchased as *a number* times *a number*: "7x19", for example. The first number refers to the number of strands in the cable; the second refers to the number of wires in each strand. Taking 7x19 as our example, we know that this cable has seven strands, each of which with 19 wires (Figure 10.7). This particular construction of cable is better known as "aircraft cable" and when also galvanized is referred to as "GAC". This construction became popular on small aircraft to tie the control surfaces to the yoke (hence the moniker) and is a very popular construction within the entertainment industry as it is readily available from most suppliers.

There are often also a couple of series of letters associated with these two numbers explaining in further detail what the rope you are buying is. *HC*, *FC*, and *IWRC* are commonly seen, and refer to the construction of the core of the rope. *HC* stands for *hollow core*, *FC* for *fiber core*, and *IWRC*

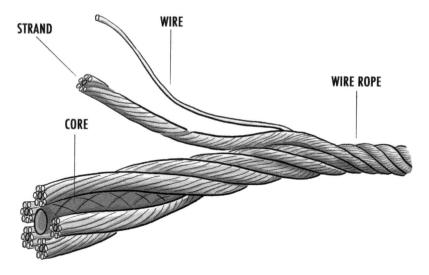

STRAND

WIRE

WIRE ROPE

CORE

Figure 10.7   Wire Rope Construction

for *independent wire rope core. Hollow core*, as you might guess, means there is no core. It is common in 6x19 construction where the outer strands are arranged similarly to 7x19, but there is no strand down the center. Fiber core is similar to this except, you guessed it, there is a fiber material running down the center of the rope instead of any steel wires. 7x19 IWRC has six strands twisted around the outside forming a jacket around another strand of the same composition running down the core of the rope's construction. These variants have an effect on the overall strength of the rope and the rope's twisting characteristics. This can become very important when selecting a rope for use with a swivel, which we will cover in more depth later on in this chapter. Other abbreviations that will be run into frequently are *IPS, XIPS, XXIPS*, and so on, all the way up to *XXXXXIPS*. The *IPS* stands for *improved plow steel*, and each *X* stands for one use of the word "Extra". Obviously, the more *Extras* in the abbreviation, the higher the quality of the steel used to make the rope. Why is rope so "extra" these days? Well, remember two things. First, wire rope was invented a long time ago; around 1831 in Germany for the mining industry. Material sciences have come a long way since then, begetting improvement after improvement. The second thing to remember about all these "extras" is that material scientists and wire rope product people are not very creative with their naming, apparently.

The other common rope construction used in performer flying is 19x7 (Figure 10.9). This rope has 19 strands, each with seven threads. Unfortunately, this just so happens to be the opposite of 7x19, which can and does lead to confusion with suppliers and technicians alike. To paraphrase a great song from *Avenue Q*, everyone's a little bit dyslexic, and this is not helping!

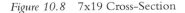

Figure 10.8   7x19 Cross-Section   *Figure 10.9*   19x7 Cross-Section

They are, however, very different ropes, as you can see by comparing the two cross-section images (Figures 10.8 and 10.9). 19x7 rope has a very different lay pattern from 7x19. This gives these two rope constructions very different twisting characteristics. 19x7 is often referred to as "non-rotational"; however, this is completely incorrect. It is in fact "semi-rotation-resistant", a fact that has huge impacts on how swivels affect this rope's construction. This misunderstanding can lead to some very bad consequences.

Swivels Effects on Wire Rope

Attached as an addendum to the ESTA Performer Flying Standard (ANSI E1.43–2016) is a study by R. Verreet called "The Use of Swivels with Steel Wire Ropes". It is absolutely worth a read if you want to better understand what is going on within your wire rope when you introduce a swivel into the system. Mr. Verreet breaks down wire rope into three broad categories: rotation-resistant, semi-rotation-resistant, and non-rotation-resistant. He explains that using a swivel with non-rotation-resistant rope causes the rope to unlay, reducing its breaking strength and life expectancy. He says that this rope used with a swivel will only be 85% efficient, as you will overload the center strand as the outer strands elongate during this unlaying process. The same action with semi-rotation-resistant rope might, logically, be expected to produce similar, but not quite as bad, results; however, the opposite is shown to be true. Because the rope is laid in such a way as to reduce, but not eliminate, rotational forces, the introduction of a swivel actually weakens the cable more than that of non-rotation-resistant rope and grossly shortens the rope's life expectancy. Mr. Verreet reports that this class of rope will only be 63% efficient. True rotation-resistant rope, on the other hand, is shown to have no ill effects of a swivel, as the rope is (nearly) inherently balanced.

From our common rope types, 7x19 is firmly in the non–rotation-resistant category. 19x7, as mentioned above, is in fact semi-rotation-resistant rope. The difference here is crucial. Without fully understanding the product you are using you might think that you have no swivel-based degradation of your rope, when in fact you have selected the rope type most susceptible to such failure modes! This is another lesson in making sure you fully understand every component of your system and how they all interact with each other.

All this being said, it seems there is no good answer for us and our love of swivels, and by the letter of the law that is true. But we can, as we are ever wont to do, make the best of a bad situation. We now know that 19x7 and a swivel is the worst of all of our options, so that clearly should be avoided. In a sealed system, which is to say one without a swivel, 19x7 is a great option and should definitely be considered. But if a swivel is an unavoidable part of your rig – like in most acrobatics, for example – 19x7 should be avoided. We know that 7x19 with a swivel is slightly better, so we should lean that way unless there is a compelling reason not to. This hazard, however, should make its way into our RA/RR paperwork, discussed in Chapter 1, and reacted to in the same way any other known hazard would be. We should classify how likely and bad a scenario could be caused by this hazard and mitigate it accordingly. In this case, with 7x19, this could take the form of additional inspections and a more frequent rope-change-out schedule. These kinds of preventive actions can reduce this known risk to something manageable and unlikely; exactly where we want all our known hazards to be.

But why not just get true rotation-resistant rope? Well, those are mostly made for the crane industry and as such are not manufactured in diameters that disappear into the background. If such a product existed, it would be the gold standard of all performer flying. There are manufacturers starting to make 35x7 as thin as 9 mm (or nearly 3/8 inch in Freedom Units) which is almost down to the range we usually work in. Here's hoping that downsizing trend continues, as 35x7 would be an amazing thing to have! There are some other exotic rope constructions out there, like XLT-4 and others, but they all have their drawbacks too. XLT-4, for example, requires the use of a special swage from Nicopress, which is coated in an adhesive on the inside. The big downside here, besides having to buy and stock more unique bits, is that these special sleeves look exactly like their non-special brothers at a quick glance. If you dump your swage organizer over on the floor by accident the subsequent resorting is both critical and a detailed job. Additionally, let's not forget the reason for the introduction of a swivel is usually because we have an acrobat on the line. Acrobats are almost always more technically in tune with the mechanics of the rig they are flying on than their performer-flying-only brothers and sisters. Thanks to XLT-4's construction, which is four large steel threads, an acrobat will almost always complain of feeling the rope "jump" as it runs up and down. It is a noticeable feeling when running XLT-4 through a sheave and can be unnerving for the person on the end of the line, depending on what they are doing. (Think about hanging from a Lyra by your neck and feeling little vibrations through your hoop!) This chattering is particularly exacerbated at low speeds, which is when we are usually doing our most delicate work. Lastly, XLT-4 is much rarer than our common 7x19 or 19x7 constructions. As such, you need to have more in stock at all times if you're using it, since getting more can have a substantial lead time associated with it depending on where in the world you might be. This can be a real problem for a touring production, for example. It often also has large minimum lengths you will have to order if you want any at all, as it is not very common in the wild.

There is, sadly, no slam-dunk answer here. All of the above rope types have their moments to be top dog, and all of them are the wrong choice in others. This can seem like an intimidating choice to the novice, and it should. But remember, there are lots of people out there in the world who are more than willing to help you! There are also tons of books written on this topic, to say nothing of the mountain of scholarly essays that can be found with a simple Google search. Your wire rope supplier will also be happy to help find a unique solution to your unique problem. The moral of the story is to know your gear, select it for a reason, know its shortcomings, and plan to mitigate them.

Types of 12-strand

Twelve-strand ropes are referred to by many different names. Technora, Vectran, Dyneema, Spectra, and Plasma are some of the most common names you've likely heard thrown around. They are often used interchangeably to mean simply "12-strand rope" but they are in fact very different from each other, with different strengths and weaknesses based on their exact chemical composition. These names are all brand names of particular chemical compositions owned by different corporations. A similar list would be like saying "Craftsman, Husky, DeWalt, or Milwaukee", when you're really just talking about a generic pair of pliers. It's an important distinction to use a particular brand name when you intend to for a reason, and instead say "12-strand rope" when you're talking about the whole family of ropes.

Technora

Technora is an aramid fiber (which is actually a shortened version of saying "aromatic polyamide") whose composition is owned by the Teijin Corporation. Aramid fibers are the same family that Kevlar comes from. Technora has a great strength-to-weight ratio, and in fact is the strongest rope at a given diameter in the world (at the time of this book's publication). It is the best of the 12-strand ropes at dealing with heat, its critical temperature being approximately 520 degrees Fahrenheit. ("Critical temperature" is not the point at which the rope melts, as so many assume. It is the point at which the rope is no longer as strong due only to temperature.) While it is the best of the 12-strand ropes at dealing with heat, don't let that sentence lull you into thinking it is anywhere near as good with heat as steel wire rope. Pyro will still go straight through Technora, and as the optics on moving lights get better and better, more and more moving lights can melt it when it is placed in the light's focal range. Technora is the worst at stretch, or creep, within the family of 12-strand ropes. It will stretch approximately 2% linearly as it is loaded from zero to its breaking strength. Technora, or Tech-12 as it is often referred to, is the most common of the 12-strands and the most readily available in the US.

Vectran

Vectran is a liquid crystal polymer owned by the Calanese Corporation. Vectran is similarly good at dealing with heat as Technora, although not quite as awesome; its critical temperature is approximately 300 degrees Fahrenheit. Vectran is particularly bad at dealing with UV among the 12-strand family and it is almost the most prone to fraying. Vectran fiber was used to make the airbags on the Mars Pathfinder Rover, which really underscores its great strength-to-weight ratio.

Dyneema/Spectra

While two different compositions, Dyneema and Spectra share many attributes. They are both made from ultra-high-molecular-weight polyethylene, better known as UHMWPE. They are both extraordinary at stretch, which is to say they don't stretch much at all. They are both quite bad at dealing with heat, their critical temperatures being approximately 250 degrees Fahrenheit. Anything that could be significantly damaged with boiling water should be used carefully out in the wild! Both ropes' real-world application is tugboat rope, as they both float and do not absorb water. They are both also very common in high-end sailboat racing thanks to their low stretch. Dyneema is owned by DSM Dyneema, while Spectra is owned by Honeywell International.

Plasma

Plasma is a high-modulus polyethylene, or HMPE. It is owned by Cortland Rope and is the strongest rope in the world by weight. Duly note: Technora is stronger per diameter; Plasma is just lighter at those diameters. Plasma has the least stretch of any of the common 12-strand ropes, clocking in at 1.25% from zero to its breaking strength. It is the worst at dealing with heat of any of the 12-strands, its critical temperature being 150 degrees Fahrenheit. It will be of no use to you before you even get the water to a boil!

Now that you've read all that, Figure 10.10 shows all that information in chart form for your future quick reference.

Just like the swivel situation with wire rope, it's important to know the characteristics of the rope you're selecting and how you intend to mitigate any outstanding risks. At the very least it is important to know you don't know enough about the different kinds of 12-strand ropes, and remember to brush up before making a rash decision. It is a common occurrence for a given rig to have one kind of rope, only for that rope to not be available

Rope Common Name	Fiber Type	Who Owns It	Fun Fact	Mutant Power	Bad At
Technora	Aramid	Teijin Corporation	Same family as Kevlar	strongest at diameter, best at heat (520F)	Most stretch (1.8%)
Vectran	Liquid Crystal Polymer	Celanese Corporation	Airbags on Pathfinder Rover	heat resistance	UV, frays easily
Dyneema	Ultra-High-Molecular-Weight Polyethylene (UHMWPE)	DSM Dyneema	tugboat rope, floats	low stretch, abrasion	Heat (250F)
Spectra	Ultra-High-Molecular-Weight Polyethylene (UHMWPE)	Honeywell International	tugboat rope, floats	even less stretch	Heat (250F)
Plasma	High-Modulus Polyethylene (HMPE)	Cortland Rope	strongest in world by weight	least stretch (1.25%)	Heat (150F)

Figure 10.10 12-Strand Rope Chart

later in the timeframe when it is needed. A substitution of another kind of 12-strand will be suggested. It is important to make that choice intentionally and armed with information, not flippantly. Twelve-strand ropes have no ill effects from adding a swivel to the system. That said, it is important to make sure that the swivel is spinning, and you are not, instead, twisting the rope over-and-over! It is also critically important to remember to never tie knots in 12-strand ropes. This degrades their breaking strength by far larger margins than their more traditionally constructed rope brothers. Much like steel cable, if you want to really geek out on rope materials and constructions, there are countless books and scholarly essays on these topics. The manufactures of these ropes also have a wealth of free information on their websites for your reference pleasure.

Conclusion

Quite intentionally, there are no specific endorsements of steel over fabric ropes, or flavors of steel over others, or flavors of 12-strands over others either. There are no "the way we always do it" kind of shortcuts to take when selecting your lifting media. All of these factors listed here, and likely several others based on your specific use case, need to be taken into account when making this important decision. The goal here is for you to be better educated to make this decision for yourself, or at the very least to now know what you don't know. Don't forget that there are many resources to get further educated on this topic! Your favorite lifting media supplier is likely a great place to start.

Takeaways: Beginners

- Steel is more resilient than fabric ropes. This resiliency gives you more margin of error in inspections, reeving, and repetitive use damage.
- Not all ropes are created equal. Make sure you have picked the one you are using for a reason!

Takeaways: Professionals

- If using a swivel on steel wire rope make sure you fully understand its impact on your rope.
- If using a swivel on fabric ropes, make sure the swivel is spinning and not the rope.
- When using 12-strand ropes make sure you have suitably designed the system to accommodate the rope's fragility when compared to steel.
- With either steel or fabric ropes make sure you fully understand all the characteristics of the rope when selecting it for your effect.

11   Harnesses and Flying Apparatuses

The correct approach to some parts of designing and executing a performer flying effect is to hit it with the biggest hammer you've got, metaphorically. For other parts it is better to sharpen your pencil and really consider what you are trying to achieve. Harness selection is definitely the latter. While it can be easiest to pack your fanciest, spinniest, flippiest harness for every show, this can add complication and risk that could have been avoided with some proper prior planning. Let's start with a discussion of the most common styles of harnesses used today. There is no finer example out there than the fine handiwork of the team at Climbing Sutra. They are the best commercially available harnesses for performer flying, and as such more than merit inclusion here. While there are many other safe and reputable harness manufacturers out there, most are also providers of whole rigging solutions. The team at Climbing Sutra are exclusively focused on harnesses and the work speaks for itself. Some of the below notes are specific to their equipment, but a vast majority will apply to any similar harness. As with any part of a performer flying rig, make sure to know, understand, and act on any manufacturer guidelines, especially those regarding inspections.

Bungee Harness

This is, sadly, the most forgotten harness. It is often overlooked for the next harness on our list, the Ultra Swivel. The Bungee Harness is as simple as it gets: two leg straps, one waist belt, and a point at each hip to connect to a fly system (Figure 11.1). It's very similar to a simple rock-climbing sit harness. As a result it's easy to forget about this style of harness when packing for a gig. But the fact that it will only hold a performer upright, or darn near upright, can be a godsend on shows where that it all that is required and you are working with inexperienced flyers. You can still get some movement around the hip axis, but you've really got to want it. The flip side to that coin is that you don't have to worry about anyone coming in for a landing head-first by mistake.

Figure 11.1 Bungee Harness
Photo: Paige Durborow, model: Genevieve Berube

As one of the simpler constructed harnesses, it is also one of the easiest to fit. That said, the fundamentals here apply to all the more complicated harnesses to follow. So, as with so many things in life, just because it is "easy" does not excuse the fitter for not paying attention to every detail and not knowing every cause and effect of every adjustment. Adjusting any harness is mainly about finding the performer's center of gravity. Unfortunately for us as fitters we cannot simply tell people to put the waist belt around their natural waist, tighten, and get out there. This is because not everyone is proportioned the same way. Don't believe that? Try giving the same instructions on harness fit to a Rockette who is 6 ft and by definition all legs, and a Cirque du Soleil acrobat who is 4 ft 9 in and a walking ab. Given the same neutral instructions the Rockette will be very bottom-heavy, what with all those legs, and the Cirque acrobat will be very top-heavy, what with all those shoulders. To have them be comfortable and upright we must adjust the harness up and down their bodies to achieve balance. Given that the goal of the Bungee Harness is to keep the performer upright, it is better to be bottom-heavy than top-heavy. Of course, the goal is always equilibrium, but if you had to pick one, and the performer only needs to go straight up and down, bottom-heavy is better. If the performer will also need to lean forward during their flight, then bottom-heavy is suddenly just as bad as top-heavy. Again, the remedy for this is to move the harness up and down the performer's body, while also remembering that there are limits in both directions to how far you can go.

In Figure 11.2 we see a harness that has been adjusted too low. Multiple problems will result from a harness fit thusly. First of all, the point of the leg straps is to keep the performer from falling out the bottom of the harness. As such, they are there to support the weight of the body from the crotch. When the leg straps are as flat as shown in Figure 11.2, you will no longer be supporting the performer's weight appropriately. When fitted like this and the harness lifts the performer, it will slide up. Important note here then: just because the harness was where you wanted it when the performer was standing on the ground doesn't mean it will be in the same place after you load them onto the rig. When a harness is adjusted low like this the performer will more than likely experience numbness in their legs. This is because all the tightening of the leg straps you can do in this scenario only serves to squeeze the around the leg, instead of adjusting the height of the harness, as intended (Figure 11.3). Tightening the leg straps at this location on the body will likely result in the performer experiencing suspension trauma. We will discuss suspension trauma further in Chapter 12, but to make a long story short, this condition causes un-oxygenated blood to pool in the legs, the results of which can be tunnel vision, blackouts, or even death. It is to be avoided at all costs!

In Figure 11.4 the harness has the opposite problem: it is too high. Telltale signs here are how vertical the leg straps are and just how high the waistband

Figure 11.2   Harness Too Low

Photo: Paige Durborow, model: Genevieve Berube

Figure 11.3   Harness Too Low (Annotated)
Photo: Paige Durborow, model: Genevieve Berube

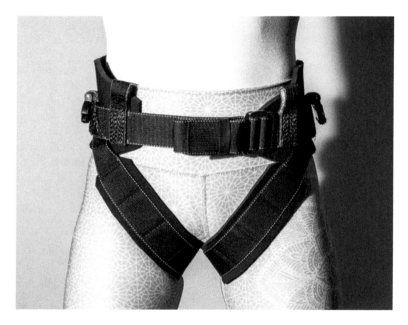

Figure 11.4   Harness Too High
Photo: Paige Durborow, model: Genevieve Berube

is on the performer's body. The two main problems here, aside from that fact that the performer will certainly be bottom-heavy, will be pain in the crotch and pinched ribs. With the leg straps this vertical too much of the weight of the performer will be supported by too little of the crotch region. This will result, rightly, in complaints of pain, bruising, and an inability to spend much time in the harness. Assuming you are on a compressed timetable (because when aren't we, really?) the performer will have a harder and harder time as the days go by getting back in harness as the bruising never has time to heal between harness usages. The other issue here will be that the harness waistband, when tightened, will crunch down on the performer's floating ribs (Figure 11.5). These are your lowest ribs that start on your spine but do not come all the way around to your front to meet at your sternum. This will cause difficulty breathing, pain in said floating ribs, and in the event of a shock load, could also cause those ribs to break. Needless to say, all of that should be avoided at all costs! Simply not tightening the waistband appropriately to alleviate this pain is also not a sufficient solution. Remember, the waistband is the only thing keeping a performer in the harness should they end up inverted. It is absolutely crucial that the waistband be tightened sufficiently!

We want to make sure the hip points are located roughly on, you guessed it, the performer's hips (Figure 11.6). This can be achieved through adjusting both the back and front halves of the waistband in a balanced dance. This can often be a guess-and-check situation as you will not be sure until you get the performer in the air how much they will tighten the front part of their waistband, which is the only adjustment of the two they can reach. If the points are too far around the front of their body they will always hang slightly backwards or be constantly fighting to stay upright with their core. If they are too far around the back of the performer they will always be tilted forward, Superman style. To avoid this we want to start the hip connections under the spot the performer's arms touch their hips when they stand relaxed and naturally. From here, after test-picking the performer, we can then adjust forward or backwards as needed to suit this particular performer with their specific proportions and their specific costume or props. Never underestimate how much a costume or prop can throw off one's center of gravity, as we will discuss in more depth later in this chapter.

Those are instructions for how to have someone balanced, as is often the goal. However, if your effect calls for someone to be leaning forward, like

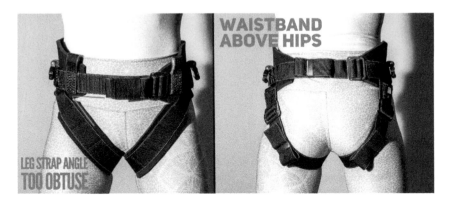

Figure 11.5 Harness Too High (Annotated)

Photo: Paige Durborow, model: Genevieve Berube

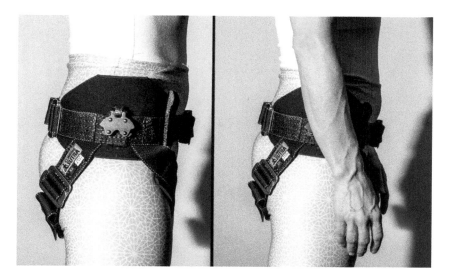

Figure 11.6   Harness Side View

Photo: Paige Durborow, model: Genevieve Berube

Superman, it might be easier to cheat their hip connections around their back slightly instead of requiring them to constantly use their core to achieve this angle. This can be particularly helpful with inexperienced flyers; this is where harness fitting becomes an art. The best way for you to understand how these adjustments can affect a performer and/or work to your favor when creating an effect is to spend some time in a harness yourself.

In Figure 11.7 we have, finally, a properly adjusted harness. The waistband is above the top of the butt and tightened appropriately, ensuring the performer will not fall out if inverted. It is not, however, so high as to start crushing ribs. The leg straps are at a good angle for supporting the weight of the performer without crushing around the leg. The hip points are located on the performer's hips, roughly where his or her arms fall naturally, but are then adjusted for that person's shape. All the extra webbing is cleaned up so as not to get tangled in costuming or get in the way of first responders if something was to go wrong. Important note: in the case of the Bungee Harness, both hip connections must be used at all times. This is never to be used a single-point harness.

Now we can test-hang the performer to see how the fit is off the ground. We certainly don't want the first time the performer hangs in their harness to be dozens of feet off the ground, or connected to a very fast flying machine! Instead, we can have a set of static cables ready from which we can hang a performer. The best move here is to make the cables short enough that you need to be standing on a milk crate, apple box, or your favorite food-named platform, to connect to the lines. Have the performer step up onto the box, connect them, and then have them lower their weight into the harness. You will be shocked by

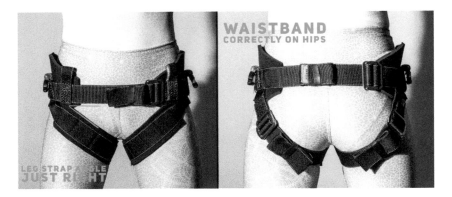

Figure 11.7   Harness Just Right
Photo: Paige Durborow, model: Genevieve Berube

how much slack is produced by doing just this! Adjust the harness as needed, and when you're done, bring the box back and ask the performer to stand up. Now you can disconnect them and re-evaluate if the harness is still fit appropriately.

Now to the oft-asked question of "How tight is correct?" As previously stated, over-tightening leg straps can lead to suspension trauma and over-tightening waistbands can lead to problems breathing, but this does not mean we want to be loose either. Of course in both cases improper harness placement plays a big role in those issues. In the case of a fall-protection harness, the rule is usually said to be that you want to be able to slide a hand between your body and the webbing, as though you were putting your hand in your pocket, but not be able to do the same thing when making a fist. While this is a great tool for fitting your fall-protection harness, this is way too loose for a performer flying harness. When the harness is in the correct position on a performer's body you want to tighten the webbing enough that the harness does not then move when actually supporting a performer's weight. Put differently, you want it to be as tight as is comfortable, and then just a little more. This can often be quite tight, and is why Climbing Sutra makes a special tool to then loosen the harness (Figure 11.8).

These are not harnesses that are designed to be there just in case something goes wrong, like a fall-protection harness is. They are designed to be the only thing briefly winning the fight with gravity. As such they should be tight. These harness are designed to save your life. That doesn't mean they should be 100% comfortable. This is why they come with padding. Think about an airbag in your car. If you need it, it might break your nose. You'll be alive, but you'll be in some pain. Now, in our case we are trying to avoid injury, but *some* pain in exchange for the gift of safe flight is a small price to pay. Let's note the emphasis on "some" in that last sentence. We don't want our performers to be in constant or unbearable pain, but some toughness is needed to do a performer flying stunt day-in and day-out.

Throughout this section the Bungee Harness has been discussed as being best for keeping a performer upright, without inverting. Based on its construction, it is fabulous at this task. You can, however, use a Bungee Harness for inversions

Figure 11.8 Sutra Harness Tool
Photo: Paige Durborow, model: Genevieve Berube

too, but it requires additional hardware in your system to accommodate it, most notably swivels. The Bungee Harness can be a fine compromise of harness visual impact and the desire to invert. That said, Climbing Sutra also makes a harness specifically designed to deal with some of the challenges and concerns around inverting: the Ultra Swivel (Figure 11.9).

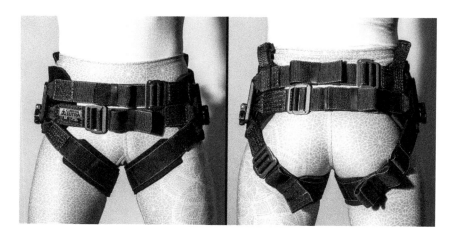

Figure 11.9 Ultra Swivel Harness
Photo: Paige Durborow, model: Genevieve Berube

Ultra Swivel Harness

The most go-to harness out there right now. While slightly bulkier than the Bungee, it allows for more effects to be executed, and more personalized adjustment. This is thanks to do the adjustable hip pick points (Figure 11.10).

Thanks to the attachment point being adjustable up and down independent of the harness placement, we have the ability to really dial in the center of gravity for each individual performer. But with great power comes great responsibility: we've also introduced an additional variable with this adjustment, which is another thing we need to keep in mind to make sure is done right. Think of the position of the harness on the performer, as discussed in length during the Bungee Harness section, as the coarse adjustment, and these hip points as the fine adjustment. We need all this adjustment so that the performer can be balanced well enough to control a full rotation about their hips; the purpose for an Ultra Swivel in the first place.

All of the same adjustment techniques that we discussed about the Bungee Harness apply to the Ultra Swivel. You may have noticed the Ultra Swivel has two waist belts. This is for multiple reasons. They allow for better placement of the hip points on the performer. It also is an extra insurance policy for keeping an inverted performer in the harness. When properly placed on the body one back waistband should be on the top curve of the butt with the other comfortably on the small of the performer's back. This placement also allows the harness to give some lower back support. This helps the performer mightily, as the act of controlled flipping can take quite a toll on an unsupported back. If you find many of your performers complaining of sore lower backs, have another round of harness fitting with them. They will more than likely have been sliding their harnesses too low on their bodies, thereby removing this additional support.

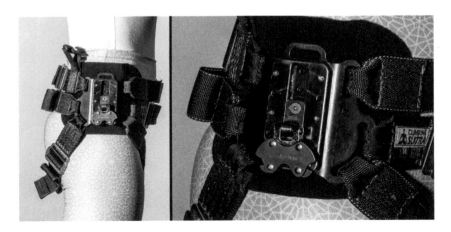

Figure 11.10   Ultra Swivel Pick Points
Photo: Paige Durborow, model: Genevieve Berube

When an Ultra Swivel is properly adjusted on the performer they should be able to have their head at any of the compass rose positions in Figure 11.11 without engaging their core to stay *rotated* there. They should be able to be straight up, straight down, flat forward, or lying back without having to work to stay there. The more acrobatic reader will likely be saying, "In both planking positions they will need their core to stay as flat as a table", and that is true, but they shouldn't need to be using additional core work to stay at that location, rotationally, about the compass rose. That said, to get from one of these positions to another will, and should, require core engagement. Getting the performer hanging off the ground in their adjusted harness can test this. Make sure you have them high enough that their head will not slam into the floor if they are wildly imbalanced! Also make sure there are no obstructions in the entire path their body can make. These test-hang points are often put in corners of buildings without remembering that the performer will need to make a complete 360-degree flip. Have them hang straight up, then put your arms out in front of them and have them try to fly forward, like Superman. As soon as they begin to tip you will know if they are balanced or not. Assuming they are not, because they never will be on the first try, simply land them back on the ground and make the adjustment you deem necessary. If they are top-heavy that means that most of their weight is above their pivot point, so you would want to move the hip points up. If they are bottom-heavy then too much of their weight is below their pivot point, so you will want to move the

Figure 11.11 Performer Compass Rose

hip points down. Eventually you will get to where the performer can easily hit the four compass rose positions and use minimal effort to get between them. At this point they can then begin working on a controlled front and back flip, assuming of course that's part of this show. The performer, when in proper control, should be able to get all the way around the circle in both directions slowly. A sign of a poorly adjusted harness is someone who needs momentum, or a big wind-up, to achieve a full flip.

Just as with the Bungee, we also need to be aware of the hip points placement around the body. Especially with the Ultra Swivel, the hip points tend to cheat forward around the body as the center of gravity adjustment goes on. This is because the performer will, rightly, continue to tighten the front waistbands. This will result in them resting in a slightly leaned back position. They will also have a hard time initiating a front flip, but once they overcome that initial difficulty, they will snap the rest of the way around the circle, albeit a bit uncontrolled. The opposite is true in the much rarer case of the hip points being too far behind the performer. They will always lean forward and be overly able to begin a front flip but will have difficulty getting back to upright. As with the Bungee Harness the best starting point is to have the hip points under the location where the performer's arms meet their hips when they are standing naturally and relaxed.

Just as with the Bungee Harness these instructions have been designed to get a harness fit for equilibrium. Intentionally throwing the adjustment to cause an imbalance in your or the performer's favor is perfectly acceptable. For example, if you have an inexperienced flyer who needs to do a backflip while pendulum flying on the stage it might behoove you to make the performer intentionally bottom-heavy. The initial pull of the flight will overcome their imbalance and their center of gravity will almost always right them during the flight. Now your inexperienced flyer can get the flip in every time and you don't have to worry about him or her coming down for a landing head-first.

The side plates of the Ultra Swivel also allow for add-ons to help performers. There is a shoulder strap attachment that can be added to the top eyelet. This can be used for any performer for whom you might be concerned about sliding out of the harness, or if your RA/RR, as discussed in Chapter 1, mandates it. This can be particularly helpful for new performers who might be afraid of falling out of the harness while inverted, for performers who don't have much hip shape to them, or for anyone who might be going at a high speed while inverted. They can also be a peace-of-mind item for you in case a performer ever passes out while inverted. While you will want to get to them quickly to make sure their blood isn't pooling in their head, at least you will not have to worry about them sliding out of the harness. There is another add-on to help with the effects of suspension trauma: foot loops. These can be added to the hip plates of an Ultra Swivel and hidden in the pants of a costume. The performer can then slide their feet into the loops and stand in them, taking some of their weight off the leg straps. This can be particularly useful for long flights or flights where the performer has a heavy prop strapped to them. The leg straps can make the performer more comfortable and you more relaxed knowing you have done something to mitigate the risk of suspension trauma.

Jerk Vest

We are now moving from common theatrical flying into more stunt equipment; enter the jerk vest. Despite initial reactions it is not named for the people who made it or the people who wear them, but rather for the action you can create with them. These are commonly used in movie stunts to "jerk" a performer in reaction to a kick, punch, explosion, or similar event. The upper part has countless loops sewn into it, each of which is rated for performer flying. Now obviously we can't load all the loops to 5000 pounds at the same time but this feature allows you to lift a performer from one loop and then jerk them sideways from another to pull them away in reaction to some event like an explosion. While this is the main reason for a Jerk Vest it can also be used for more traditional flying. For example, if you want someone to take off for flight like Superman, finding the perfect loop on their back so they naturally hang at the angle desired might be easier on the performer, and more readily repeatable, than putting them in an Ultra Swivel and asking them to control that position with their core. Now you know they will always hang at the desired angle and you don't have to worry about

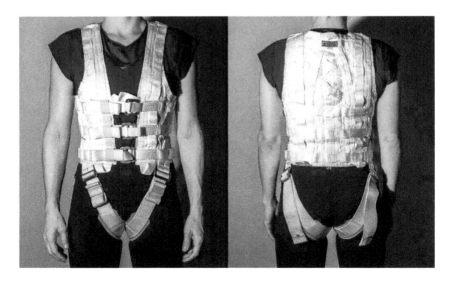

Figure 11.12 Jerk Vest
Photo: Paige Durborow, model: Genevieve Berube

them losing control, ending up inverted for a landing. There are countless conceivable ways to connect to this harness. In that way it's very much a Swiss Army knife; it can get you out of a lot of jams. Obviously, costuming choices can very much affect this harness' viability as an option. A similar design is made as a corset for a lower costuming impact. This comes in particular handy when working with female costumes. The Jerk concept is also made as stand-alone shorts, or as a full Jerk Suit, where the Jerk Vest and Jerk Shorts are combined into a single item.

Fit is critical when using a Jerk anything, especially when stunt work is being considered. Unfortunately, these harnesses have less adjustment to fit various shapes of performers. As a result, these are often made to suit a particular performer although they can be bought off-the-shelf in Small, Medium, Large, and so on.

Martial Arts Harness

Somewhere between the Bungee and the Jerk Vest is the Martial Arts Harness. This is effectively a Bungee Harness which has had load-bearing loops sewn into the waist belt and leg straps. This allows for similar effects as the Jerk Vest in a lower-profile package. This harness is particularly well suited for a common movie stunt where the performer is lifted and then spins rapidly, usually in reaction to a kick of some kind. One winch lifts the performer into the air while another winch, or other suitable machine, pulls on a line that has been wrapped around the performer's waist and connected to one of the extra load-bearing loops.

All the tips, tricks, and rules we've discussed earlier in this chapter in regard to harness fit apply to all the Jerk products. That said, it is not uncommon for stunt performers to wear their harnesses much tighter than those in theatrical productions. For one, stunt performers are often being exposed to much higher forces, and as such don't want their harness to come loose while being jerked about. Secondly, stunt performers are rarely expected to dance, act, or really do anything other than be jerked about while in their harness. As such, there is no need to balance one's ability to move gracefully with the fit of the harness.

Twisty Belt

For the flippiest, twistiest of effects there is only one harness that will do the job: the Twisty Belt (Figure 11.13). This is best known for being connected to P!NK, as this is the harness she used for her famous 3D flight over the audience on her recent tours. It is two large aluminum rings connected by a big bearing. The performer is then attached to the inner ring with an Ultra Swivel harness. The harness has been stripped of all the swiveling bits so that the underlying steel plate at the hip can have one of three sizes of blocks

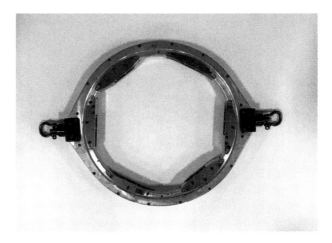

Figure 11.13 Twisty Belt

attached to it to be received by the ring. This allows the performer to rotate around two axes, one horizontal and one vertical. Most commonly known for being attached at each hip, like the Ultra Swivel harness, it can also be used with a single pick point. In this configuration the Twisty Belt can be used with a single line on the side of a building to aerial dance, or connected to a robot arm to simulate space flight. While this harness is best known for being used in 3D flight it can also be used in any other kind of flight. When the performer is not in a 3D rig and is instead being picked straight up from the two hip points, it does require a great deal of control for the performer to spin themselves and not send all that energy up the lines, causing them to cross. In a 3D situation, the geometry of the rig causes the ring to be far more stable in space, allowing for finer control with less experience. The Twisty Belt is rarely used in shows when a story is being told because it is very visually impactful on the scene. Put differently: it's big and it's hard to hide with costuming. As such, it is far better deployed on effects where the point of the rig is the spectacle of it all. In those scenarios the utilitarian design of the Twisty Belt is often accepted as a necessary evil.

The fit of the harness portion of the Twisty Belt should be identical to the Ultra Swivel. Just as with the Ultra Swivel, the correct positioning of the harness up and down on the performer's body will be critical to their ability to control the Twisty Belt.

Control about the horizontal axis also works exactly the same as an Ultra Swivel. The performer should be able to hang at the cardinal directions of the compass rose about the axis without any core input. They should then have to engage their core to get from one cardinal position to another. Given that your performer, unless it's P!NK herself, is probably inexperienced at rotational flight it might behoove you to intentionally imbalance the performer to help them get around and it's better to have the performer be bottom-heavy in these situations. They will need to "wind up" with their core and throw themselves forward to initiate the flip but once they get there their imbalance will throw them the rest of the way around the rotation, ending up straight up, right where you want them. This is of course a situational decision based on your performer's level of experience and the time you have to train them properly.

Control about the vertical axis can be described as being akin to a Hula-Hoop. By undulating one's hips you can control which direction you're facing. Instead of the ring moving around the performer, as would happen with a Hula-Hoop, the performer rotates him or herself. It's really that simple. That said, making it look smooth and being able to stop on a dime take time and practice. Alternatively, one can "wind up" for a spin with one's legs in this situation by swinging one's legs in the direction one wants to spin. Most first-time performers, not having enough time to practice these techniques, end up just grabbing the outside ring and dragging themselves around the circle. The more time one spends in a Twisty Belt the more one really appreciates how easy P!NK makes it look!

Inspections

Most important with regard to inspection is to follow any and all manufacturer's recommendations. That cannot be overstated. Everything that follows here is a general suggestion and should not be interpreted as designed to supersede anything the people who actually make your harness recommend. That said, inspecting a performer flying harness is very similar to inspecting a general fall-protection harness. As such, it can be broken into four main categories.

Webbing

We want to inspect all the webbing that makes up the harness. We are looking for any cuts, tears, fraying, burns from heat or chemicals, or any other surface or internal damage. We want to inspect *all* of each piece of webbing. This means being thorough enough to move webbing trapped by buckles or other hardware through that piece of hardware so that we can inspect that small part of the webbing. This is often the most likely part of the webbing to be damaged! Don't sleep on chemical burns either. As we will discuss later in this chapter, costuming departments across the world are constantly coming up with new and creative ways to destroy harnesses. Never assume that you and your performer are the only two who have come into contact with your equipment. They best way to check webbing for burns of any kind is to roll it between your hands, almost like a Slinky. The webbing will take a turn it is comfortable with from one hand to the next. If it suddenly flattens out and doesn't want to take that same curve, this is an indication that the webbing has been burned. You should also be looking for UV or bleach damage. In both cases a discoloration or lightening of the color of the webbing is the best indication.

Stitching

Now that we've made sure the webbing is in good condition, we want to make sure all the webbing terminations are holding up. First, it's important to be able to tell which stitching is structural and which is not. Structural stitching is integral to the harness' function, while non-structural stitching is simply attaching an extra feature – one not critical to the harness keeping a person in the air – to the harness. Examples of non-structural stitching would be that which holds any padding on the harness, or that which holds any labels on the harness. While these features are important, and this stitching should be inspected for wear, this stitching failing will not cause the harness to drop a person from the sky and as such is not reason alone to fail a harness. Damage to structural stitching, on the other hand, is very much a reason to fail a harness. Structural stitching can most rapidly be found by noticing that it is a contrasting color to the harness. This is to call your attention to it and make it easier to inspect. Structural stitching is also a much heavier thread and almost always in a box-style pattern (Figure 11.14).

Figure 11.14 Stitching Comparison
Photo: Paige Durborow

Now that we've established what we're looking at and why, let's discuss what we're looking for. We want to see that all the stitching the harness began life with is still intact. This means no cuts, abrasions, burns, or fraying. The cord used for these stitches is very susceptible to heat damage, so we want to be extra vigilant in looking for those effects. Heat guns to deal with fuzzies on the harness webbing, or half-baked dye jobs by the costume department, are among common causes of stitching damage from heat. We want to check both visible sides of all the stitch patterns, in all locations. If done properly, you will come across one or two little fuzzballs per pattern. Many people assume these are cut strands, but this is not necessarily so. This is often, although not always, simply the beginning or the end of the thread used to sew this location (Figure 11.15).

The best trick to ensuring that this is what you've found is to grab the fuzzball and pull it away from the stitching. If nothing happens, you've just found the end of the thread, and that's okay. If, however, the strand begins to run or pull out of the pattern you've found a cut strand and the harness should be failed and retired.

Hardware

Next we want to make sure all the metal bits of the harness are still playing nicely with their softer friends. The first thing we should be looking for is

Figure 11.15 Stitching End
Photo: Paige Durborow

any sharp edges the hardware may have developed since the last inspection, particularly on the parts that interact with webbing. It is possible, over time, for some pieces of hardware to develop edges as sharp as knife blades! After this we should be looking for any rusting, pitting, or discoloration. Any of these can be a sign of reduced strength or an exposure to elements we'd rather not see our performer flying harnesses in. We should also be checking on the hardware's general shape as it compares to the day it was new. We want to make sure nothing looks as though it has been overloaded. Overloading hardware usually causes it to elongate in shape and possibly even show cracks. Any of these kinds of findings are, of course, grounds to fail the harness and retire it.

Function and Condition

Lastly, we want to be evaluating the harness' condition and function. It's great that all these individual parts still *look* new, but do they also function as new? This is particularly important for the hardware. Do the buckles hold tension? Do the clips snap into their locking position? This is also an opportunity to take a moment and evaluate if this harness is the right one for the job it's being asked to do. Shows can evolve over time and while perhaps this was the right harness on Day 1 of rehearsals, the show may have changed and now there is a better solution. A great example of this might be how the rig connects to the harness. Perhaps there was a reason to use a particular kind of carabiner in the beginning, but now a new carabiner that has just come out would solve some other problem you're having periodically. Or even more likely, you've discovered the magic of Climbing Sutra's quick-release (QR) clips, seen in all the pictures of their harness contained herein, and want to move to those. The point is, while you're hyper-focusing on the small details of the harness also take this time to think about how the whole harness system is being used, and don't be afraid to try and make it better!

The kind of inspection prescribed here should be done weekly for any normal show. If you work on a particularly high-volume show, like a short theme park show that runs over 15 times a day, then perhaps more frequent inspections would be a good idea. The RA/RR paperwork you made during the design phase should help with those decisions. These inspections should be documented on a standard form you create and saved, at least digitally, somewhere safe. While the act of performing the inspection is the most important part, if you were ever to end up in court over an accident you would really want to be able to prove you were as diligent with your inspection as you took the time to be.

These weekly formal inspections do not absolve the end user of their responsibility to do a pre-use check. As the name might suggest, yes, that means before *every* use. If the performer takes their harness off to go for their dinner break, they should perform a brief pre-use inspection before putting it back on for the evening session, for example. By putting the harness on, the performer is agreeing that they too have inspected the harness and found it to be acceptable for use. This is a cultural issue that has to be stressed at every level of the organization, but most importantly the last rigger a performer checks in with before flying should ask the performer if they inspected their harness.

Costuming Challenges

As alluded to earlier in this chapter costumers across the world continue to invent new ways to destroy performer flying harnesses. This usually comes out of the process of wanting to build the harness into a costume or to otherwise camouflage it. No matter how many times the following "cant's" are enumerated, they almost always seem to be forgotten until the first batch of harnesses have been destroyed.

- You cannot paint, dye, or otherwise alter the color of the webbing.
- The harness can, however, be made in a variety of colors!
- You cannot sew fabric to the webbing of the harness.
- You cannot paint, powder-coat, or otherwise alter the surface of the bearing parts of the hardware.
  ○ This means any hardware that contacts the webbing.
  ○ This also means you cannot alter the parts of the connecting hardware from the harness to the rig.
    – This usually gets asked of the QR hardware (Figure 11.16).
    – You can, however, paint, nail-polish, buff, shine, or do anything else to, the parts of the QR hardware that do not interact with each other.

Shortly after you have told the costuming department this they will sew directly to the harness, spray-paint the webbing, or have the whole connecting hardware nail-polished green. You will then have the unpleasant conversation of explaining to them that they just bought a very expensive harness. While this is an unfortunate and all-too-frequent event it can be avoided sometimes by suggesting some common ideas to achieve what they want to do without destroying the harness. The absolute best way to make a harness match the costume without destroying it is to simply make a sock, or socks, that Velcro on to cover the harness. This will allow it to completely match the costume without endangering the structural integrity of the webbing *and* it will allow you to remove the socks for washing of the socks and inspection of the harness. It's just the best! Also, as shown in Figure 11.16, you *can* alter the color of the parts of the QR hardware that can still be seen after being connected, which should be the only parts the costumers need to concern themselves with in the first place.

Figure 11.16 Annotated QR Hardware
Photo: Paige Durborow

Also previously alluded to, a key message of this chapter is to not underestimate how much the weight of a costume or prop can throw off a performer's center of gravity. Some examples include large hats or headpieces, giant angel wings, masks, heavy or large skirts, fins for mermaids, or prop instruments. If some of those seem so specific that they must have come from a particular experience, you're right! If anything like this is to be in your flying life make sure you know about it as early as possible and plan for it while fitting your performers into harnesses. Do not forget to inspect the quality of the build of this thing the costuming or prop department just handed you. Make sure it is of sufficient build quality to be hoisted above the stage or the audience as the case may be. Take time to decide if it needs a backup loop connected to the performer, their harness, or directly to the rig. Once you get over that hump you will want to make sure you are rehearsing and training with the actual prop or costuming piece or at the very least a stand-in piece that has the same weight distribution as the actual piece. It can be a common mistake to swap for the "real" one in the middle of a day of rehearsals, seemingly innocuously, only to have the performer end up in a dangerous position (think: head down coming in for landing) because the real piece is weighted so very differently from the rehearsal one. If the prop or costume piece is making a performer who needs to do flips particularly bottom-heavy the desire can exist, particularly on the part of the performer, to want to lower their whole harness. As long as you are respecting the correct positioning laid out earlier in this chapter that can be an acceptable fix, but remember two main points here:

1. The hip points are independently adjustable from the harness location.
2. Lowering the harness beyond the correct guidelines is *never* the correct solution. You are increasing the risk of the performer falling out of the harness in an inverted state, and you are increasing their risk of repetitive stress injuries to their lower back.

The moral of the story is not to let any variable, and certainly not this one, slide by as a "no big deal" situation. Any change to what you have been doing regularly warrants a special rehearsal to test the effects this might have on what has become normal.

Ride-on Props

Another common way to get a performer in the air is riding on a prop. This can be Glinda showing up for the first time in *Wicked*, or a pop star that wants to get out over the audience without also learning how to be an acrobat. In either case we need to secure the performer to the rig in some way. Almost invariably someone will ask if the performer can be legally safe with just a handrail around him or her. The short answer is almost always no. While the handrail is likely sufficient when everything goes right, imagine what might happen if one of the two lines supporting the prop broke, or became slack for some other reason, and the prop was suddenly hanging at a 45 degree angle. A handrail alone doesn't seem so sufficient in that case, does it? But surely we don't have to fit the performer into one of the harnesses we spoke about previously, right? You are in fact correct. If you can limit the free-fall distance, a waist belt is an acceptable means of safety.

In Figure 11.17 we see the Climbing Sutra Quad Release Belt. It has a doubled-up version of the QR connector as the belt closure, and can be made with many rated loops for connecting the belt to the rig. The belt should be tightened around the performer to the standard we previously discussed for fall-protection harnesses: tight enough that you can still fit a flat hand between the belt and the body, as if you were putting your hand in your jeans' pocket, but not so loose so that you could fit a fist. Remember that this belt needs to catch the performer and keep them in the air if something goes very wrong. You don't want the belt to be able to slide past the performer's shoulders or hips in the course of a violent event like the abrupt stop at the end of a fall. The leash that connects the performer to the rig should be as tight as is reasonably possible, and might even want to include a small, rated, shock pack to dampen the forces on the performer's body. All the same inspection criteria and costuming guidelines we've discussed previously in this chapter also apply to belts. The Velcro-on sock

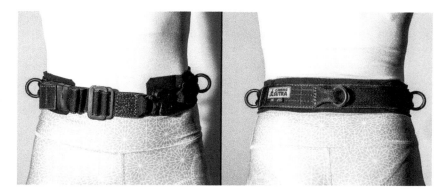

Figure 11.17 Waist Belt
Photo: Paige Durborow, model: Genevieve Berube

is the go-to move for camouflaging a waist belt. The costume department will resist this idea initially, ruining at least one belt by bedazzling directly to the belt's webbing, but then they'll catch on to the brilliance of your suggestion.

So, where do we attach the leash to the prop? ANSI E1.43–2016, better known as the ESTA Performer Flying Standard, says that the performer must be tethered directly to the load path. This has been read to mean a couple of different things. At its most basic reading this would mean you need to attach the performer to the rig independent of the prop. So, at one of the connection points from your system to the prop you would want to also attach a leash to the performer. This makes logical sense in that if the prop totally fails and falls from the sky, at least the flying performer is still in the air. However, this can prove to be challenging to execute if the performer needs to be able to move about on the prop or if they intend to turn around many times. Also, the appearance of this longer leash can be visually unappealing, to say nothing of the increased fall distance the length of the leash might cause. Remember, there's a reason waist belts have been banned for industrial fall protection since 1992. Falling a great distance into them is not at all comfortable or safe, to say nothing of what happens to you while you hang in one waiting to be rescued. This is why we want to have the shortest-length leash that is reasonably possible. Enter the other reading of the ESTA mandate: that the point on the prop you want to attach the performer to should be engineered as part of the load path of the prop. Now, if you have your pop star on your prop, you can have a pole come right up behind them for them to lean on and connect them directly to it with nothing but a piece of connecting hardware between the prop and the belt. That's a short leash! Unfortunately, if the prop falls out of the sky the performer will ride it all the way down, but thanks to the fact that you've gotten it engineered and you're doing regular, thorough, inspections that will never happen. To that point: all performer flying props must be engineered. You may find that someone else will build the prop that the performer will ride on your rig. The fact that you must have it engineered is a policy to make clear early and often, and is one hill worth dying on. Small prop companies who are sometimes hired to make these elements can be very irked by this demand but an argument about it is a non-starter and should be treated as such. You have gone through all the trouble of engineering every inch of your system. To then put the performer on a non-engineered platform made by It'll Hold Industries.com is simply irresponsible.

QR Clip Tips

Training performers to operate QR clips can be a tricky thing. It is always a good idea to have a few extra stand-alone male and female clips that you can give the performers to practice with. If you are flying few enough people, you can even give the clips to them as key chains. The key to disconnecting them is simply to pinch the ears on the female towards the male. When this is done fully, the male clip will simply fall out of the female receiver. When you first teach the performers this they will instantly get it. And then, little by little, it will fade away. This is because they will begin to pinch less than all the way and instead try to pull the male out of the female. Simply remind them that all they have to do is pinch and the rest will happen for them. Eventually they will realize you're right. The Quad Release clip can be even more daunting as it has four ears that all need to be pinched. The reason for the added ears is that this connection provides sufficient redundancy to be used as a single connection for life safety. (This is why it is the connecting latch of the waist belt, for example.) Ergonomically it's very well designed and happens quite easily. That said, performers can have a hard time in the beginning with them, particularly those with small fingers. Again though, reminding them simply to pinch, and having a few extras for them to have in their dressing room, will eventually get you there.

Both styles of QR clips, those that must be used in pairs and those that can be stand-alone, meet the ESTA standard of auto-locking, auto-closing connections which require two independent actions to open. While very popular 20 years ago, screw-gate carabiners, snap shackles, and other similar pieces of hardware are no longer considered safe enough for performer flying. There are quite simply too many ways for them to end up open without someone intentionally causing them to open. As such they are out!

Circus Elements

Not quite harnesses, but also elements that can connect people to rigs are the various common, and not so common, circus apparatuses. The issue with trying to write about them in general is that very little is standard about them. Circus elements are usually made on a per-act basis or, even worse from a tractability standpoint, handed down from generation to generation. Being aware of their point of origin can be near impossible, to say nothing of their engineering or modification history. That said, with the rise of aerial yoga studios and Instagram acrobats there are companies that have started to have standard offerings for some of these. The following list is by no means exhaustive but these are the more common elements you are likely to run into. The key thing is to remember to treat these apparatuses like any other ride-on prop. Know where they came from, make sure that source is reputable, and make sure you've seen an engineer stamp for what your rig can do to the apparatus. Always remember: the Cat-0 E-stop of your winch will likely put far more force through the element than the day-to-day at the aerial yoga studio from which it came.

Straps

Straps are one of the most common circus elements in use today. There is no faster way to lock an acrobat to a winch and swing them around for the crowd's amusement. Straps are composed of two long pieces of fabric, usually with hand loops at one end and an eye at the other (Figure 11.18). These two straps are then connected to a delta plate, which is then connected to the winch, usually with a swivel between the delta and the winch. This allows the performer to spin wildly as they are raised and lowered. The locking mechanism at the performer falls into one of two main categories. Either they

Figure 11.18 Straps
Photo: Genevieve Berube

will have a locking loop that the acrobat will use to synch the hand loop onto their wrist and then grab over the top of, or the hand loop will feed back over the main length of the strap, creating an auto-synching loop. Either one is perfectly acceptable for an experienced acrobat to fly with. It comes down to the acrobat's preference.

A common mistake when programming a strap act is having rehearsal straps that are a different length than the "real" straps, or not having the hardware stack-up between the straps and the plate, or the plate and the winch, decided on as final. Either situation has the same result: screwing up your programming. It's a problem that can be overcome; you can simply re-zero the winch to deal with the incorrect values in your programming and be ready to fly again after sandbag testing. But when you're dealing with pendulum flights, and you almost always will be with straps, the change in length of the apparatus will affect the flights. They will need to be re-cued to make them as beautiful as you had them dialed in before the swap. Straps should be washed periodically in a No Tears kind of soap or something equally gentle, in room-temperature water. (Always consult the manufacturer before deciding how to wash the straps.) They should be air-dried, *never* machine-dried. Inspecting straps is exactly the same as inspecting a harness. We are checking all the same elements in the same way.

Cerceau

Next on the list of popular circus elements is the cerceau, pronounced *sir-so*. It is also commonly referred to as a lyra or aerial hoop. As that last name suggests, this is a hoop that is usually 33 or 36 inches in diameter and has a welded-on eye on the outside of the ring (Figure 11.19). Performers who are using this as a ride-on prop will connect the hoop directly to the cable of a winch with a swivel and some connecting hardware. A common acrobatic attachment will have a 3 or 6 foot rope connected to the welded eye; the winch will then connect to the other end of the rope. The rope will be a three-strand cotton wrapped around a steel cable, which is the actual load path. This has all been assuming a single-point attachment to the cerceau. There are also formats in which a roundsling (or two) is/are choked around the hoop itself. This is a stronger connection method, as you are not relying solely on a weld in tension to hold the prop in the air. As with any apparatus, make sure you get engineering approval of the prop's construction method before hanging a person from it!

A proper acrobatic routine will use the cerceau very similarly to straps. It can used to fly pendulum flights while making various shapes and spins. Others will use it as an interesting-looking seat to ride up and down on while occasionally making an interesting shape while on it. In either case they are usually wrapped hockey-stick style with athletic tape, or if your performer is very fancy, Guidoline. This is a French cycling tape used for the handlebars on very expensive racing bikes. It is also, as you might expect, very expensive.

Figure 11.19   Cerceau
Photo: Genevieve Berube

At the even higher end you can find them wrapped in PPT Tape, which is a 3M product for protecting the leading edge of airplane wings. This is also, as you might imagine, very expensive. Inspecting the welded-on load-bearing eye often is critical to making sure the cerceau remains safe. This can sometimes be costly, both monetarily and in time, when the cerceau is wrapped in tape. Nonetheless, it is crucial that it be done thoroughly and at regular intervals. As mentioned above, relying on a weld in tension is always a dangerous place to be.

Trapeze

It is rare to see a trapeze, particularly swinging trapeze, on the night club circuit, so if you see one you must be doing some proper circus. At its most basic level a trapeze is a bar with two ropes attached to it. What most people don't notice is that a swinging trapeze bar usually has two weights attached to the bar on the outside of where the ropes pick up said bar (Figure 11.20). The size of these weights is at that acrobat's discretion. For a static trapeze number this is to help dampen any swing the routine might begin to cause. For a swinging trapeze number these weights are to help keep the momentum of the swing going once it is in motion. All that being said, some trapeze bars have no weights at all on them. It really comes down to what the acrobat

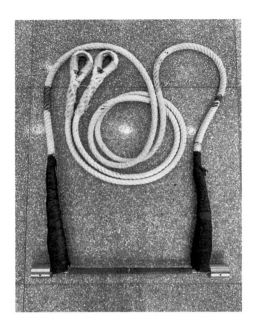

Figure 11.20 Trapeze
Photo: Genevieve Berube

using the bar needs/wants to make the act happen reliably. The connection to a trapeze is similar to the cerceau. There will usually be a thick cotton rope on either end of the bar. It is thick for two reasons: (1) it is a nice diameter for the acrobat to grab and hold on to, and (2) it is thick enough to hide the wire rope, or synthetic rope, inside it doing the actual lifting. The bar has a welded-on eye on either end to catch this cable. The trapeze bar will be taped similarly to the cerceau. For swinging trapeze, the location where rope meets the bar will be wrapped and hand-stitched with thin leather pads. This is to add additional friction for the tricks performed on it. The inside of these leather pads is a fun place to leave your future self, or people who have your job in the future, notes about how much fun you are having! All this padding and taping can make inspecting the welded eyes quite a chore, but it still must be done thoroughly, and at regular intervals.

Tissue

Along with straps, tissue is the most common apparatus you will run across. Also known as silks, these are often what you see in an aerial yoga studio. As a result, many feel qualified to jump on a performer flying rig and swing around with their trusty tissue. Be wary of these people. This is not to say none of them are qualified, but there is a big difference between being 3 feet

Figure 11.21   Tissue 8
Photo: Genevieve Berube

off the ground, above a mat, in a well-lit, temperature-controlled studio, and being 60 feet in the air, waiting for a cue, in the dark, above hot lighting units, in a theatre. Proper tissues are produced to a Military Specification. They are made from polyester Lycra or more commonly from nylon tricot. In either case they have some good elasticity to them. They are commonly woven through a Rescue 8 belay device in a particular knot so the performer has two lengths of tissue hanging down.

There are many YouTube videos from reputable sources on how to achieve this knot. The Rescue 8 is then connected to a rig, often with a swivel and a carabiner as the connecting hardware. When inspecting tissue we need to really take our time and look at every inch of the fabric. If there is even the smallest hole in the fabric the tissue must be retired. Nylon tricot is very strong fabric when solid, but the tiniest hole can cause a run in the fabric that could take your performer all the way to the ground! This is seriously not the time to decide it can make it one more show like that. Just as we discussed earlier regarding webbing on harnesses interacting with hardware, make sure you loosen the knot at the Rescue 8 and inspect the fabric that has been locked to the 8, and the condition of the 8 itself. These apparatuses will often show up with aluminum Rescue 8s. While there is technically nothing wrong with this, steel Rescue 8s are preferred. In a yoga studio setting, where the tissues will be rigged once, aluminum is likely okay. But in entertainment, where we are going to hook it up over and over again, throw it in a box in between uses, and bounce it around in a truck, steel *feels* better. Emphasis on "feels" in that last sentence. There isn't necessarily anything flagrantly wrong with aluminum in this case, but if it's steel it's one less thing you might consider fragile.

Conclusion

How a performer is attached to the rig is clearly no small decision. In the case of harnesses, making sure you have selected the right tool for the job is just as important as making sure you know how to fit it on a performer. Knowing that props and costuming can grossly affect the performer's control, thinking through these obstacles early and often is paramount. For circus-style apparatuses and ride-on props it is most important to stress that you must have engineering paperwork for the specific piece you are using. In all cases making sure your performer is comfortable but safe is crucially important. Educating them not only on the "whats" of their connection to the system but also the "whys" will go a long way towards being a team with your performers.

Takeaways: Beginners

- There are many different kinds of harnesses. Make sure you have the right one for your specific use case!
- Just because a performer shows up with their own circus apparatus does not mean it is strong enough to survive the forces your rig can produce.
- Regular inspections by the technical team and pre-use inspections by the performer are equally important to ensure everyone goes home at the end of the show.

Takeaways: Professionals

- Precise harness fitting is a skill to be practiced. Don't be afraid to work by yourself in a static rig to better understand your performers' notes on this topic.
- Regardless of who provides the ride-on prop or the circus apparatus, proper engineering documentation must exist before it is used on your rig.
- Don't forget to consider the effects of costuming and props on your performers' ability to control their position in flight. Think through these challenges early and often.

12   Rescue

The fourth of the Cardinal Rules of Performer Flying, as discussed in the Introduction, is:

> If you don't know how to get down, don't go up.

It seems obvious, but it is often overlooked. In the excitement of realizing a performer flying effect, we often forget to make sure we have a plan, and the materials to execute that plan, to get someone down in the event of an emergency. Quite simply, if you are going to put someone up in the air you must know you know how to get them down regardless of anything that could happen next. When *standing* on the stage there is nothing stopping a performer from getting themselves out of the building in the event of an emergency. Once the performer is suspended in the air, this is no longer the case. Having a plan to get our performers back to ground safely regardless of the circumstance is a key element towards building trust with your performers. It is crucial that we take this responsibility seriously and have thought through the issues this presents before it happens. Enter rescue planning.

How do we end up needing a rescue in the first place? Most people assume an injury to the performer in the normal course of events constitutes a rescue. While that scenario can and should result in different procedures beyond just continuing the show, it does not necessarily constitute a rescue. A rescue is needed when the mechanism flying the person becomes inoperable, leaving the performer stranded in the air. In a manually operated system this could be caused by the reeving of the system becoming tangled, or the operator having a medical emergency. In an automated system this can also be caused by the system becoming tangled or by the loss of power or a loss of control of the electrical system.

OHSA (the Occupational Safety and Health Administration), says of rescuing personnel from heights that the rescue must be "prompt", and that's pretty much it. It's understandably vague; OSHA's statements need to cover *all* industries. If they were to put a time limit on executing a rescue it could instantly put an entire industry, like the radio tower inspection/repair industry, into a state of non-compliance. We are therefore left to interpret what "prompt" means in our situation. "The Golden Hour" is a concept among first responders which states that a traumatically injured person's odds of survival dramatically increase if they get to professional medical care within one hour of their injury. Clearly then we should be planning on completing our rescue within an hour. Given that in a theatre, or an arena, or a stadium, we control a great deal of the variables that would otherwise slow down a rescue (such as weather, new surroundings, or appropriately trained personnel) we should be able to clock in well under this goal. Even on a touring production we can eliminate a huge number of variables that would otherwise cause a rescue to take longer than it needs to. A well-thought-out, written, rehearsed, and executed rescue plan in almost any entertainment setting should have the stranded performer on the ground and in the hands of medical care well within the golden hour. Given that the effects of suspension trauma (discussed in more detail later in this chapter) can start to become serious in as little as 20 minutes, we should be aiming to keep our rescue times below that whenever practically possible.

The Hierarchy of Rescue

A critical flaw in rescue planning among riggers is the desire to have Plan A be the most aggressive rescue of all: rappel in wearing the full Petzl catalog on your harness, SWAT team-esque, pick-off rescue. This plan, however, should always be the last resort. While very cool looking, and hero-worship-worthy, there are so many easier ways that do not put any additional member, or members, of your team in the air or at risk. When planning a rescue system from scratch we should always make sure we thought through the Hierarchy of Rescue:

1.   Recover the System
2.   Ground Rescue
3.   Self-Rescue
4.   Brake-Release Rescue
5.   Pick-Off Rescue

No one of these options can be the only option on paper or rehearsed; rather, they are escalating steps to be taken in the course of any emergency.

1. Recover the System

While it is good to be prepared to execute a full-blown rescue, it is equally important to give the operator a few moments to try and get the system back up and running in full, if not just enough to get the performer to the ground. For this to be possible it's important to practice not only the actions of a rescue, but also the communication surrounding the rescue. If there is not a clear point person calling the shots your headset traffic will rapidly degrade to a whomever-can-talk-loudest format, which is not conducive to good decision-making. Step 1 of a good rescue plan is to identify who will be in charge of the rescue. This does not have to be the calling Stage Manager (SM), and in fact is often better that it not be. This way the SM can continue to try to keep the show moving, or be coordinating the show stopping, while others focus solely on the stranded performer.

The Rescue Leader (or the Incident Leader as stated in ANSI E.143–2016) should spend their free moments during the show contemplating what they would say, to whom, and in what order to manage a highly stressful moment like a live-fire rescue. The person leading the rescue should think of this responsibility like Derice, the captain in *Cool Runnings*: always studying the turns even when the others are having fun. 1990s movie references aside, thinking through these scenarios often does lead to cleaner, more efficient rescues. If the person in charge has thought through the situation many times before, they will be more likely to be able to give the operator a few extra moments to assess the situation properly. Never forget that the stranded performer also needs to be communicated with. They are likely to be embarrassed, if not shocked, by what has just happened. In the age of the smartphone, the audience will likely by now be videoing the scene, further adding to the performer's emotional state. It is important for the person in charge of the rescue to get in eyesight of the performer and explain to them, succinctly, what happened and what will be happening next. It is also critical that the performer be told before they start moving again, be that from a recovered system, a brake release, or a full-blown pick-off rescue.

Giving the operator 60 to 90 seconds to determine the cause of the stop can often lead to a solution to that problem. The operator's solution may only take an additional 60 to 90 seconds to execute. That would mean the whole event could be moved on from in as little as three minutes! This requires restraint on the part of the person calling the ball, and confidence in your operator. This does not mean we have to sit idly by and wait for 60 to 90 seconds. Instead we can be preparing for the following steps in the Hierarchy while the operator tries to diagnose the problem.

It is important to involve your automation team in your rescue planning, as they will be the first line of defense. It is important to think through your whole system to give them the best chance to recover the system, or at least get the performer on the ground. For example, in a single-axis rig if the one flying machine is dead there is very little the operator will be able to do to help. But in a two-axes, electrically compensated rig, the lifting axis being dead is not the only way to get the performer to the ground. If you plan far enough ahead, and your operator knows how to run the traverse axis independent of the lift axis, then you can use the traverse axis to get the performer down! Similarly, in a 3D rig, depending on where in the rig you are and which axis went down, you can likely use the other live axes to get the performer down. The lesson here is simple: take the time to diagnose not only what is dead, but also what is still functioning. These extra few seconds may save you from having to make your rescue any more dramatic than using your automation system to get your performer to safety.

2. Ground Rescue

Sadly, giving the operator their moment doesn't always result in a magically fixed system. In the event of a power outage the "unrecoverable" answer can come quickly. At other times the problem can be diagnosed quickly, but may be not corrected quickly enough to be *the* solution in the moment. In that case we need to escalate to the next level. This solution does not work for all rigs but is often forgotten about on rigs where it *could* work. Before you send a rigger to the roof to deploy a rescue system ask yourself, "Can we just get a ladder out here?" All kidding aside, if the flight is close enough to the ground, this is your best, quickest, safest, most-repeatable rescue. This is also the go-to rescue for manual systems used in smaller and one-off performances. Simply dispatch your team to the backstage to get *the* ladder for the rescue. There is a reason the word "the" is italicized in that last sentence. If this is to be one of your rescue plans it is crucial that there be a dedicated ladder for this purpose, that it have a clear path to the stage during any performer flying rehearsal or performance, and that it be checked for being where it is supposed to be prior to beginning either. Given that it will be *the* rescue ladder you can even paint it black, label it specifically, or decorate it to match the scene's surroundings, abiding by the ladder manufacturer's recommendations of course. Similarly, depending on your situation could a Genie lift or a scissor lift be used in place of a ladder? Of course! While having a dedicated machine for this purpose is recommended it is not always financially realistic, and that's okay. The lift should be always be plugged in prior to any rehearsal or performance, and during the flying routine must have a clear path to the stage. The latter point there can be difficult thing to get even in the beginning of a production, and even harder to maintain as people become comfortable with the reliability of the equipment. That said, the point of the ground-based rescue is to be quick and easy. The clear path must be maintained during the routine. If the lift is trapped behind heavy set pieces and countless props you will have negated the reason you have the lift backstage in the first place. If you are intending on sending a technician up in the lift, or on the ladder for that matter, it is important to make sure the lift or ladder is rated for both your technician and the performer(s) you are going to add to it. Just because it is a rescue situation does not mean we can willfully ignore the manufacturer's limitations. Never forget: if the plan involves a machine, like a lift, we also need a backup plan for the day the lift wasn't plugged in or decides not to work.

The ground rescue is the prime rescue answer for manual systems. While unlikely, there are scenarios where the operators could end up needing to hold the performer's weight entirely on their own. Obviously, this is not a situation we want any operator to be in for a long time. Recognizing this risk, we should always have a staff member identified as the person to jump on the operating line if the main operator suddenly ends up in this scenario. We also want to make sure neither of these people are assigned to bring the rescue ladder out on stage! We want those people to be able to react quickly and in parallel with our team keeping the performer in the air.

3. Self-Rescue

Perhaps there is a large prop or set piece directly under the performer. Perhaps they are just too high for a ladder or a lift. Or perhaps they are swinging to and fro wildly. Any of these issues, and many others, would make a ground-based rescue implausible. Enter the self-rescue. This is a plan that is often better deployed for acrobatic rigging than for performer flying, the definitions for which can be found back in the Preface. If the performer is using an acrobatic element in which they are hanging from their arms, then having a self-rescue plan is an absolute must. In fact, it might need to be deployed even while you are giving the operator his or her time to recover the system. For elements such as straps, a common acrobatic device, the performer is hanging by their arms as their main support. As such, they cannot hang there indefinitely while you mobilize a rescue. Acts such as this also usually involve large pendulum flights, which means the performer will be swinging when the errant stop occurs. The best way to alleviate both problems is to give the experienced acrobat something to take the load off their arms and climb down. The most common thing to use here is another circus element, a tissue or silk. These are stretchy fabric panels that most circus performers, and an ever-increasing number of yoga enthusiasts, are familiar with. If you have one of these pre-rigged above each performer and stowed in a bag, then in this moment you can simply deploy the fabric down to the ground and let the performer grab it with their legs. With the help of a friend on the ground their swing can then be killed. They can then take their weight off their arms, release themselves from their straps, and climb down the tissue. This is a quick and relatively easy rescue that doesn't put anyone else at risk of a fall.

When it comes to performer flying and self-rescue, it really is a situational decision. If your performer has an acrobatic background perhaps this would be a good choice. But if your performer is new to the whole concept of flying this might be adding more risk than it's worth. This is because you will be asking the performer to unclip him or herself from the offending machine. That means you will be trusting them to transfer their weight to the new system, free a hand to unclip themselves, and then climb down. Why though would we consider this okay for an acrobat and not a flyer? As discussed in the Preface, in acrobatic rigging we take more risks because we know the performer is trained and experienced to be participating in such an act. In performer flying all too often we are flying people who have never left the ground before. This doesn't mean we have to lower them a tissue; we could lower a ladder (like a truss ladder) from above and let the performer climb onto that. The warning still stands though: make sure your performers are experienced and ready to perform such a self-rescue before committing to it as a main plan.

One other option for self-rescue for a flyer would to pick them off their winch without sending someone over the edge to help them. If you've purchased harnesses with rescue loops built in, and have practiced this plan with your performers, this can be a great rescue method. In this scenario your riggers in the grid or roof would rig a rescue-rated lifting/lowering device and lower the hook down to your performer. The performer would then clip him or herself in as you practiced. Your riggers would then raise them up with the device to get their weight off the offending machine. The performer would then unclip themselves from the winch and your riggers would lower them to the stage. This plan clearly requires a lot of practice and a lot of trust between you and your performer that they will clip themselves correctly. It also requires a lot of clear communication between you, your team, and the performer. All that said, when executed properly this will get your performer down without putting anyone else at risk of a fall.

4. Brake-Release Rescue

As discussed in Chapter 6, all performer flying winches are equipped with two independent brakes, each of which can be manually bypassed. The reason for the manual bypass feature is for this exact scenario. During this procedure we will intentionally defeat both brakes, resulting in us slowly lowering the performer to the stage. It is absolutely crucial that this skill be practiced regularly with an inanimate object like a sandbag. The exact procedure will vary from specific winch to winch, but to speak broadly about the steps, it goes like this:

1.   Completely bypass the primary, or motor, brake.

We start with the primary, or motor, brake as it is usually the more coawrse of the two brakes. Put differently, it has the least adjustment of the two between fully closed and fully open. As a result, we completely bypass this one first so that we are now only dealing with the holding power of one of the fully redundant brakes. The process for bypassing the primary brake will vary but generally speaking it falls into one of two methods. Either there will be a lever to pull or the brake will require electrical energy to open. In the case of the lever you will want a synch strap of some kind that you can wrap around, or through an eye on, the handle and around another part of the winch. This will allow you to move the lever to the open position and hold it there, so you can focus completely on operating the secondary brake safely. (Some organizations may instead insist on two people at the winch to perform a brake release. In such cases the synch strap is not needed, as the second person would operate the primary brake.) In the case of a brake that requires electricity, you will need a battery source of power and a means to get it into the brake. These are often created by modifying flashlights from cordless tool sets, adding a cable coming off the device with the appropriate plug to hit the winch. Building it into a flashlight is very handy given that one of your likely causes for needing to perform this rescue is a power outage in the building. This will allow you to find the correct location on the winch to plug your flashlight/power source into the winch and turn that circuit on. This will, when wired correctly, push 24 volts (usually) directly to the brake, thereby opening it completely. This will then, just as with the synch strap, allow you to focus completely on the correct operation of the secondary brake.

2. Slowly and carefully open the secondary, or output, brake until the weight of the performer overcomes the remaining friction and the winch slowly starts to spin.

It is important for the technician performing the rescue to understand that in this moment they are now defeating the only remaining system keeping the performer safely arrested in the air. As such, it is important not to attack the bypassing of this brake harshly or quickly. We want to very slowly apply more and more pressure to the lever on the secondary, or output, brake until the weight on the end of the line begins to pull the drum through the brake. The technician should then continue to apply the same amount of pressure to the lever until the performer reaches the ground in a controlled manner. Given the realities of how this rescue is performed, it is a very good idea to have a crash mat of some kind that gets deployed below the performer before beginning this step. The person performing the brake release will rarely have line of sight on the performer as they lower them. As such, this is another point in the rescue when communication is absolutely critical, and another example of why the person in charge of the rescue should have thought through what they will say, how, and when, before this moment comes to pass in a show scenario. Never forget: the performer must be informed before they start to move as a result of this maneuver being executed.

In Figure 12.1 we have an example of a written rescue plan. Notice how it lays out roles, responsibilities, definitions, and procedures. Said procedures start before the rescue begins and end after it is finished. These are hallmarks of a well-written rescue plan. Remember: this document isn't only for you and your team; it is also for all future teams who come after you. While we have a proud tradition of oral training in the entertainment industry, the less we leave to a game of telephone through the years, the less there is to forget or mis-hand-down.

If a brake-release rescue is to be the only method for an acrobatic performance (meaning that there is no self-rescue plan) then technicians must

Scope

- The purpose of this document will be to lay out stock procedures for a brake release rescue for the T-Winch. This procedure assumes the reason for the rescue is a mechanical, electrical, or similar failure of the winch and that the performer is not injured.

Definitions

- **Primary Break** – Break built in to the drive motor of the T-Winch.
- **Secondary Break** – Break attached to the drive axel of the drum.
- **Rescue Kit** – Pelican 1610 case outfitted by Tait Towers with all necessary gear for aerial rescues. Designed to
- live on the truss with the Performer Flying Winch(es).
- **Sinch Strap** – Black 1" webbing with locking buckle. Used to bypass one brake by holding the handle in tension
- for the Rescuer.
- **Rescuer 1** – Performs the brake release.
- **Rescuer 2** – Makes contact with the Performer, Clears landing area.

Procedure

1) The first person to notice a winch is not behaving normally calls on radio and/or headset "We have a problem with Winch XXX".
2) Rescuer 1, using appropriate fall protection, safely accesses the location of the disabled T-Winch.
3) Rescuer 1 isolates the power to the T-Winch via the On/Off Switch on the side of the Winch.
4) Rescuer 1 retrieves one "Sinch Strap" from the Rescue Kit located on the Truss.
5) Rescuer 2 makes contact with the Artist to inform them they will be coming down shortly. Constant contact should be maintained to help avoid the Performer going into shock.
   ○ Given the nature of this type of rescue we are not anticipating any injuries to the Artist on the disabled Winch. As a result, no extra steps are taken to evaluate them for injury prior to the rescue. The individual circumstances of the moment will dictate whether such steps are necessary. This will be at the discretion of Rescuer 1.
6) Using the "Sinch Strap", Rescuer 1 bypasses the Primary Brake.
   ○ This is accomplished by running the strap between the eye on the Brake Handle and the eye built in to the T-Winch, and tightening it.
7) Rescuer 1 removes the Secondary Brake Release Handle from its mounting bracket in the T-Winch and screws it into the Brake Release Mount.
8) Rescuer 1 calls on radio and/or headset that they are ready to lower the Performer.
9) Rescuer 2 tells the Performer they are coming down and gives Rescuer 1 a clear to lower.
10) Rescuer 1 slowly releases the Secondary Brake to control the speed of the descent.
11) Rescuer 2 helps the Performer to the floor.

If the Performer has been in suspension for 15 minutes or more it is *crucial* that the Performer not be allowed to stand up or removes their harness immediately. This must be done slowly over a period of time equal to the time they were in suspension to avoid the effects of Suspension Trauma.

Figure 12.1 Brake–Release Rescue Plan

be at the winch and at the ready to perform this rescue. This is crucially important for acrobatic routines where the performer is using their strength to stay connected to the acrobatic element. This would be elements like tissue or straps. This importance comes from the fact that they only have so long they can continue to hold on and therefore stay airborne. We cannot be spending time on the ground getting to the offending axis or fumbling around near it to be ready to lower a performer in this condition. This required readiness does not, however, excuse us from making sure the performer is aware they are going to start moving before the brake release begins.

5. Pick-Off Rescue

If we can always perform a brake release, why would there need to be step above that? Well, because you can't always perform a brake release, of course! For example, the winch could be thoroughly cross-grooved to the point of not being able to spin the drum. Similarly, some other part of the reeving of the system could be gummed up. The cable could be sitting outside a sheave on a sharp edge, making moving the cable dangerous. You quite simply may have forgotten to charge the battery to open the primary brake or lost the flashlight all together. What if we are suddenly missing one of the brake-release handles (as they are often removable)? For all of these reasons, and countless others, we need a nuclear option. A pick-off rescue can take many different forms depending on the training of your staff and the equipment you have. The example we discussed in the Self-Rescue section of lowering a rescue lifting/lowering device to the performer is technically a pick-off rescue, for example. We will discuss two versions that, unlike the Self-Rescue example, involve sending additional personnel over the edge to go get the stranded performer.

Industrial Access, or the Crew-Assisted Rescue

In this example a technician accesses the stranded performer by means of an additionally rigged system. The technician then connects the stranded performer to himself or herself or the aforementioned additional system. The stranded performer is then lifted to take weight off their connection to the offending machine and is unclipped from it. The technician then calls for the system to lower him or her to the ground with the performer. In this crew-assisted rescue, the technician needs only a rope access harness, two slings, and four carabiners to perform the rescue. The rescue-rated raising/lowering device in question is most often, currently, a DBI Sala RPD (Figure 12.2) or a DBI Sala Rollgliss R500 (Figure 12.3).

These two devices work slightly differently to accomplish the same goal. The RPD is an auto-locking block and fall. The mechanical advantage makes it easier for you to haul the weight of the technician up to the performer and then to handle the load of two people. The auto-locking feature works like a

Figure 12.2   An RPD

Figure 12.3   A Rollgliss

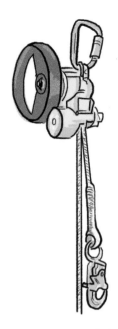

seatbelt in that if you try to lower the load too quickly, or drop it altogether, it will lock the block and fall from further movement until you slowly lift the load a small distance off the brake. The Rollgliss is quite simply a rope running through a gear reducer. As a result, you can easily lift a large load, like two people, via the flip-out handle on the body of the device. To lower a load you simply let go of the rope and let it pull through the system. The exact speeds vary based on exactly how much load is applied, but the system runs at about 2ft/sec. This is a nice leisurely pace, but sometimes needs to be managed slightly as the ground approaches.

With either device, or a different one altogether, the process goes similarly to a brake release. When the Rescue Leader says so, riggers are deployed to install the rescue device. If, through your many rescue practices, you decide that the load of two people on one device is too unruly for your staff to handle, then simply have the riggers hang two systems, one for the rescuer and one for the stranded performer. When the riggers call on headsets that the system(s) is (are) ready, the rescuer can attach themselves to the device. Whether they come from above or below is at the discretion of the Rescue Leader and will likely be determined by where exactly the performer is stuck and which way will be shorter trip. After the Rescue Leader informs the performer that their rescuer is coming, he or she clears the rescuer to head for the performer. Once they arrive at the performer, after quickly evaluating

Scope

- The purpose of this document will be to show a general rescue template for a performer stranded on a Winch at height where a Brake Release Rescue is not possible. This procedure assumes the reason for the rescue is a mechanical, electrical, or similar failure of the winch and that the performer is not injured.

Definitions

- **Rescuer 1** – Performs the Aerial Rescue.
- **Rescuer 2** – Ground Rigs the Rescue.
- **Rescuer 3** – Assists Rescuer 2.
- **Rescue Kit** – Pelican 1610 case outfitted by Tait Towers with all necessary gear for aerial rescues. Designed to live on the truss with the Performer Flying Winch(es).
- **Rollgliss R500** – Capital Safety Controlled Decent Rescue Device.

Equipment Needed

- 1 – Capital Safety Rollgliss R500
    - ○ 1 – 3' Daisy Chain Strap Choked to the Top Block
    - ○ 1 – Omega Aluminum Carabiner Clipped to the Daisy Chain

Procedure

1) The first person to notice a winch is not behaving normally calls on radio and/or headset "We might have a problem with Winch XXX".
2) Rescuer 1, using appropriate fall protection, traverses the Truss to the disabled Winch.
3) Rescuer 1 isolates the power to the Winch via the On/Off Switch on the side of the Winch.
    - During this time Rescuer 2 retrieves a mat and places it under the disabled Winch.
4) Rescuer 1 or Rescuer 2, whoever is closer to the Performer, makes verbal contact with the Performer to inform him/her of the Rescue Plan. Constant contact should be maintained to help avoid the Performer going into shock.
5) Rescuer 1 retrieves the Rollgliss from the Rescue Kit and hangs it on a main structural rung of the Truss with the attached Daisy Chain and Carabiner.
6) Rescuer 1 communicates to Rescuer 2 that the Rollgliss is Rigged and Safe for Load.
7) Rescuers 2 and 3 pull on one side of the rope from the Rollgliss to bring the other side up to the Performer.
    - Given the nature of this type of rescue we are not anticipating any injuries to the Performer on the disabled Winch. As a result, no extra steps are taken to evaluate them for injury prior to the rescue. The individual circumstances of the moment will dictate whether such steps are necessary. This will be at the discretion of Rescuer 1.
8. When the hook is at an appropriate height the Performer clips him/herself into the Rollgliss through the Rescue Loops built in to the Harness.
9. The Performer gives Rescuer 1 or 2 (whoever is closer) a Thumbs Up that they are clipped in properly.
10. Rescuers 2 and 3 pull the remaining slack out of the line.
11. Rescuer 1 uses the Winch function of the Rollgliss to raise the Performer enough that they can disconnect from the disabled Winch.
12. The Performer disconnects him/herself from the disabled Winch and gives Rescuer 1 or 2 (whoever is closer) and Thumbs Up that they are disconnected from the Winch.
13. Rescuers 2 and 3 operate the line as needed to control the decent of the Performer.
    - This should be very minimal as the Rollgliss is designed to perform a controlled decent without any input from an operator.

If the Performer has been in suspension for 20 minutes or more it is crucial that the Performer not be allowed to stand up or remove their harness immediately. This must be done slowly over a period of time eequal to the time they were in suspension to avoid the effects of Suspension Trauma.

Figure 12.4 Rollgliss Rescue Plan

Figure 12.5   Z-Rig

him or her for injuries, they connect the performer to the device with one sling, and to their own center waist ring with another. This is so that the performer still has two independent points of failure holding them in the air throughout the rescue. The rescuer then calls on a headset or gives "the signal" to take weight on the performer. Once the performer's weight is off the offending machine, the technician disconnects the performer from the winch line(s). The technician then calls over a headset or gives the signal to be lowered to the ground with the performer.

Rope Access, or the Solo Rescue

A rope-access rescue plays out nearly identically except it is performed by a technician accessing the performer on two climbing ropes. It must be pointed out that rope access techniques should only be performed by someone who has been trained and certified by IRATA (the Industrial Ropes Access Trade Association) or SPRAT (the Society of Professional Ropes Access Technicians). To speak broadly about the rescue, when the Rescue Leader says so, riggers are deployed to hang two ropes of sufficient and compatible diameter. The technician then rappels down to the stranded performer and quickly evaluates them for injury. The technician then connects the performer to the technician's rappel device with one sling, and to their central waist ring with another. This double clipping is again to ensure the performer has two independent points of failure during the rescue. The technician then creates a small block and fall with the dead side of their rappel rope, also called a "Z-rig" (Figure 12.5).

This is to give him or her the mechanical advantage to lift his or her own weight along with the performer's weight. The Z-rig is used and re-rigged as needed until the performer's weight is off the offending machine. The technician then disconnects the performer from the machine and slowly lowers himself or herself to the ground with the performer attached. This is not done without redirecting the rappel line through an extra carabiner, or similar, to allow for additional control of the higher load through the rappel device. The rappel device being used, being an ISO Type 3 device, will not be rated for a two-person load during normal usage but is allowed to belay such loads in a rescue scenario.

Suspension Trauma

According a technical bulletin published by OSHA (SHIB 03–24-2004, Updated 2011) the effects of suspension trauma can lead to death in as little as 30 minutes if left unmitigated by rescue. Due to the way harnesses keep us off the ground, supporting the user's weight by their crotch, they can cause a serious health concern. When we hang all our weight on the leg straps of a harness, we can cut off blood flow to and from our legs. The pooled blood in our legs becomes un-oxygenated as it can no longer circulate through our veins. If that large amount of un-oxygenated blood is then rapidly reintroduced to the rest of our system, by pressure being taken off the clamped veins, it can cause blackouts or even death. While OSHA states that 30 minutes of this condition can cause death, we should always be aware of the potential for these lesser symptoms to take hold in much shorter periods of time. What factors make our situation different from those OSHA studied? For starters, 30 minutes is based on a fall-protection harness which was not previously supporting the person's weight before the fall occurred. In performer flying the person has been supported by their legs the whole time they've been off the ground. Also consider that the leg straps for performer flying are much tighter than a correctly adjusted fall-protection harness. Given these factors, we want to be as efficient as we can to avoid the effects of suspension trauma.

It is true that suspension trauma sets on most quickly when the stranded person is unconscious, but given the factors we've just talked about it's important for us to be concerned about it after even a few conscious minutes in suspension. If our performer is conscious we want to make sure they are moving their legs and even inverting themselves periodically, if their harness allows and they feel comfortable to do so of course. The goal is to keep the blood in their legs circulating, at least a little. That said, when landing a person who has been in extended suspension, conscious or not, it is important not to let all that blood go rushing back into their system all at once. We want to slowly reintroduce the un-oxygenated blood back into their system so the performer doesn't lose consciousness. This is achieved by slowly letting the pressure off the harness. If suspension trauma is suspected, we do not under any circumstances want to lay the person down flat immediately after landing and totally loosen their harness. This is particularly important to remember if the performer has also been injured and first responders are called. The emergency medical technicians (EMTs) are legally responsible for the person's health once they can access them. That said, don't be afraid to tell the EMTs that this person likely has suspension trauma as you are landing them. That way the EMTs know everything you know about the situation before you rightfully hand the performer over to them.

That is all quite dramatic and very much a worst-case scenario. What is more likely is that your performer is not injured and has simply been stranded for some time in the air. If you suspect they might have suspension trauma simply land them in a chair and slowly lower their weight into the chair over several minutes, or land them on the ground with their legs out straight and slowly lower their weight onto the floor. Then slowly loosen the harness over several minutes. This will allow the un-oxygenated blood to reenter their system without harm to them.

Conclusion

As you can see from reading these procedures, they can be complicated and have a lot of moving parts. As a result, the only way to know you're ready and to be confident that you can get the performer down inside of 20 minutes is to practice, and practice often. You should practice so often that you have to start inventing more and more unlikely scenarios to keep you and your staff entertained. The more these procedures are second nature to everyone involved, the less likely a critical mistake will be made in a stressful moment should it ever actually be needed to be performed. Spend those bored moments during long-running shows, or during the 400th rehearsal of the same scene in a short-running one, to think through what you would say and do, to whom, in what order, and when during a rescue. Always plan for the worst and hope for the best. The opposite is far worse.

Takeaways: Beginners

- Don't go up if you don't know how to get down.
- Having a written rescue plan, with clear roles and responsibilities, is only half the battle.
  - The rescue plan must also be practiced often.
- Your Rescue Leader should be thinking through the rescue plans often, even when that is not what is most pressing in the moment.

Takeaways: Professionals

- Having a single rescue plan is often not enough. Make sure to have an answer for each step of the Hierarchy of Rescue.
- Make sure your staff is trained in any skills they will need to execute the written rescue plans.
- Remember the possible catastrophic effects of suspension trauma when planning and executing rescues.

13   Code Compliance

Throughout this book there have been references to various codes with the promise we would go over them later. OSHA, ANSI, ESTA, NYC DOL, D8, BGV-C1, and others can be a confusing alphabet soup of acronyms and expectations to navigate. They are often incorrectly used interchangeably, their specific requirements mixed and jumbled. The wrong codes, geographically, can also be cited by Authorities Having Jurisdiction (AHJs) as being required in places they quite simply are not. Don't beat yourself up for finding this terribly confusing. In fact, so many people are in that boat that a whole cottage industry has sprung up around consulting on the topic of code compliance in the entertainment industry. The first and most important weapon you have in your arsenal is knowing where the show is being performed. The biggest mistake often made in regard to code compliance is struggling to make a system conform to a code you aren't even required to meet.

Domestic Codes

If you know your effect will only be operating domestically in the US, then there are fewer codes you have to worry about. OSHA (the Occupational Safety and Health Administration) is the only organization in American life that can enforce or change laws related to workplace safety. Everything else we have in the US is a code of best practice, also known as a "standard". OSHA has no laws on the books specific to performer flying during a performance. In fact, OSHA has almost no laws specifically written for the entertainment industry. Until recently that last sentence could have read that OSHA has *no* laws specific to our industry. In 2017, among other updates having nothing to do with the entertainment industry, OSHA updated one line in 1910.28 about the need for handrails on raised platforms to specifically address stages! 1910.28(a)(2)(iii) says that stages for performance are officially considered as part of "General Industry", thus finally putting to bed the debate of whether stages should be regulated in the construction industry (1926) or the general industry (1910) codes. Aside from this one line, though, nothing applies uniquely and distinctly to the entertainment industry. This is mainly because we are such a small industry when compared to total people employed and therefore workers affected. As such, OSHA doesn't pay much attention to us. If you were to research some of the recent fatal performer flying accidents and the subsequent OSHA investigations, you would find that the fines OSHA gave the producers of those performances mainly relate to their documentation of their safety plans and how they cleaned up the blood of the injured or killed performers. This is not out of a lack of caring on OSHA's part; it simply doesn't have any other laws on the books to go after negligence on the part of our industry.

In an effort to keep OSHA from passing unnecessarily restrictive or simply uninformed laws, the entertainment industry in the US has created its own code of best practice. This has, after rigorous peer review, manifested itself in ESTA's E1.43–2016 Entertainment Technology – Performer Flying Systems. ESTA is the Entertainment Services and Technology Association, which, thankfully, makes all its codes available to the public for free through support from Prosight Specialty Insurance. You can read the full text of this code on its website, or by Googling "ESTA Performer Flying Standard", which will get you to its website. Since ESTA writes all its codes under the guidance and supervision of ANSI (the American National Standards Institute), E1.43 was adopted in full by ANSI in February of 2016. While ESTA and ANSI do not create laws, willful ignorance of the suggestions in E1.43–2016 would reflect poorly on you and your system in a court of law. Little by little adherence to ESTA's standard is becoming mandatory as more and more producing organizations are citing compliance with E1.43–2016 as a contract deliverable. The good news is the E1.43–2016 does an excellent job of defining its scope and being clear with its expectations. While it does cover performer flying design, manufacture, use, and inspection, it explicitly does not cover connections where the performer is responsible for keeping himself or herself attached to the system (like most circus acts) and flying the general public (rides). You should read the code cover-to-cover if you intend to design a system that is compliant, but the highlights are as follows:

- Structural Design (like support frames that are not in the direct load path)
  - 6.67:1 safety factor against working load limit (WLL)
  - 4:1 safety factor against characteristic loading
  - 2:1 safety factor against peak loading
- Machine Design
  - Two independent fail-safe brakes, each capable of holding 125% of WLL.
    - Brakes must be able to open without facility power
  - 10:1 safety factor against WLL
  - 6:1 safety factor against characteristic loading
  - 3:1 safety factor against peak loads
- Dynamic Loading
  - No more than 2.8G for 0.2 seconds in peak loading without regard for body position
  - Any system using multiple axes to move one object must have those individual axes grouped and monitoring each other in the control software

The ESTA standard also does a great job of defining required roles when executing a performer flying effect without mandating a minimum number of people to fill those roles. While many roles are cited as required to the safe and successful production of a performer flying system, E1.43–2016 does not say that a single person cannot fill multiple roles. This has the benefit of enumerating all the things we need to be paying attention to in order to realize one of these effects, without mandating a minimum crew number to be considered "safe". As a result, the code can effectively educate the smaller productions or less experienced riggers out there on what they should be paying attention to without handcuffing these systems into being unduly expensive from a staffing point of view. Please do take the time to read ESTA's E1.43–2016 cover-to-cover if you are trying to create a flying effect, regardless of your experience level or your production's budget.

The only other US-based law of note worth calling out explicitly is that of New York City's Cultural Affairs Law, specifically 37.09 Part 41. This is a New York City law that applies specifically to aerial performers. The text of the code seems to go out of its way to not specify measurable criteria to comply with, instead saying things like "Every safety device shall be of such strength … as to withstand the impact due to the fall of any and all persons who depend on it for safety." You might think to yourself, "That's great! It's all up for interpretation!" Unfortunately, you are exactly correct about that. The openness to interpretation means that the NYC Department of Labor (DOL), which is the AHJ to enforce this law, has broad authority to decide if your rig meets its standard or not. The good news though is that it is increasingly deferring to the ESTA standard. If you can prove compliance with ESTA E1.43, you should be in the clear. The most important thing when touring through, or producing in, New York City is to know the details of your rig and be prepared to demonstrate compliance with E1.43. In almost all cases, between your knowledge during DOL's visit and your beautiful paperwork you sent them in advance, you will breeze through your inspection.

International Codes

If your show will be traveling overseas you will need to be familiar with the flying codes of every country the show will visit. This can be a daunting process indeed. Instead most organizations make it their business to know which code is the most stringent in the world, and design to meet that one. The theory being that if you can clear the hurdle of the most stringent code out there, you will be able to get past any other code. For the most part this is a wise train of thought. The only drama then is keeping up with which is the most stringent code. The frontrunners these days (in 2018) are England's BS 7905–2:2001 and Germany's DIN 56,950:2012 and BGV D8+. But the current blue-ribbon holder, the most stringent code out there, is Germany's BGV-C1.

BGV-C1, often referred to as just "C1", can be a difficult code to read for clear information. For starters, it's written in German! That said, even if you get a translated version you will notice that the code itself does not call out many measurables to design your system to. Instead it refers to a variety of other German codes where you can find the measurables you seek. Now you need to go find translated versions of all those codes too! This is one of the many reasons why there are companies springing up all over Europe to consult on C1 compliance. Again, just as above with ESTA, you should make sure you fully understand the whole code cover-to-cover before setting off on designing a compliant system, but the highlights are as follows:

- Structural Design
    - Supporting structures must comply with DIN 15 560–47
    - Minimum of 10:1 safety factor for all load-bearing elements
- Machine Design
    - Minimum drum D:d ratio of 18:1
    - Minimum pulley D:d ratio of 20:1
    - Lifting media must have 10:1 safety factor against peak loading
    - Connecting hardware must have 12:1 safety factor
    - Must have overload protection, actuating at 120% of WLL
    - Must have underload sensing
    - Two independent fail-safe brakes each capable of holding 125% of WLL
        - System must be equipped with emergency lowering device
- Dynamic Loading
    - Max speed allowed 1 meter per second

But wait, how on Earth can you do all those huge flights across stadiums and arenas with a max speed of 1 meter per second!? It's a great question. The simple, real, honest answer is that inspectors are often satisfied with your compliance with the rest of the law; they do not hold many feet to the fire on the issue of speed. As far as the rest of law goes though, the inspectors really do look for strict adherence, not only in physical reality but also in documentation of compliance. The German inspectors will expect you to be able to submit paperwork proving you have met their code well in advance of arriving for the show, and then they will inspect your rig before your performance to make sure your paperwork matches reality.

An important thing to note here is that you are only required to meet C1's code if you are performing in Germany, or any other country in the European Union which has decided to enforce Germany's law. If you are in Canada, for example, and your system is not designed to meet C1, that's okay! This will not stop an AHJ in Canada from asking you for C1 compliance documentation. At that point, you may have to find a polite way to explain to the gentleman or gentlewoman from the AHJ that they are trying to enforce a law that doesn't exist in their country, and then go on to explain why your rig is in fact compliant on the soil you are currently standing on. It's a difficult needle to thread, but sometimes it has to be done.

Conclusion

Code compliance can be intimidating and daunting. The important thing to remember is that all of these codes are written down and generally very available. Equally important to remember is that there are subject matter experts on these codes out there who would be more than happy to help you out, for a fee of course, if you are still unsure of your system's compliance. While this can be seen as cutting into profits, getting some good advice in advance is almost always better than the possibility of getting shut down on the day of the show! And don't forget as long as you're paying someone for their advice and knowledge it's okay to learn from them too. You are not required to go back to them every time if you no longer need their help. Code compliance can also be seen as a waste of time. You know what you're doing after all, right? It is fair to say that some codes are written without the full knowledge of what they are legislating. Others can assign too much focus on parts of the system you don't see as the most worrisome, requiring you to spend more time on that part instead of the issue you are most concerned with. The important thing to remember is that all these codes were written with the right idea at heart, even if they weren't executed quite perfectly to that mission. Know the codes you need to meet, clear their hurdles, and design a system you believe in. The rest will fall into place.

Takeaways: Beginners

- Make sure you know what codes you are required to meet by geographic location and contract.
- Any code needing to be met should be read cover-to-cover for a full understanding.
- ESTA's E1.43–2016 Entertainment Technology – Performer Flying Systems is a great resource not only for information on the standard but also for performer flying best practices in general.

Takeaways: Professionals

- Don't be afraid to hire consulting help if needed to better understand the requirements of the various codes, particularly if they are written in languages you don't read/speak.
- Don't get stuck in a design trap where you are only designing to clear the hurdle of a given code. Instead, make sure your design is code-compliant and continue focusing your design efforts on creating as inherently safe a system as possible.
- These codes change with some regularity. Don't forget to make sure you have the most up-to-date information!

Part 5

Performer Relationships

While there is only one chapter in the part that follows, it covers a distinct-enough skillset to warrant being sequestered from the rest of the information presented here. Every decision or challenge presented to this point can be overcome by increasing one's hard skills in a variety of areas. Managing performers, however, is far more reliant on soft skills. Soft skills, of course, can also be learned but only if we are willing to admit there is a deficiency to be supplemented. Some of the most brilliant technical minds are less-than-awesome at some of the soft skills that follows. It's important to remember: that's okay! It is not critical that any one person on your staff be brilliant at every phase of a performer flying effect. Instead, it is critical that we have an expert at every phase on our staff. Planning for the challenges of interacting with performers is equally as important as any decision that has come before it!

14 Performer Relationships

What a gauntlet we have run to get to this moment. We did all our pre-planning. We thought about what kind of effect we wanted. We sought out qualified people to answer questions we had about things we knew we didn't know well enough. We designed a great system and got third-party engineering review. We built our system and tested our machines. We set limits and completed a thorough SAT process. We wrote and practiced our rescue plans. We're finally ready to fly performers! Right?

Wrong!

We did all this homework to make sure that the machines and the system won't fail us; let's put that same effort into making sure we look good in front of the performers on Day 1. In the world of performer flying perception is nine-tenths of the law. (This turn of phrase is an intentional play on "possession is nine-tenths of the law" for comedic flair. The attempted reference aside, it is a critical point to wrap your head around when regularly interacting with performers.) While it is of course critical that your system be safe, it is irrelevant how safe it factually is if the performers riding it perceive it to be unsafe. It is one of our primary jobs to make sure our performers always *feel* safe, while also actually *being* safe. This is an absolutely critical concept to understand and cannot be overstated. We want to make sure we already know everything that is going to happen any time a performer is on the line.

Day 1 Prep

What kind of work is left to achieve these goals? We've already thought all the way through our system, early and often. What could possibly be left to do? We still have a small amount of proper prior planning to do to ensure our success. For starters, we never want to fly a person on a machine in any manner other than with a practiced and tested cue. While all modern automation systems have the ability to jog an axis (that is, the ability to move the axis via a joystick) and to give custom move commands on the fly, this should never be done with a performer connected to the machine. There are simply too many variables that could easily result in an unintended move. Your joystick settings could be too jerky and startle the performer. You could enter an incorrect position or speed into your custom move window. Either will result in your team yelling "*STOP!*" and hitting the E-Stop button. This is one of the quickest ways to have your performers lose confidence in you, your team, and your rig. The same can be said of manually operated systems. The first time we start flying around the space, working to match our technical choreography with the artistic expectations, should absolutely not be with a performer on the end of the system.

So how do we avoid these situations? Simple: we do our homework.

First, we want to have a meeting with the artistic staff to determine what the goals for the first day are. It's important to get the artistic staff's buy-in on the plan so that no one is trying to push the envelope on what is achievable or what the order of operations will be on Day 1. Having stretch goals is always okay, but it's better to hard plan on doing less than you expect as these first-time introductions can take a lot of time. How long exactly these first introductions to the rig can take vary wildly from situation to situation and rig to rig. The correct strategy here is to under-promise and over-deliver. Plan on getting very little done that day, recognizing though that the "very little" you're going to get done is excruciatingly important and the foundation of trust on which you are going to build the rest of your show. Framed and planned as such, you will definitely have enough time to take your time. Time of course is the only commodity rarer in the entrainment industry than talent. If you get further than you planned, wonderful! But that's a way-better situation to be in than trying to rush through too long a punch list with new, baby-giraffe-esque performers.

Before we start running performers on show cues we want to make sure they are comfortable with everywhere they could end up while connected to the rig. This is especially important for inexperienced aerialists, as they may be more afraid of height or speed than they let on or know. The best way to achieve this is to write a series of cues building up to the max speed and height of your rig, and test them with sandbags in advance. Put differently: Day 1 with your performers is really *your* first show. You wouldn't run head-first into a performance with no cues written, would you? Of course not! We should treat our planning for Day 1 exactly the same.

So, therefore, we need a cue stack of programmed events, but where to begin? We should write all our cues to start and/or end with the performer on the ground. We also know we want to take them as high as the rig can safely go within its limits. So, we want to write a cue that goes from the ground up to the full trim of the rig, and then a separate cue that brings them back to the ground, both moves at a comfortable walking pace. If there is a traverse axis in our system, we then want to traverse them the full available length of travel, again at a walking pace. If there is a loading/unloading grid, or other designated area where they will be clipped into the rig, we should load/unload them there at least once. Again, we do not want to do any of this on the fly, or for the first time, with a performer connected to our machines, so we will write cues that do all these moves as separate segments. Then, before Day 1 ever begins, we will test those cues with a sandbag to make sure the cues do what we think they will do. Sandy, our anthropomorphized sandbag, is way better at being slammed around than our performers; she has a very high pain tolerance. This means that by the time we get to Day 1 we already know we are going to ace this first crucial test. We know exactly what is going to happen every time our automation operator hits the G-O button.

It is often beneficial to show the performer the cues they are about to ride with Sandy on the line first. This gives them an opportunity to see what is going to happen before they are strapped in. Once we have had the performer ride the rig everywhere they can end up at a walking pace, we will want to make sure they are also comfortable with the max speeds they could encounter. You will want to have also written and tested cues that take the performer from the stage to the top of the flight envelope at max speed. The introduction of speed is very important to everyone's comfort, especially if your rig can go fast enough to generate the "pit in the stomach" feeling.

Fun fact: accelerating at 6ft/sec squared going down is all it takes to make someone feel like they are falling. If your rig can achieve this, or more, you can expect performers, particularly inexperienced ones, to let out a decent yelp when accelerated down at that speed for the first time.

Now, on Day 1 we have everything we need canned and tested to introduce the performers to the rig. This should be the technical staff's only goal for Day 1. Often Artistic also wants to see the performers ride the show cues on Day 1. This is completely acceptable and a good plan, time permitting. The opportunities to have performers ride cues in (relative) quiet and work lights are few and far between, and should always be taken advantage of.

A common mistake on Day 1, however, is thinking that the heights of the show cues cannot be set *without* the performers on the line. This leads to a situation where we are jogging the winch with the performer attached until the Director says, "Yes! There! Perfect!" We then end up writing cues with the performer still in the air, and running those cues without testing them with Sandy first. This is very bad and wholly unsafe. Instead we should get the Director, and anyone else with an opinion, in the room and fly Sandy around to get those positions. We can then do our cuing homework and test the cues with Sandy. Then on Day 1 we are ready to look organized, professional, and in control in front of our performers.

Over the course of Day 1, you will of course end up with artistic notes. It is important that the leader of the technical rehearsal, be it the Head of Automation, the Stage Manager, the Flying Director, or someone else, be very receptive to the notes from Artistic, but similarly firm that those notes will be done after the conclusion of the technical rehearsal and not during it. Changing cues on the fly with performers in the rig is an easy way to end up in a completely avoidable dangerous situation. You, as the Flying Director, are the only one in charge of making sure all the flying performers are safe.

Do not take that responsibility lightly, and do not let others pressure you to cut your process short. With proper prior planning everyone will be on the same page. From time to time, representing the safety of the performer will put you at odds with someone who has a bigger bat to swing. If you are not prepared to stand up to anyone in the name of safety, being the Flying Director might not be the right role for you.

Day 1 Execution

Now that we've prepared all our cues, got Artistic's buy-in as to the day's plan, and got a good night's sleep, we're ready to throw the kids on the rig, right?

Wrong, again!

As the saying goes, "You only get one shot at first impressions." From the moment our new performers walk into the room we want to be presenting an air of knowledge and control, even if neither is true! Remember: "Perception is nine-tenths of the law." If we are having self-doubts about our knowledge base, abilities, or anything else, we need to check that at the door this morning. Your new performers are looking to you to make them feel safe. Let's emphasize that point, because it warrants repeating: they need you to make them *feel* safe. We need to build trust between the technical staff and the performers. The rig may well be expertly designed, immaculately executed, and thoroughly inspected regularly, but if the performers don't *feel* safe, none of that aforementioned flawlessness will matter. Equally important to *making* a safe rig is *representing* a safe rig. Now, this doesn't mean we need to be as stiff as a board or behave like a drill sergeant. In fact, being personable and friendly will work better every time. However, while being friendly and affable we also want to be knowledgeable and in control. On the "knowledgeable" front, make sure whoever is representing the team is ready to answer questions the performers might have. On the "in control" front, make sure the team know who is in charge. As the day goes on, and various participants start to get the rhythm of the day, there is a tendency for control to become distributed and as a result important steps are missed. It is crucial that throughout this Day 1 that all communications and decisions run through one person to make sure we are not missing a possible hazard. It is of the utmost importance that one person, usually the Flying Director, be the choke point of information. One single person needs to be the narrow part of the hourglass. This is how we ensure that we are always doing every single step of the process, and that we don't end up with someone with inadequate authority giving a "G-O" command errantly.

Before Getting on the Rig

When the new performers arrive we, of course, want to start with introductions. Look people in the eye, shake their hands, and attempt to remember their names. A great ice-breaking activity is to have a roll of gaff tape and a Sharpie handy. When someone tells you their name you have them turn around and you put a stripe of gaff tape across their shoulders like a football jersey. You then write their name on the gaff tape, explaining that you are terrible with names. This does two things very well. It loosens up the room with a large silly gesture and gets people laughing. It also breaks an important barrier that we need to get over: touching. A lot of performer flying involves holding onto people, or strapping people into devices, all of which involves touching. This gets that out of the way early with a benign, safe, gesture. Don't forget though about the concept of consent when crossing this touching barrier. Performer flying harnesses cover, or hover near, some very sensitive areas of the body, to say nothing of how revealing some costuming can be. Always make sure the performer is aware of how you are about to physically interact with them before it happens, especially, though not exclusively, when those interactions are happening near said sensitive areas. This has two benefits. One, you will be seen as polite and overly sensitive to their personal space, which is a great way to start building trust. Two, if you are about to tug on some part of a harness the performer has ample time to be ready for that so as not to fall over from your tugging.

Next talk about the machines we will be connecting the performers to. It is worth noting that a vast majority of this information will likely go over the performers' heads, or not be retained. That said, this is a *huge* opportunity to show how much you know about your system, and to make them feel safe. This should be an abbreviated rundown of the information covered in Chapter 6, related to making our "Safe Sandbox". Take them to a winch and point at it while you go over these features. Go over the breaking strength of the cable. Explain the 10:1 safety factor and what "fail-safe" means. This will start to make them understand how much thought has gone into the design of everything. Explain, broadly, some of the sensors on the winch. The main point to hit with them is that there are redundancies built into every sensor and that each sensor is monitored hundreds of times per second. Drive home the idea that all those sensors have to be reporting correctly at all times for the winch to move at all. Put another way: if the winch is moving, hundreds and hundreds of things are going right every second. It's actually very difficult to get these machines to move at all! Pointing this out usually gets a laugh, and makes performers feel very safe with the equipment.

Then wander over to your control station. Show them the console. Broadly explain how cues are written in advance and run from this position. Show them how small a unit of measurement they are flown to. For example, if your system is running metric and is displaying numbers down to the millimeter, explain to them that those numbers will be the same every time the operator presses the G-O button. Showing them how refined the system is, and how precise we expect it to be, is often a great way to calm nerves as to the quality of the equipment. This is also a great time to start talking about how to announce there is a problem should one arise.

Stopping a Flight in Motion

It is important to impress upon the performers that they have the final say in whether or not a flight starts, continues, or ends. Yes, we have put in place many processes to make sure everything is perfect every time, but if the performer feels uncomfortable for any reason they are in charge and can stop it at any time. Impress upon them that they don't even need to have a "good" reason. Their ability to stop what is going on is not limited to thinking something might be mechanically wrong, it is not limited to thinking they might pass out, and it is not limited to feeling their harness might be loose. They can stop the flight for any reason at all. These reasons can include, but are not limited to, lightheadedness, becoming disoriented, realizing they are not in a proper mental state to continue, becoming distracted, or literally *any* other reason. With newer performers in smaller productions it is particularly important to stress that just because Great Aunt Sue is in the audience is not a reason to push through a dangerous situation. Just stop the flight. All we are doing here is telling stories; the most important thing is that everyone gets to go home at the end of the day. Many of us in the live entertainment industry have had "the show must go on" pounded into us. This is *not* one of those times to be an adherent to that philosophy. Even if your show is a one-off event, it is far better to stop for any reason the performer needs to than to continue into a potentially dangerous situation. Verbalizing these core principles is a great way to show your performers that their safety is your number one priority.

Next you will need to tell them how to stop a flight. The first method, and one we will be using for our Day 1 exercises, is to say "STOP" loudly and clearly, and to keep saying it until such a stop is achieved. Not "Whoa", not "Pause", not "Wait", not "Hold", and definitely not "*Iiiieeeeeeeeeeeeee*". "STOP" is the only word that we, the flying team, will react to. This is sometimes particularly important to stress to stage managers, who may have become accustomed to saying something like "Hold" to make an action stop. Given that we are talking about a stop that needs to occur because of an imminent emergency, "STOP" is the only word that will do. "STOP" works great in work-light-style conditions but its usefulness decreases once we start adding sound to the mix. For show situations you will want to teach your performers to put their arms in an X position above their heads (Figure 14.1).

It is important to stress that when we make this symbol it needs to be as clear as yelling "Stop" at the top of your lungs. It should not be attempted to be made pretty by inserting it into choreography, as performers might be wont to do. The hand signal needs to be made loud and proud. Remind the performers that while we will be watching like hawks for any sign of trouble, we too have mitigating circumstances, such as shifting lighting conditions, to deal with. If they need the flight to stop, we need their communication to be very clear. The next logical question that may be asked of you by your performers, particularly in acrobatic situations, will be "But what if my hands/arms are busy holding my weight in the air?" In this situation

Figure 14.1   Arms X

it will be important for you and the acrobatic choreographer to agree on a body signal that will be able to be executed at all times during the routine. At the end of the day, it doesn't matter what the signal is as long as everyone knows what it is and anyone who needs to show it can do so at any time. It should be obtuse and obvious. This signal is meant to be used in the event of an impending emergency. It should not be designed to deceive the audience of its implication. If we are throwing this signal, the magic is over. Make it an obvious gesture to the technical staff.

Harness Fittings

Now we can start to get our performers fitted to their harnesses. It is strongly recommended that each performer have their own harness. This greatly reduces the chance of there being a mistake in fitting the shared harness to performers on a nightly basis. This may not be a viable option for smaller productions, and that's okay too. Be familiar with the risks of harness sharing and make sure you have taken steps to mitigate those risks. How many performers can be fitted at once really depends on how big your staff is. It is best practice to start with everyone watching one performer get fit up. This gives you the opportunity to explain how a harness is fit correctly in front of everyone. This will in turn speed up the fittings of everyone else. For precise and detailed instructions on how to fit a performer into a harness please see

Chapter 11. Also, again, remember the discussion of consent earlier in this chapter. Make sure each performer understands how you will interact with them before it happens and make sure they are okay with that.

Once correctly fitted, we are ready for a test pick. While this can be done on the rig it is better to do it with a static system that is nearby. These are sometimes noisy moments as everyone is excited to finally be in a harness, so the static situation is a better choice since it removes the need for communication with an automation operator. For this kind of rig simply hang two points, one for each hip, with the appropriate connecting hardware. Make sure the lines are terminated high enough to allow the performer's feet to dangle off the ground when in the rig. You may want it higher if you intend to have the performer practice flips on this static rig. You then simply have an apple box or similar to get the performer up to a clip-in height. Then have them sit in the rig and remove the box. Voila! You have a performer hanging in their harness and you didn't need a machine!

At this point you want to look at the performer's waist. There will more than likely be some slack. You want to readjust the harness for fit and position again, removing all the slack. You will also want to take note of how high up the performer's body the harness has ridden. If we are now in the performer's ribs with the waist belts, the leg straps were likely too loose. No problem; this happens all the time. Simply bring the box back, have the performer take their weight off the rig by stepping on said box, and adjust accordingly. We keep repeating this process until the performer is comfortable and the flying team is happy with the fit. Again, a more detailed discussion of the harness-fitting process can be found in Chapter 11.

An important note here about harness fit: some people will be 100% comfortable in a properly fit harness. Others will never be 100% comfortable. This has to do with biological factors such as where different individuals have padding on their bodies. While the goal should always be to have every performer be 100% comfy in their harness, it is sometimes unachievable. Sometimes even after adding extra padding to a harness the person is still not comfy. At these times it's helpful to point out that the harness is a piece of life-safety equipment. While comfy is a goal, it is not a 100% necessity. This device is designed to keep you alive in the air, while being as low-profile as possible for the show. "No pain, no gain", as the saying goes. If the person is so uncomfortable they can't fly, it would be time to have a meeting with the artistic team and the acrobatic choreographer about what options exist; perhaps this isn't the right person for this role.

First Rides

We are finally ready to put performers on the rig! Depending on your group's dynamics you can choose to either explain the cues to the performers, or show them the cues running with Sandy before clipping them in. When explaining the cues to the performers try to stay succinct and only talk about what is going to happen immediately next. Don't overwhelm them with the full rundown of every cue you're going to run. So, you might say something like,

> Okay everyone, now we are going to ride the winch all the way up and all the way back down. So one of you will come up here, we will clip you in, and take you to tension. Then I'll ask if you're ready. I'll tell Vinny at the desk you're ready. Then I'll say 'Moving!' and you will go the way up. When you're there we will ask if you're ready to come down. Then I'll say 'Moving!' again and you'll come back down here. We'll do this at a nice walking pace and then we'll build up to the max speed. Sound good?

Ask for a volunteer to go first. By now you should know who is the most stressed, worried, or scared about flying. It will have been made obvious during the tour or the harness fitting. While that person doesn't need to go first, do not let them go last either. You will find the performers will cheer each other on as each one gets to fly. But the performers will also get distracted as the rides become normal over the course of getting through the whole group. Don't let the most worried person fly when they don't have the support or attention of their friends. Always try to work them in the first half of the total rides.

The last piece of information we want to stress to your flying performers before takeoff is to always land with their knees bent. The performer needs to absorb the last bit of deceleration at the ground with their legs. There are two main reasons for this. First, we always want weight on the system when it's running. As such, when a performer is landing, if they straight-leg the landing the winch will continue to pay out slack to the end of the cue (usually enough for them to unclip themselves) without the expected load on the winch. This could result in a cross-groove or similar issue! Second, straight-legging a landing is a quick way to really hurt oneself. Even when everything is going as planned and the winch is decelerating in the landing moment, coming in with your knees locked can lead to serious injury. Now, imagine that same scenario except something has gone wrong and we're coming in for a landing way too fast. The risk of serious injury has jumped ten-fold. So, we want to drill into our performers to always absorb the landing at the deck with their knees bent. We want them to keep their full weight on the rig until it comes to a complete stop.

As we discussed earlier in this chapter, you will then work your way through your Day 1 cue stack, taking each performer to the extents of the rig slowly at first, then working up to full speed. If you have any loading or unloading scenarios to practice with the performers, now is also the time to go through that. This is also a prime opportunity to once again drill into them that they have the final say on a flight. The last thing that happens before anyone begins a flight is a technician checks that the performer is ready and then clears the flight to begin.

Once each performer has completed these runs you get to say to them as a group, "Here's the good news guys: you've now been everywhere this rig can go, as fast as we can get you there. So everything from here on out will be something you've done before!" This is usually a huge confidence booster for the team.

You now have a decision to make about how you want to introduce your performers to the rescue plans. Depending on your situation you can elect to simply explain the plan to them, make them watch a member of your team rescue a dummy or Sandy, or have each performer experience a rescue. This is entirely up to you and is situation-dependent. The most important thing is to have the performers walk away from this understanding that there are written rescue plans, which they may read at any time, and which are practiced regularly by the full team. This is another opportunity for you and your team to show that you have thought of everything and have a plan for it! It also worth stressing with them that the odds of needing to act out a rescue are very low.

Acrobats will often also want a self-rescue option, particularly those who specialize in routines that involve hanging from one's arms. Fortunately, you already read Chapter 12 and were prepared for such a request! It is always worth going through a full self-rescue with any acrobat who will be expected to perform such a maneuver. Further, this is the rare example of a rescue plan that should be practiced in both work lights and show conditions with each performer.

Keeping Communication Lines Open

At the end of Day 1 it is important to stress a few closing points to your newly minted flyers. You will want to thank them for their time and ask if they have any questions. After that you should re-stress that *anyone* can stop a flight at *any* time for *any* reason. Make sure they understand that you would rather stop a flight than deal with the consequences of pushing through an unsafe situation, perceived or otherwise. Make sure they know that you want open communication between your team and them. We have to see ourselves as one family executing these flying routines. Just like a family, that means we have to be comfortable enough with each other to say difficult things to each other when warranted. Your team will be checking in with each flyer after each flight, every night. Make sure they know that no detail is too small to report back on or to ask a question about. Reiterate that we are only telling stories here in this building and that it's more important that everyone gets to go home at the end of the night than it is to risk an accident.

Keeping communication lines open is the single most important soft skill that you and your team need to maintain with the performers. This is achieved by checking in after every flight and being honest with each other.

If/when something goes wrong do not stonewall the performers and tell them everything is fine. This is one of the quickest ways to lose their trust. Be honest, be clear, be succinct.

Breaking the Ice with Experienced Performers

So far we've really focused on new performers with very little, if any, experience. But what should we do differently if we are blessed to be working with performers who have done this before? Frankly, very little. The more experienced the performer is, particularly with acrobats, the more we should treat them as a peer and less as a student. We likely have an opportunity to learn a trick or two from an experienced acrobat that we might otherwise ignore if we treated them like a brand new performer. Equally and oppositely though, it is still worth going over all the same information on Day 1 about how the system works and how safe it is; the performer might learn something from you! Even if the performer is experienced with gear from the company which produced this particular rig, we should still go over the finer points of this particular setup. We need to be prepared for more detailed and technical questions from an experienced performer. These should not be hard to answer given the long and winding road we walked to get to this moment, but should the performer stump you don't just make something up. Remember: they have experience that is causing them to ask you this question, and your made-up answer might be the way you lose their trust. Instead, simply say something like, "Oh, good one! I'll have to get back to you that." We must also not then leave it at that. We have to go find the answer and report back to that performer. This exercise will build huge trust between you and your experienced performer. Don't be afraid of not knowing everything in the moment; be afraid of causing your performers to not trust you.

You may think that experienced performers require less handholding than your newbies, but this is not true. The only way to maintain trust in these relationships is to work at them! You still need to check in with your experienced performers after each flight. Look them in the eyes, speak frankly but politely, and take notes. The point of these quick chats is not only to talk about obvious issues, but also to be a pressure-release valve on your relationship. If the performer wants to give you a note it is best to get it quickly rather than let that thought fester with them for hours, overnight, or until the next time you see them. You need to create an environment and a relationship where you are being honest and fair with each other.

Conclusion

Perception is nine-tenths of the law. We must always be a few steps ahead of the situation to make sure that everything is safe. We must work diligently to make sure that everything is not only factually safe, but also appears and feels safe. We must embrace the fact that sometimes those two things are not self-evidentially the same. We must be ready to defend our timetable and needs to directors, producers, or others who may want to (incorrectly) accelerate the process. We must make it clear to the performers that we are on their team and want to not only keep them safe, but also see them succeed. Managing the relationship with your performers is a mostly soft-skill project, but one we must be just as good at as we are at design, fabrication, administration, or any other part of the process.

This chapter lays out what might seem like a lengthy performer break-in process. You might be saying to yourself, "We don't have that kind of time." Much like the roles laid out in ESTA's E1.43, which states all the various roles without prescribing how many people must fill those roles, think about these suggestions as a process that must occur and not how much time must be invested. If you and your team can safely and successfully execute these steps in half a day, so be it! What is important is to understand how critical these steps are and to make sure you've successfully advocated for all the time you reasonably think they will take.

Takeaways: Beginners

- Day 1 with performers on the machines is really your first show day.
- The goal of projecting intelligence and safe control of any situation is not to be taken lightly. It involves as much planning as a successful performance.
- Building trust with the performers is paramount.
- Consent before touching goes a very long way very quickly towards building trust.

Takeaways: Professionals

- The soft skills to manage a healthy relationship with performers are paramount to success.
- "Perception is nine-tenths of the law." Think about this often as you plan your interactions with your performers throughout the lifecycle of a flying effect.
- Consent before touching goes a very long way very quickly towards building trust.

In Summation

First and foremost, thank you for reading! This book is the result of a wealth of experience from a career in progress and two years of edits, revisions, and changes due to the desire to get all these lessons down on paper. Countless friends had the misfortune of reading earlier drafts and setting me back on the correct path, for which I will be forever grateful. This book is meant to be primary source material. As such, there are very few citations except where absolutely critical. Similarly, that means this book is a collection of one man's opinions. It is worth noting that these opinions have been arrived at after 15 years of focusing almost exclusively on performer flying at every level of our industry. The other side of that coin, though, is that they have been formed exclusively in the space between *my* ears.

I hope this book inspires debate among professionals and beginners alike as to where we want to go as an industry, and how to get there safely. I hope this helps underscore the need for a new certification in our industry relating specifically to automated rigging. Most of all, though, I hope this effort helps lay bare a process and way of thinking that, to this point, has mainly been handed down through an oral tradition. Some of the suggestions contained herein may seem too expensive, time consuming, or otherwise unachievable at your organization. As is stressed at many points throughout this book, doing exactly what is prescribed here is not always the answer. Understanding the motivations laid out here, though, is critical, and executing *your* version of those ideas is completely acceptable. There are very few absolutes in performer flying. As the title of Part 4 says, "It Depends".

Remember these fundamental ideas:

Proper prior planning.
Thinking through the entire system early and often.
Knowing what you don't know.
Asking for help when you need it.

Thank you for your time. I hope you got out of this as much as I did.

Index